STUDIES IN SCIENCE AND THEOLOGY
Volume 5 (1997)

STUDIES IN SCIENCE AND THEOLOGY (SSTh)

Yearbook of the
European Society for the Study of Science and Theology

in connection with
Willem B. Drees, Botond Gáal,
Michael Heller, Jürgen Hübner, Michael W.S. Parsons,
Xavier Sallantin, Karl Schmitz-Moormann[†]
and Jaqueline Stewart

Managing editor: Christoph Wassermann

Volume 5 (1997)
The Interplay Between Scientific and Theological Worldviews, Part I

Edited by
Niels H. Gregersen, Ulf Görman
and Christoph Wassermann

This volume has been sponsored by the
Committee for Scientific Research in Poland (KBN).

LABOR ET FIDES, S.A.
Geneva, Switzerland

Studies in Science and Theology

ISBN 2-8309-0915-1

Contents

SECTION 2
Biology and Theology

SECTION 3
Mind and Nature

INTRODUCTION

Since its foundation in 1990, the *European Society for the Study of Science and Theology* (ESSSAT) has organized biennial conferences in Europe on the still growing field of science and theology.

The *Sixth European Conference on Science and Theology* (ESCT VI) took place in Cracow from March 26 to 31, 1996 at the Pontifical Academy of Theology. 180 scholars from five continents, specialists in all fields of science, theology, philosophy, and other relevant disciplines such as history, psychology and ethics took part in the event. Five invited lectures were delivered, and additionally no less than 92 workshop papers.

Of course, interest does not guarantee validity, and quantity does not necessarily imply quality. However, we are quite confident that this new field is on a fertile track, and we acknowledge the importance of insights coming from other continents. The issue of debate cannot be but international.

In this volume we present some of the invited lectures, and a selection of the workshop papers. The overall theme of the conference was "The Interplay Between Scientific and Theological Worldviews", which is also the title of this and the next Yearbook of ESSSAT, *Studies in Science and Theology*, Volumes 5 and 6 (1997 and 1998).

This first part is dedicated to the more general agenda that constantly reappears in the discussion: The relationships between physics and theology (Section 1), between biology and theology (Section 2), as well as between mind and nature (Section 3). The last section of this virst volume (Section 4) is devoted to methdological issues at stake in interdisciplinary research.

The second part, to be published in 1998, will address ethical issues, science and theology from Orthodox perspectives, world views of science and theology, world views in public culture as well as natural theology and revelation.

The organizing committee of the Cracow Conference is deeply indebted to the sponsors of the conference: *The Templeton Foundation*, and for the administrative support given by the *Pontifical Academy of Theology*. Without these sponsors, a conference of this size could not have been organized and completed. And without the conference, we would not be able to present this volume of Studies in Science and Theology (SSTh 5).

Special thanks are also due to Miss Barbara Runkel for her diligent work in correcting the manuscripts.

The idea of publishing the *Studies of Science and Theology* is not only to provide a suitable place for publication of the papers of the biennial European conferences. The volumes of SSTh are *not* intended to be "proceedings" of conferences. Space restrictions only allow for a smaller selection of workshop papers to be published here. In addition our Yearbooks are also open for contributions that have not been presented at the European conferences.

May 1997

Niels Henrik Gregersen
Ulf Görman
Christoph Wassermann

Section 1

Physics and Theology

THE LAWS OF NATURE
AND THE IMMANENCE OF GOD
IN THE EVOLVING UNIVERSE

Templeton Lecture delivered by
JOSEPH M. ZYCINSKI
(*Cracow, Poland*)

Abstract: The paper critically assesses new attempts to interpret God's interaction with nature on the level of microphenomena. God should not be placed in the gaps of our knowledge that are consistent with Heisenberg's uncertainty principle, He rather manifests his immanence in nature both in the cosmic order and in evolutionary processes. After critical evaluation of Hawking's philosophy of creation, the author tries to justify the notion of a cosmic Logos implicitly assumed in philosophical presuppositions of modern cosmology. The Logos at stake can be understood either in a neo-Platonic way or in the philosophical framework proposed by Nicholas of Cusa. Its acceptance fosters these theological interpretations in which God interacts with nature in the process of creatio continua not in special interventions dependent on microgaps.

Keywords: chaos, creation, determinism, evolution, immanence, laws of nature, logos, necessity, novelty, order, panentheism, possible worlds, universe.

The problem of God's action in nature arises in the context of contemporary quantum cosmology as it did in the 18th century comments to Laplace's mechanics and in the 19th century controversies on Darwin's theory of natural selection. Certainly, nobody would defend today Samuel Clarke's concept of a God who was supposed to fill up gaps in Laplacean physics. There are, however, new attempts in which Clarke's old ideas return in a new subtler form without reference to his deistic image of God. Instead of classical gaps in Newton's mechanics we find now stochastic gaps or quantum microgaps in the new metaphysical comments to the theories of physical chaos or to the models of quantum creation out of nothing. In these comments, one distinguishes between the traditional concept of the upward causality dependent on the laws of Nature and the so called downward causality where various forms of God's action in the world are involved. The latter develops the classical idea of *creatio continua* by presenting a God who interacts with the physical world as a principle of its organisation. In this framework God is to bring new information to the domain of natural phenomena (Polkinghorne 1995).

William Alston, in his model of the divine action in nature, refers to the indeterministic character of the physical processes in the microworld. He seems to regard God's agency on an equal footing with the action of natural causes when he claims: "perhaps God designed the universe to operate in accordance with probabilistic laws so as to give room for God to enter the process as an agent" (Alston 1993, 189; Alston 1989, 197-222). In his attempt to justify an analogous approach, John Polkinghorne argues that in Clarke's physico-theology "the gaps were epistemic, and thus extrinsic to nature, mere patches of current scientific ignorance. As they disappeared with the advance of knowledge, the 'god' associated with them faded away as well. No one need regret his passing, for the true God is related to the whole creation, not just the puzzling bits of its" (Polkinghorne 1993, 446). Contrary to the approach proposed by Clarke, Polkinghorne argues that God cannot be treated "as a cause among other causes" because his interaction with natural phenomena "is not energetic but informational". A form of intrinsic microgaps is necessary in this suggestion because "we are unashamedly 'people of the gaps' in this intrinsic sense and there is nothing unfitting in a God of the gaps in this sense either" (Polkinghorne 1993, 446n).

Leaving aside terminology in which the nature of various types of gaps is discussed, I argue that the main defect of the interpretation proposed is that in it nature cannot be understood as a physically closed system, i.e. a system in which physical phenomena should be explained only by reference to another physical phenomena. Only on the level of human existence, when conscious processes are involved, does God interact by bringing new information into human consciousness. The content of our consciousness cannot be explained by reference to purely physical determinants. This distinguishes mental systems from physical ones. In the latter, the so called principle of methodological positivism, underlying the growth of modern science, does not permit the scientist to refer to any extranatural factors to explain natural processes. For methodological reasons, when the chain of causal dependencies is examined on the level of the natural sciences, one cannot introduce into this chain either radical discontinuity, by assuming a special divine intervention, or a sequence of microdiscontinuities in which God's presence would be described in the language of information increase. Certainly, the principle at stake is methodological in nature. It does not preclude the existence of an extranatural agent that can be referred to in philosophical research. It only brackets his role in the cognitive framework of natural sciences.

In Polkinghorne's proposal this bracketed divine action does not imply physical falsifiable consequences. As a result, the God of the microgaps cannot be eliminated from nature in the process of growth of natural sciences. This differentiates essentially Polkinghorne's interpretation from the approach defended by Samuel Clarke in the past.

In this paper, after assessing critically certain new models of God's interaction with nature on the microcosmic level, I will try to defend the thesis that God's immanence in nature is expressed by cosmic order and evolutionary novelty. Among many physical forms of manifestations of the divine immanence we have to notice in particular:

1. the very existence of the laws of nature in a world that would exist as a lawless disorder;

2. the emergence of new attributes that constituted the domain of pure possibilities in the earlier stages of the cosmic evolution.

The presented essay is written in epistemological framework of philosophy. For this reason I do not discuss the status of such theological facts as Incarnation or Resurrection. The revealed truth concerning the latter facts introduces a radically new perspective, in which one transcends purely rational philosophical inquiry and discovers a God so different from intellectual schemes provided by human logic.

LAWS OF PHYSICS AND THE ABSENCE OF GOD

In 1889 Aubrey L. Moore, in his comments to the Darwinian theory of evolution, wrote that this theory is more Christian than the theory of 'special creation' because it implies the permanent immanence of God in the evolving nature. He argued: "Those who oppose the doctrine of evolution in defence of a 'continued intervention' of God, seem to have failed to notice that a theory of occasional intervention implies as its correlative a theory of ordinary absence" (Moore 1989, 73). A century later, this lack of logical consequence in explaining God's immanence in nature has still been a real problem. In 1991, when undertaking the same issue, Owen Thomas admitted sarcastically: "Theologians continue to talk a great deal about God's activity in the world, and there continue to be only a very few who pause to consider some of the many problems involved in such talk" (Thomas 1991, 35-50).

In traditional attempts to answer the question dealing with interaction between God and nature, God's action was referred to when scientists could not determine any natural phenomena to explain empirically confirmed effects. Such a procedure appeared risky from the standpoint of the scientific development because many phenomena that were supposed to be explained theistically later found natural explanation. God who was introduced initially as a necessary cause became a useless hypothesis when gaps in scientific outlook were filled.

The reference to the God of the gaps who enters into world history mainly by occasional interventions was clearly inconsistent with methodological principles of modern science adopted already by Galileo. Though he never denied the value of theological explanation, Galileo argued in the *Dialogo* that, for methodological reasons, any theological factors must be excluded from the domain of astronomical research. If, in the spirit of medieval astronomy, one refers to the role of angels to explain the motion of planets, one could always introduce the hypothesis of angels to explain any set of empirical data. As a result, in such an approach, astronomy would remain merely a branch of an applied angelology (Galileo Galilei 1890, VII, 263; VII, 325; V, 316).

Galileo's methodological distinctions implied what we call now the principle of methodological positivism. At the beginning of modern science this method seemed unacceptable to Gabriel Naude when he accused Girolamo Borro of being an atheist because the latter denied the existence of the empyrean heavens (Spini 1966, 56). Naude's main argument can be presented in the form: "When there is no empyreum, there is no God." Contemporarily, combining theories of the empyreum with atheism may seem extravagant. We find, however, a new version of Naude's philosophy in Stephen Hawking's model of quantum creation out of nothing (Hartle, Hawking 1983, 2960-2975). Hawking's dictum "if there is no edge, there is no God, the Creator" expresses the essence of the same philosophy which we find in Clarke's gaps and in Naude's empyreum. Regardless of terminological preferences, the reference to the "the edge", "the gap", or to "the empyreum" implies the breakdown of natural laws and makes the search for the supernatural psychologically easier.

Hawking himself in his justification of the "no edge" argument tries to make his reasoning more rational not by reference to the psychological but to the methodological factor. When replying that in his model there is no God and the very edge plays the role of God-like principle, he claims: "if we could show that we can explain everything in the universe on the hypothesis that there is no edge, I think that would be a much more natural and economical theory" (Weber 1986, 214). Many authors share the same views and do not accept Moore's concept of God hidden in natural laws because they worry that any attempt at theological interpretation of the laws of nature would be regarded as contrary to the basic principles of interpretive economy. Why refer to a God immanent in ordered nature when the very notion of physical order is enough to explain investigated phenomena? This methodology seems justified on the level of physical investigations. It cannot however be justified on the level of philosophical explanation.

Our belief in epistemological simplicity and economy of explanation resulted in the well-known principle of Ockham's razor. This very principle, however, is methodological in nature, not doctrinal. It could inspire an effective research procedure but it cannot provide simple answers to complicated metaphysical questions. Even on the level of physical research, this principle often played a heuristically negative role. Its critics indicate many examples of the disadvantageous consequences of its application in science. It is true that in the 19th century the appeal to Ockham's razor retarded the development of extragalactic astronomy by nearly one hundred years. Dogmatic adherents of the Ockham's principle argued at that time that there are no extragalactic objects because all observed astronomical phenomena can be explained more economically by reference to the objects in our galaxy. This search for simplicity resulted in a false cosmological model. As a result, in the contemporary philosophy of science a special "de-Ockhamization" program has been promoted in which the Ockham's principle has a relative, not an absolute value.

Can this very principle justify the absence of God in a philosophical interpretation of nature? Can our reference to natural laws make useless any reference to God, the Creator? My answers to these questions are negative because the basic notions of the laws of physics and the laws of nature remain unclear insofar as we do not refer to God as the ultimate basis of physical order.

GOD AS THE BASIS OF COSMIC ORDER

While modern technology provides spectacular confirmation for practical application of the laws of nature, contemporary philosophy of science still cannot explain the status of the laws of nature. Two main interpretive proposals are found in the so called *regularity theory* and in the *necessitarian explanation* of the laws of nature. The former is defended in the empiricist tradition, the latter — mainly in various versions of the neo-Platonic philosophy. According to regularity theorists, the laws of nature are nothing but regularities observed in nature. In the spirit of Humean critique of causality, they argue that all law-like statements of the form $(x) (Fx \Rightarrow Gx)$ assert merely a constant conjunction of the determined phenomena F and G. In this approach, one avoids referring to a vague concept of physical necessity and regards psychological intuitions or commonplace evidence as the ultimate criterion in explaining the observed order in nature. The necessitarian theory holds that the essence of the laws of nature cannot be reduced to the level of observed regularities, because the latter presuppose the existence of hidden necessary links that consti-

tute the order of nature, even if in a specific situation no empirical procedures reveal physical instantiation of these links.

The simple identification of the laws of nature with observed regularities cannot explain at least two important elements:

1. that the regularity itself is not a sufficient condition for being a
law of nature, since we have many uniformities which cannot be regarded
as laws of nature (e.g. no lake contains pure Pepsi Cola);

2. that the observed regularity is not a necessary condition for being
a law of nature, because there are probabilistic laws that permit local
irregularities, e.g. in stochastic processes when only on the large scale
we discover statistical regularities.

If we try to answer the question, what does the expression "the laws
of nature" mean? we must raise the questions: What does the implication
operator $=$ mean when we present the law of nature in the form: (x)
$(Fx=>Gx)$? How does one explain the relationship of physical necessity
between F and G, when it would be psychologically easier to conceive
of the universe as uncoordinated chaos with no necessary links between
phenomena, no order and no universal laws? Certainly, positivistically
minded authors can reject all similar questions as meaningless and sterile.
Such a practice seems, however, neither intellectually satisfactory nor
heuristically useful for the growth of science. Contrary to this practice,
many contemporary physicists go beyond the level of empirically confirmed theories and formulate the questions:

1. Why at all there are universal laws of physics?

2. Why this particular set of physical laws is instantiated in nature?
Are these laws absolute in the sense that no alternative laws could have
been instantiated?

3. Why we can describe complex physical processes using simple
mathematical formulae?

Similar questions cannot be answered on the level of scientific explanation. They require philosophical answers which must not be submitted to Ockham's razor, which is effective only on the level of research
characteristic of the natural sciences. The questions dealing with the order,
necessity and lawfulness belong to the classical questions of metaphysics.
Science cannot answer them for the same reasons that it cannot provide
mathematical description of human goodness. Nonetheless, we can find
rational answers if we treat seriously the philosophical doctrine of God
immanent in nature. Paul C. Davies adopts such a doctrine when he argues
in his Templeton Lecture: "The idea of God who is just another force or
agency at work in nature, moving atoms here and there in competition
with physical forces, is profoundly uninspiring. To me, the true miracle
of nature is to be found in the ingenious and unswerving lawfulness of
the cosmos, a lawfulness that permits complex order to emerge from

chaos, life to emerge from inanimate matter, and consciousness to emerge from life, without the need for the occasional supernatural prod; a lawfulness that produces beings who not only ask great questions of existence, but who, through science and other methods of enquiry, are even beginning to find answers" (Davies 1995 no 55, 34).

Certainly, not all authors must follow Davies in his theological comments to lawfulness (Davies 1995, 2-6). Not all physicists share his amazement that there is order rather than mess in nature. Statistical unanimity never remains the ultimate criterion of truth either in science or in philosophy. In the long tradition of European metaphysics there are many authors who found intellectual inspiration in the question: Why does something exist when there could have been nothing? This question, criticised as trivial by positivists, can be expressed in physical terms: Why are there the laws of physics at all, while nature could have been only an uncoordinated mess?

Dependent on philosophical preferences, various authors, in replying to this question, refer to God's immanence in nature or to the divine mind underlying physical laws. They speak of the Neo-platonic Logos or the philosophers' Absolute to present the cosmic order as a different name for the immanent God. Those who committed to agnosticism, as Heinz Pagels, refer only to the cosmic code (Pagels, 1983). All these expressions refer to the same reality, which in the neo-Platonic tradition was called a cosmic Logos and understood as a principle of cosmic order immanent in the laws of nature. This principle should be ontologically prior to any physical process, which is only an instantiation of the relationships determined by the laws in question. The existence of the Logos, conceived in this way, seems to be assumed implicitly even by these authors who develop ideas explicitly opposed to any form of theistic interpretation. For instance, Hawking in his famous proposal of the creation of the universe as a quantum object does assume implicitly that in the neighbourhood of the "no boundary state" our logical principles and the basic concept of rationality hold. If these assumptions are not accepted, one could not eliminate the possibility that before the boundary state S_i there existed different universes with laws different than our laws of Nature, different principles of mathematics, etc. Such universes could have been submitted to laws of physics unknown to our science. Their evolution could have been developed, for instance, according to the logic of our dreams while the edgeless "initial" boundary state would be just a state that happens from time to time in the discontinuous process of the cosmic growth. In this approach, Hawking's "no boundary" state of creation would be regarded only as a relative beginning of a new stage in cosmic evolution, not the absolute beginning. Without auxiliary assumptions it seems methodologically impossible to prove that in a discontinuously evolving universe this state could not have been anteceded by another physical state subject to different physical and logical laws. The pre-existence of the cosmic Logos, defining a set of basic principles of scientific rationality, seems thus necessary to prove that the state Si can be regarded as the boundary state not preceded by any physical phenomena.

One can try to defend Hawking against the former objection by arguing that in his model we cannot meaningfully ask what was *before* the "no boundary" time because to the time described by imaginary co-ordinates one cannot apply the very concept of temporal precedence in its classical understanding. To assess the value of such an objection one has to answer the question whether Hawking assumes the epistemology of realism in his cosmology or is he only an instrumentalist who constructs mathematical models and avoids the question of their correspondence with real processes in the physical world. In his *Brief History of Time: From the Big Bang to the Black Holes*, several statements suggest that the author rejects scientific realism in favour of cognitive instrumentalism. For instance, he describes as "meaningless" the question whether the time of our physical experience corresponds to the real or imaginary co-ordinates of the space-time representation of relativity theory. He argues that scientific theories do not describe reality but are merely useful mathematical models which describe regularities that exist "only in our minds" (Hawking 1988, 139). After such a strong declaration, one is amazed to read, two pages later, that physical cosmology is so successful in "describing events" and cosmic laws and that in the cosmological picture of the completely self-contained universe without boundaries there is no place either for a Creator or for theological explanations. Such arguments are mutually inconsistent. When one rejects realism in discussing the nature of time one cannot argue that objectively God does not exist. One can only claim that there is no place for God either "in our mind" or in a particular model. Such a claim scarcely could be called inventive. Cosmological models with a physical place for God would namely imply nothing but the well-known regress to methodology of the pre-Galilean epoch.

In various philosophical schools the cosmic Logos mentioned above is described as the Absolute, the field of rationality, the formal field, etc. To avoid terminological debates and to shed new light on the nature of this Logos, we can define its nature in the language of relationships determining both cosmic evolution and its scientific study. In this class of relationships one may distinguish a proper subset of relations that are instantiated in the physical processes as well as in the actual scientific procedures. In our physical world, e.g. in the hadron epoch, no law of the evolution of galaxies was instantiated since there were no galaxies at that time. In research practice of medieval physics no normalisation procedure was accepted because the quantum phenomena were unknown at that period. Consistently, we are entitled to claim that the initial Logos containing all scientific principles and physical laws is only partially instantiated in the actually existing cosmic structures and in the process of scientific growth. Its reality is disclosed in the observed physical phenomena through their conformity to the principles of theoretical physics which implies the effectiveness of this physics in predicting new facts as well as the effectiveness of the language of mathematics in describing physical phenomena.

When describing God's presence in the evolving universe one may refer to various modes of existence in various cosmic epochs. At our level of phylogenetic development the species *homo sapiens* remains especially attracted by interaction between individual macro-objects as well as by the aesthetic experience of the beauty of nature. The evolutionary processes played the decisive role in making the human eye sensitive to the electromagnetic waves in the band 8×10^{-5} - 4×10^{-5} cm and the human ear to the sounds of frequency in the band 16×10^3 - 20×10^3 Hz. These biological predispositions were formed in human organisms only in the recent period of cosmic evolution. Combining God's immanence with the psychologically strong experience of the beauty of nature appears thus a late invention that was impossible in billions of years of the earlier cosmic evolution. When we explore these earlier stages of evolution, we come to the epoch when no individual macro-objects existed. For instance, in the lepton era there were no planets, no rocks, flowers and birds. Can we speak of God's immanence of nature when we try to write off the anthropocentric vision of the universe? In what sense can we speak of God's immanence when cosmic space was filled with electrons, mesons and neutrinos? In metaphysical terms we can regard all these particles as contingent beings and relate them to the divine Absolute as an ultimate ground of *creatio continua*. In the novel cosmological proposals dealing with the initial creation out of nothing we find solutions where originally no particles and no physical substratum exist. For instance, in the already mentioned Hawking-Hartle model of creation at the original no-boundary state there are no physical objects except for laws of quantum cosmology, universal principles of logic and the wave function of the universe. When we speak of God's immanence in this universe we can refer only to His existence in the universally valid links that appear physically or logically necessary. The subsequent cosmic evolution can be described on the basis of these laws. They are thus regarded by philosophers as an expression of the cosmic Logos ultimately grounded in the divine Absolute. Since all physical events which constitute the later stages of the cosmic evolution are submitted to these laws, it is justified to speak of God's immanent presence in all physical processes.

TWO BASIC FORMS OF GOD'S IMMANENCE IN NATURE

When explaining God's immanence in nature, Thomas Aquinas distinguished God's presence by His power, essence and all-embracing knowledge (S.Th. q.VIII, a.3). This theory of immanence was developed almost five centuries before the discovery of the basic principles of Newton's dynamics. At that period mathematics was already applied to describe the orbits of planets, but its role in terrestrial physics was still unclear, especially after the breakdown of Nicholas Oresme's attempts to describe human emotions mathematically. The astonishing role of rational elements in exploration of physical processes was demonstrated by Newton when on the basis of his mathematical account he called into question the adequacy of empirical data provided by John Flamsteed on the basis of telescopic evidence. This procedure might have been regarded as controversial by adherents of empiricist methodology who stress the role of inductive reasoning in science. As a matter of fact, it merely expressed the basic conviction that scientific research aims not at simple description of the observed facts but at the discovery of hidden stable relations that are instantiated in physical processes.

These stable relations in nature, which justify speaking of rational cosmic structures, are often described in terms of physical necessity. Thanks to Alvin Plantinga's profound analysis one can no longer defend the positivists' opposition between logically necessary propositions and contingent physical laws (Plantinga 1978). Explanations provided by modern theoretical physics cannot be regarded satisfactory unless we re-establish the scholastic notion of the necessity *de re*.

The physically necessary connection of natural events is expressed in nature in two basic forms: i) in the actually observed set of physical and biological laws; ii) in the theoretically possible evolution of physical systems predetermined by the laws of nature even if the latter remain uninstantiated at given stages of the cosmic evolution. For psychological reasons, the study of the second indicated possibility seems more interesting because it discloses the failure of empiricist philosophies to explain the nature of the cosmic order. On the one hand, God manifested in evolutionary novelty, which in earlier epochs remained merely a pure possibility, brought so many ardent controversies after Darwin. On the other hand, the same God of cosmic novelty was described by Augustine and Nicholas of Cusa as the ultimate ground of cosmic changes.

GOD'S IMMANENCE AS THE UNINSTANTIATED POSSIBILITIES

Why were the adherents of the doctrine of God's immanence in nature not predisposed to regard laws of nature as an expression of His immanence? Why did they tend to look for God rather in special events, especially when the latter appeared inconsistent with the laws of nature? How can one explain why the concept of the *creatio continua* has remained so fuzzy even now when various physical "mechanisms" of creation out of nothing are described in many scientific theories?

Certainly, the present state of the philosophy of God's immanence depends on clashes between explanations proposed in theology and in the natural sciences. In scholarly practice of the growing science, the reference to the laws of nature very often resulted in eliminating earlier theological as well as pseudotheological explanations. It inspired a mentality in which God was pursued either in the absence of any physical laws (the God of the gaps) or in capricious behaviour contrary to the laws of physical determinism. While Baruch Spinoza in his philosophy of pantheism tried to equate God and nature, his critics developed an opposite approach in which God was opposed to natural causes. As a result, instead of Spinoza's adage *Deus sive Natura*, we received the dictum *aut Deus aut Natura* – either God or nature. This new opposition prevailed in the long-lasting tradition of Christian authors who were inspired by the phrase "order, number and measure" (*Wisdom* 11:20) as well as by the Vulgate translation of *The Letter to the Romans* 13:1 "quae a Deo sunt, ordinata sunt". This tradition resulted in the idea of the universe as an "ordinata collectio creaturarum" which was developed at the School of Chartres in the 12th century.

Why should we abandon as ungrounded this tradition in which one looked for God's immanence in unpredictable events rather than in the order of causal regularities? Probably it resulted from an improper form of respect for the thesis of God's transcendence to nature. It seemed more justifiable to search for this transcendence in miraculous events than in constant regularities submitted to the universal laws of nature. We find all unusual events psychologically interesting while repeatable regularities seem trivial and obvious.

The acceptance of God's immanence in the laws of nature does not preclude the doctrine of divine transcendence. God hidden in physical and biological laws cannot be pantheistically reduced to the level of natural order. To contend that He is more than the order of nature, we must not, however, deny His immanent presence in the observed regularities. God's immanence in nature as well as His transcendence can be reconciled in the so called philosophy of panentheism. There are various versions of panentheism. In its most general form this philosophy contends that the being of God is not only immanent in nature, by including the whole universe and permeating it, but also transcendent, in the sense that the universe does not exhaust God's being. St. Paul the Apostle is regarded as its protagonist when he spoke of the world permeated by the immanent God in whom "we live, and move, and have our being" (*Acts* 17:28)

The thesis of God's immanent presence in the laws of nature should not be regarded as a result of an empiricist approach in which the observed suggestive regularities are identified with God. Contrary to such suggestions, it implies overcoming epistemological empiricism, because in the process of cosmic evolution an important role is played by these natural laws, which were uninstantiated in earlier cosmic epochs. For instance, in the early stages of the cosmic evolution there were instantiated neither Kepler's laws of the motion of planets nor biochemical laws of human metabolism because there were no planets and no human beings at that epoch. The uninstantiated laws of nature revealed their actual existence in the process of cosmic evolution when more complex structures emerged. An empiricist or an agnostic could regard this emergence either as a consequence of more fundamental laws or as a fact resulting from combination of accidental physical conditions. Moreover, for a theist the emergence in question reveals God who is involved in the process of *creatio continua*.

The immanence of God in (uninstantiated) natural laws constitutes the ultimate ground for cosmic rationality because these laws determine the realm of the possible cosmic evolution. Heinz Pagels' analogy with the genetic code seems appropriate here to explain the role of God who influences the process of cosmic evolution. In the growth of the biological sciences, for a long time the role of genetic factors was misunderstood when defenders of the theory of preformation believed that properties encoded in human embryos exist in the same manner as the physical properties of adult individuals. In this common sense empiricism they only quarrelled about whether measureless sequences of human beings pre-existed in Eve's ovary or Adam's sperm. The rise of modern genetic required overcoming common sense stereotypes and introducing new categories so remote to naive empiricism.

POSSIBLE OBJECTS IN CUSANUS' ONTOLOGY

In contemporary debates dealing with the ontological status of the so called possible worlds (resp. possible objects) the most adequate explanation of the results of contemporary science seems to be provided by the standpoint of modal actualism in its versions developed by Alvin Plantinga and Robert Stalnaker (1979). This explanation of the nature of possible objects remains especially close to the philosophical position that was developed in the 15th century by Cardinal Nicholas of Cusa. In his dialogue *De possest* the cardinal argues that through inquiry of visible objects we can discover both the invisible unactualised possibilities and their invisible Creator. The insight into the essence of the visible physical phenomena directs our attention to their creative Power, which brings them into actual being. In accordance with the teaching of St. Paul from his *Epistle to the Romans* (1:20), in the created world we discover the immanent as well as the transcendent Creator in whom there are unfolded all possibilities before their instantiation in the actual visible world (Nicolai de Cusa, De possest, 5, 3f; 14, 3-8). Since all beings are enfolded in God, the process of cosmic changes discloses the presence of an immanent God who unfolds the possible in making them the actual. God, understood by Cusanus as *posse ipsum*, constitutes the ultimate rationality of the cosmic evolution and makes the cosmic order rational not only on the level of observed regularities but also on the level of unactualised possibilities of the physical growth (Casarell 1990, 7-34). God's role cannot be reduced to the role of an additional factor filling up the newly discovered gaps in our knowledge because He himself overcomes the basic distinctions between the possible and the actual. On the one hand, by determining the domain of the possible he constitutes the final ground of cosmic rationality and defines its laws of physico-biological evolution. This form of immanence in nature can be described in universal categories. On the other hand, his creative presence can be discovered in particular processes, in which there are actualised events that originally belonged to the domain of pure possibilities. These two forms of God's immanence in cosmic order, the order understood statically as well as dynamically, represent two basic forms of God's interaction with nature. Laws of nature and evolutionary novelties can be regarded as their counterparts described in modern science.

DEUS ABSCONDITUS IN COSMIC HISTORY

Instead of God hidden in Heisenberg's uncertainty, or expressed in the so called physical chaos, we propose a model, in which the role of God immanent in cosmic history is contained in laws of nature as well as in what we metaphorically call the "boundary conditions". The expression denotes theologically conceived boundary conditions in which non-physical (i.e. biological, psychic, spiritual) factors are also taken in consideration in a system considered "from God's point of view" (again metaphor). Cosmic history as well as the history of our individual existence run as they run because, for an omnipotent, atemporal God in the moment of initial creation, all data dealing with the future physical and biological evolution were already known. He must not enter secretly in the domain of nature by remaining hidden in quantum microintervals, because as a cosmic Logos he was able to define his specific role in these "boundary conditions". In these conditions his potential answers to possible human behaviour, our free actions, prayers etc. were already contained. Attracted by the persuasion of concreteness, so suggestive for our phylogenetic propensities, we are often predisposed to look for God in special interventions and in particular gaps in the body of scientific knowledge. Contrary to our psychological biases, he is rather the God of the whole than a God of holes in our knowledge.

The model proposed must not imply any form of reductionist pandeterminism either ontologically or logically conceived. One cannot argue that in this model our prayers are useless because everything was ab aeterno pre-established by God. Such an argument would be unjust at least on 1) theological, 2) personal and 3) epistemological level. From the standpoint of theology, one cannot fancy predicting the future of cosmic and human evolution on the basis of knowing the "boundary conditions" of the evolving universe. When all theological aspects are taken into consideration, these conditions *ex definitione* are considered in the system which is envisaged only by God and as such they contain information transcendent to any human mind. In this system, God's foreknowledge remains nothing but time independent knowledge, in which all data, our prayers included, are pondered by an atemporal God in an eternal "now".

In a personal frame of reference we can distinguish the "physical" state of the praying person and certain principles concerning the reality of grace in the same manner as we distinguish the physical conditions and the laws of nature in scientific explanation. Prayer changes the status of the praying person. This change must not necessarily deal with physical properties. It may refer to mental states or spiritual motives. Prayer creates also a new possibility for grace's action in our life. This action was *ab aeterno* envisioned by God. His immanence in the life of the particular human person depends on the co-operation of this person with God's grace. One cannot thus argue that the evolving universe unfolds only possibilities predetermined by God and independent of any human action.

From the standpoint of epistemology, we must furthermore take into consideration the possibility that the universe in its logically described global structure remains a counterpart of a rich logical system in which the Gödel uncompletability theorem obtains. As a result, in such a system there must be problems that cannot be answered by using any consistent set of algorithms. In a nontrivial structure of the relationships instantiated in physical phenomena a form of *ontological incompleteness* may be manifested in such a way that any form of reductionist philosophy must collapse because certain phenomena cannot be reduced to a few basic principles in a same way as in rich logical systems certain sentences cannot be deduced from the accepted axioms. Roger Penrose provides the problem of human consciousness as an example of such problems when he argues that maybe the human brain is a kind of computer, but it has been programmed by 'the best programmer in the business'. "We cannot know this mysterious algorithm, but Got does and it was he who instilled it within us, rather than its having arisen by a process of natural selection" (Penrose 1995, 25).

While following the cited argument, I would not follow Penrose in his opposition between God and natural selection. Probably psychic phenomena cannot be reduced to their physico-biological substratum. Certainly, God instilled these phenomena within us. It would be, however, a risky theology to suggest to him that he should have done it in a special intervention and not in the process of natural selection. Leaving aside the detail of Penrose argument, I would like to stress that the argument itself suggests the interpretive possibility that the traditional distinction between physical and logical objects may be overcome in the cognitive framework of cosmology when we try to determine the deepest structure of the universe. In his comments to the contemporary search for the Theories of Everything, John D. Barrow seem to intimate such a possibility suggesting that in its deepest structure the universe is not a great symmetry but a computation. He claims: "The ultimate laws of Nature may be akin to software running upon the hardware provided by elementary particles and energy. The laws of physics might then be derived from some more basic principles governing computation and logic. This view might have radical consequences for our appreciation of the subtlety of Nature, for it seems to require that the world is at root discontinuous, like a computation, rather than a continuum" (Barrow 1995, 62).

Regarding the bedrock structure of the universe as a *continuum* is relevant for our concept of cosmic rationality as well as for the acceptable explanatory models. It does not influence, however, the essence of the presented argument for God's immanence in nature. Whether we regard the universe as a continuum of laws and symmetries or rather as a process of discontinuous computations, the immanent divine Logos manifests its presence both statically, in the already instantiated universal cosmic laws, and dynamically — in the process of actualisation of events that in earlier stages were nothing but a pure possibility. In this framework the process of ceaseless creation reveals the same Logos that was already contained in the logical structure of the "boundary conditions".

Certainly, there are many psychological questions that arise when we regard God in a purely rational way as the principle of cosmic order and evolutionary novelty. When many dramatic questions of our age are formulated, such a vision creates many problems in the context of existential experience. When we raise the problem of God's immanence in the laws of nature we cannot avoid the intriguing question: Was God present at the Auschwitz crematories? There is an irony in the fact that the crematories in question functioned according to the principles of standard thermodynamics and a silent God was present in the heart of a most tragic human experience. To understand both his presence and his silence one has to refer to the drama of Christ's crucifixion. One cannot explain the drama of Golgotha in rational terms of common-sense logic. God is not only in laws but also in love and suffering. The means chosen by him to redeem his people transcend our psychological stereotypes and our rational discourse. They seem to indicate that God present in nature is not only immanent in cosmic order but also transcends it.

REFERENCES

Alston, W.P. 1989: *Divine Nature and Human Language: Essays in Philosophical Theology*, Cornell University Press: Ithaca.

Alston, W.P. 1993: "Divine Action, Human Freedom, and the Laws of Nature", in: *Quantum Cosmology and the Laws of Nature: Scientific Perspectives on Divine Action*, ed. R.J. Russell, N. Murphy, C.J. Isham, Vatican Observatory Publications.

Barrow, J.D. 1995: "Theories of Everything", in: *Nature's Imagination. The Frontiers of Scientific Vision*, ed. J. Cornwell, Oxford: Oxford University Press.

Casarella, P.J. 1990: "Nicholas of Cusa and the Power of the Possible", *American Catholic Philosophical Quarterly*, vol. 64, no 1.

Davies, P.C. 1995: "Physics and the Mind of God", *First Things*, no 55.

Davies, P.C. 1995: "Paul Davies & Critics: An Exchange" *First Things*, no 58.

Galileo Galilei 1890: *Le Opere di Galileo Galilei*, ed. A. Favaro, Florence: G. Barbera.

Hartle, J.B., Hawking, S. 1983: "Wave Function of the universe", *Physical Review* D 28, 2960 — 2975.

Hawking, S.W. 1988: *A Brief History of Time: From the Big Bang to the Black Holes*, New York: Bantam.

Moore, A.L. 1889: "The Christian Doctrine of God", in: *Lux Mundi*, ed. C. Gore, Murray: London.

Nicolai de Cusa: *Opera omnia*, vol. 11, Hamburg: Felix Meiner Verlag 1973.

Pagels, H.R. 1983: *The Cosmic Code: Quantum Physics as the Language of Nature*, Bantam Books: New York.

Penrose, R. 1995: "Must mathematical physics be reductionist?", in: *Nature's Imagination: The Frontiers of Scientific Vision*, ed. J. Cornwell, Oxford: Oxford University Press.

Plantinga, A. 1978: *The Nature of Necessity*, Cambridge University Press.

Plantinga, A., Stalnaker, R. 1979: *The Possible and the Actual: Readings in the Metaphysics of Modality*, ed. Michael Loux, Cornell University Press: Ithaca and London.

Polkinghorne, J. 1993: "The Laws of Nature and the Laws of Physics", in: *Quantum Cosmology and the Laws of Nature: Scientific Perspectives on Divine Action*, Vatican Observatory Publications, Vatican City State.

Polkinghorne, J. 1995: "The Metaphysics of Divine Action", in: *Chaos and Complexity. Scientific Perspectives on Divine Action*, ed. R.J. Russell, N. Murphy & A.R. Peacocke, Vatican Observatory Publications, Vatican City State.

Spini, G. 1966: "The Rationale of Galileo's Religiousness", in: *Galileo Reappraised*, Berkeley: University of California Press.

Thomas, O. 1991: "Recent Thought on Divine Agency", in: *Divine Action*, ed. B. Hebblethwaite, E. Henderson, Edinburgh: T & T Clark.

Weber, R. 1986:. *Dialogues with Scientists and Sages: The Search for Unity*, London: Routledge and Kegan Paul.

THE ROLE OF
THE ELECTROMAGNETIC INTERACTION
IN DEFINING THE IMMANENCE OF GOD

LAWRENCE W. FAGG
(*Washington, D.C., USA*)

Abstract: The elementary properties of the four known forces, or interactions, of nature (nuclear, electromagnetic, weak and gravitational) are described primarily in terms of our dependence on them for our existence. It is then shown that compared to the other three interactions, how much more intimately dependent we are on the electromagnetic interaction (EMI) and its radiation (light) in all aspects of our living experience. How this interaction, and especially light, serves as a primary medium or symbol for human spirituality is then described.

Given this ubiquitous presence of the EMI in one form or another in both our secular as well as spiritual lives, I will discuss the extent to which made the EMI serves as a physical correlate for the immanence of God. As such I will argue that the EMI plays a vital role in our ability to define, sense and understand the nature of God's immanence.

Keywords: electromagnetic, immanence, indwelling, light, natural theology, quantum electrodynamics, photons.

INTRODUCTION

A vast manifold of examples of wondrous natural phenomena from the growth of plants to the operation of the human body undoubtedly runs through the minds of scholars in their contemplating God's indwelling relation to us and the world, that is, God's immanence. However, as I attempt to describe in what follows, virtually all of these phenomena and/or our awareness of them depend directly or indirectly on the electromagnetic force, or interaction. This being the case I will maintain that to fully understand God's immanence we must meaningfully interpret the electromagnetic force and its awesome universality, which plays a major role in making the apprehension of that immanence possible. This hypothesis is not only based on the premise of universality of the electromagnetic force in general, but also on the nature of the photon of electromagnetic radiation, or light, the carrier of this force, in particular. The primality of light as an indispensable element in our daily lives, as a means of communication for all humankind, and as a manifestation of divine presence suggests a uniquely proximate connection between the physical and spiritual worlds. These along with other related considerations are the basis for a second hypothesis supportive of, and concurrent with, the first: that the electromagnetic force to a remarkable extent is a physical correlate for the immanence of God. In this paper I deal only with the immanent, not the transcendent aspect of God.

To provide background and support for these hypotheses, the four forces of nature and their relative impact on our lives will be reviewed in the next section. A very brief historical survey will introduce a description of the pervasiveness of the electromagnetic interaction in the third section. In the fourth section how this interaction and especially light, its radiation, serve as a primary medium and symbol for human spirituality will be discussed. How electromagnetic phenomena may serve as a possible link between the material and spiritual worlds is treated in section five. In the final section arguments will be presented in support of the two hypotheses cited above, especially for understanding the vital role the electromagnetic interactions plays play in sensing the immanence of God.

THE FORCES OF NATURE

As far as we know today there are four known physical forces in nature. The strongest of these is the nuclear force, which, for example, keeps quarks together to form protons and neutrons and in turn keeps protons and neutrons together in a nucleus. Next in order of strength is the electromagnetic force which, as emphasised in this paper, is the fundamental mechanism that makes our operation possible and that of most of the world to which we usually relate. The third is known as the weak force, which comes into play in the radioactive decay of a nucleus and many other elementary particle phenomena. By far the weakest of the four is gravity.

Despite the difference in their strengths, the electromagnetic and gravitational forces are both distinguished by the fact that they are long range forces in contrast to the other two, which have very short ranges. In particular the electromagnetic force between two electrically charged bodies and the gravitational force between any two bodies with mass are both proportional to the inverse square of the distance between the two bodies. Although this means that these two forces become weaker the larger the distance between the bodies, it also means that however weak they become, in principle they never die out to exactly zero.

Therefore by their natures the electromagnetic and gravitational forces can lay claim to some kind of spatial universality, if only because their range can be so extensive. Indeed in the case of gravity it is its great range that renders it the dominant force cosmologically. The theory of general relativity tells us that mass and space-time are intimately interdependent, so that it is the distribution of gravitationally interacting masses in the universe that defines the limits of the space of the universe. Furthermore, it is the mutual gravitational attraction that slows the universe's expansion and controls the interaction of planets, stars and galaxies.

It is also true that the other two forces (weak and nuclear), although of very short range, play a very vital role in sustaining the balance in cosmic nature that makes possible our existence. For example, if the nuclear force were weaker, deuterium (heavy hydrogen) could not form to go on to make helium, resulting in a universe made up of hydrogen only and we would not be here. If it were stronger, there would be too much helium, and we would not be here either. The nuclear and weak forces drive the processes that form the heavier nuclei in supernova explosions, which later lead to the formation of second and third generation stars, such as our sun. It is such heavier nuclei that are at the core of the atoms and molecules making up our bodies.

So while the gravitational, nuclear and weak forces are unquestionably vital, in this paper I focus attention solely on the characteristics of the electromagnetic force because, as will be seen, this force and electromagnetic radiation (or light), its carrier, are by comparison with the other forces so much more intimately dominant and omnipresent in our lives and the way we sense the world.

THE PERVASIVENESS OF THE ELECTROMAGNETIC INTERACTION

With a set of equations of elegant simplicity and symmetry James Clerk Maxwell in 1873 showed that electricity and magnetism were simply aspects of one force, electromagnetism. This can be considered a major early step toward the realisation of just how extensive the domain of the electromagnetic force or interaction (EMI)[1] is.

One of the most important results of Maxwell's work was that the electromagnetic field predicted by the theory turned out to propagate at a speed about equal to the speed of light, as experimentally measured at that time. It was soon realised that the whole spectrum of radiations, radio waves, infrared, visible, ultraviolet, X-rays and γ-rays, were all electromagnetic radiations moving at the speed of light. "Light" has now become a generic label for all electromagnetic radiations.

Just how intimately light is associated with electro-magnetism and how universal it is in a general sense was revealed in the next major refinement of electromagnetic theory. This came soon after World War II when Richard Feynman, Julian Schwinger, Shinichiro Tomonaga and Freeman Dyson formulated quantum electrodynamics (QED). This theory reconciled Maxwell's theory for electromagnetic phenomena with the universally applicable basic theories of quantum and relativity. Although the quantum behaviour of light as photons had been known for some 40 years, the theory gave a comprehensive and consistent description of all electromagnetic phenomena, in particular photons. QED, although applicable only to electromagnetic phenomena, is by far the most accurate theory in all of physics, predicting numbers that agree with experiment to better than one part in a billion (Feynman 1985, 7).

QED showed that there are both observable and unobservable photons and that the electromagnetic force between electrically charged particles is carried by the unobservable photons, called virtual photons. Though they cannot be directly observed their existence is certified by the fact that without including them QED calculations could not yield results which are in such incredible agreement with experiments.

In part because of the accuracy of QED, but also because of the wide technological application of electromagnetic theory, the electromagnetic force or interaction is known far better than the other three forces. Its effect and presence in all aspects of our life and relation to the world is ubiquitous. Electrons are constrained to orbit around the nucleus of an atom by the electromagnetic force via its virtual photons. It is the same interactive "glue" that keeps atoms together in a molecule so that all of chemistry and biology at root operate via the electromagnetic force. For example, this force makes it possible for bacteria, the smallest living cells, to exhibit the purposeful mobility, coherent collective action, and remarkable sophistication they do in their growth and survival (Shapiro 1995, 209). Bacteria as well as all other biological organisms are from a thermodynamic viewpoint open, far-from- equilibrium systems which exchange matter and energy with their environment for their sustenance and growth.

Humans are the farthest-from-equilibrium system of all, but as with less complex organisms the coherent action making possible this dynamic balance depends on the EMI. Thus we ourselves, and all our organs, are run by this mechanism, from the interactions of blood cells to the activity of neurons in the brain firing signals to each other across the synapses that separate them. The electronic imaging techniques currently being used to locate the regions of the brain activated by thoughts or emotions are based entirely on electromagnetic phenomena.

Light from a fire, gasoline consumption and explosives (except for the nuclear bomb) all proceed via this interaction. It is the same force with its photonic "glue" that governs the incessant interplay of the molecules in air and water that collectively unite their motion to give us sound and ocean surf. While it is gravity that keeps us, all earthly objects, and the atmosphere attached to the Earth, it is the electromagnetic force with its mediating photons binding the atoms and molecules tightly together in solid objects that is the prime factor along with certain quantum effects[2] in keeping the table lamp from falling through the table, and the table from falling through the floor. It is this force that makes possible all modern communication: telephone, radio, TV, satellite, etc. The wonders of laser technology, including the ease of delicate eye surgery, are based on this force.

Furthermore, whether we are examining the microscopic realm of elementary particles with sensitive and sophisticated instruments or probing the heavens with giant telescopes, the knowledge we gain is mediated by the EMI. Virtually all experimental studies of the other three forces, whether in the microscopic or the cosmologic realm, are conducted through an electromagnetic "filter". This, of course, includes the operation of all the computers and complex electronic instruments that store and analyse the data, and that make calculations based on the data. The now-famous cesium atomic clock is based on the fact that the cesium atom in one of its transitions between energy states emits photons which oscillate at precisely 9,191,631,770 cycles per second. This has now become the time standard accepted universally throughout the world.

However, for this discussion perhaps the most relevant property of the EMI and its mediating photons of light is a multitude of very low energy, subtle, electromagnetic quantum events that make possible the life of vegetable and animate nature as well as humans and their consciousness. It is such a manifold and incredibly organised array of what Geoffrey Chew calls "gentle quantum events" (Chew 1985) that vivifies the functioning of our brains as described above as well as our body's activity and supports the presence of our consciousness.

The extreme subtlety of the events is quantified in recent experiments in microbiology which show that voltage gradients as low as 10-7 volts/cm and frequencies between 0 and 100 Hertz (cycles per second) are involved in the interaction between cells in living creatures (Adey 1993). All plant and animal life is bathed in, and interacts with, a sea of such very low frequency radiation that envelopes the earth. This is independent of the additional radiation superimposed by technology (Adey 1993).

Obviously one could go on indefinitely giving examples of how universal electromagnetism is in our internal and external experience. For no other phenomenon of physical nature so totally and intimately permeates and affects our lives and our world, providing the means by which humans can in turn sense nature and the presence the sacred.

THE ROLE OF ELECTROMAGNETISM AND ITS RADIATION IN HUMANKIND'S SPIRITUALITY

With this capacity of complete permeation, light, the radiative aspect of the EMI, has served as a primary symbol for the spirituality of men and women since the dawn of human consciousness. Moreover in the mystical experiences cited below it has actually served as some form of medium for relation to God. It has been an abiding catalyst for inspiring hope in worshippers throughout history.

Light has perennially figured prominently in characterising the nature of God's posture with respect to humankind. Scriptures of religions world-wide are replete with the use of light to symbolise God's provident and salvational relation to men and women. In the Old Testament, to cite a very few examples, God dwells in light (Ex 24:10) and is the light of Israel (Isa 10:17) and a light to the Gentiles (Isa 42:6; 49:6). Also in the New Testament Jesus is the "light of the world" (Jn 5:19; 8:12; 9:5; 12:35). He is the light for revelation to the Gentiles (Lk 2:32).

In the Quran light proceeds ahead for believers (Sura 62:12-15) and is provided by God so that believers may walk straight (Sura 62:28). The Svetasvatara Upanishad, often called Hinduism's theistic Upanishad since it synthesised traditional meditation with worship of a personal god, speaks of "the great Purusha, who is luminous like the sun, and beyond darkness" (Chap. III, vs. 8); "He is the Ruler and the Light that is imperishable" (Chap. III, vs. 12).

The spiritual goal of the adherent of most religions in one form or another is enlightenment, moksha in Hinduism, Nirvana in Buddhism, Satori in Zen. The verb enlighten has light, directly or indirectly as its derivative in many languages throughout the world (as examples in Europe: erleuchten in German, éclairer in French, iluminar in Spanish, in Russian).

In many of the spiritual paths travelled by the Christian Mystics light has been a major feature in the visions they have experienced. For example, St. Theresa of Avila speaks of a "light which knows no night" and Mechthild of Magdeburg "the flowing light of the Godhead" (Underhill 1930, 248). Christian saints are pictured with a halo of light surrounding their heads. When Yahweh spoke to Moses, it was via the burning bush. Paul's conversion on the road to Damascus was accompanied by blinding light. Many of those who have had near death experiences report finding themselves at the final stage of the episode in the presence of a "Being of Light," that exudes unquestioned warmth and love and requires unequivocally honest response (Moody 1976, 58-64).

The quiet, calm glow of a small candle has been a spiritual symbol and aid to engender a sense of divine indwelling for men and women for millennia. Such use of candles to symbolise the spirituality expressed in rituals is found in religions throughout the world.

The foregoing brief survey of various examples demonstrates how universal is the use of light as one of humankind's most intimate symbols of spirituality. Whatever God there may be has provided the photon of electromagnetic radiation as an indispensable ingredient of our daily lives, as a means of communication for all humankind, and spiritually as a symbol or manifestation of divine presence.

Although the spiritual implications of light dominate the discussion in this section, it should be noted that other aspects of the EMI provide an underlying physical grounding for other forms of spiritual experience. Many such experiences have involved hearing voices, interpreted as messages from God, messages of solace, hope or challenge (Underhill 1930, 281). But here again it is electromagnetic interactions communicating between the brain and inner ear that made these auditions possible. The spiritual sustenance received in the tactile contact that occurs in an embrace with a holy person or in laying-on-of-hands in a ritual or prayerful blessing, is also supported by the physical mechanisms of the EMI.

Thus a consideration of the EMI with its encompassing physical characteristics suggests an uniquely proximate connection between the physical and spiritual worlds.

ELECTROMAGNETIC PHENOMENA AND THE IMMANENCE OF GOD

Indeed there is no physical mechanism closer to constituting a link between the material and mental worlds of humankind than the EMI with its complete ubiquity in all aspects of experience. The exquisitely subtle electromagnetic exchanges that are the basis for the operation of the brain reveal how proximally related are mind, both conscious and unconscious, and matter in that marvellous organ and should be sufficient testimony for the EMI's potential for serving as a link between the two.

An alternative approach to the idea of a link would be to consider the possibility of some kind of interface between mind and matter. But here again, if there exists such an interface, then the domain of the EMI extends the effects of the matter it vivifies right to this border.

While it may be argued that the mind serves as a mediary between matter and spirit by virtue of the mind's consciousness of spiritual experiences, it can also be argued that spirit and matter enjoy a direct relation without such a mediary. There are certainly many sources that could be used in implying such a direct relation in the scriptures of major world religions as well as the writings of religious philosophers.

However, it must be emphasised that in speaking of matter and spirit, or mind, and their interface, there is no intention of seriously espousing or even implying any kind of dualism. All that is being claimed here is that whether there is a bridge between mind or spirit on the one hand and matter on the other, or whether they are part of some form of as yet incomprehensible continuum, the EMI is at the frontier of matter with its tendrils probing toward mind and spirit, informing them and responding to them.

Although they do not specifically treat the role that the EMI plays, there are thinkers whose approach to the physical phenomena of the natural world deliberately implies the immanence and influence of God or some sacred presence. Alfred North Whitehead's metaphysics, replete with subjective metaphors, posits that the natural world is propagated by units or quanta of experience called "actual occasions," influenced, but not determined, by God (Whitehead 1929, 158).

Teilhard de Chardin sees all matter vivified in a life-like or preconscious interaction. He speaks of the "within of things" as an inner aspect of all elements of nature. For him there is no sharp demarcation between life and non-life; life could not evolve unless inanimate matter possessed the potential for life, if not itself already possessing some form of primal, incipient life (Teilhard de Chardin 1959, 71-8).

While not based on the Western concept of God, another insightful view of the nature of indwelling can also be found in Eastern religious philosophy, for example in the Taoist and Shinto traditions. The Tao is the mysterious quiet that pervades the natural world. The Tao is the way of harmony of man and woman with the vibrant serenity of enfolding nature. The Tao is the healing way of return to enlightened passivity, genuine spontaneity and inner peace (Ta-Kao 1982, Welch 1957, Kaltenmark 1967).

In Shinto the objects of worship are sacred spirits, or kami. All beings possess spirits and can be considered potential kami. Trees and mountains are worshipped and the mystery of nature is enshrined in places of special grace and beauty (Ono 1962). The soft trickle of a fountain in a Japanese rock garden is an endearing legacy of this enshrinement. Certainly these qualities of the Tao and Shinto convey a general sense of immanence, an aura of inherent grace underlying the natural world.

Whether the world is suffused with the grace of the Tao, or Shinto, vitalised by Whitehead's actual occasions, or evolving via Teilhard's matter embodying embryonic life, I believe that all three of these concepts can be significantly supplemented by considering the universal grounding afforded by the EMI. Whitehead speaks of an actual occasion "prehending" or appropriating a certain pattern of "eternal objects" in its process of what he terms "concrescence" i.e. maturation or becoming. The eternal objects are ideal, abstract qualities such as shape, colour, number, etc. which are potentialities for realisation. But it is the subtle interaction of electrodynamic quantum events, the multitude of mostly very low energy photons, real and virtual, that "carry out the orders" in the prehension operation.

It is the EMI that is the physical grounding of Teilhard's "within of things" and that is the physical agent for the thrust toward complexity, life and consciousness that he sees in evolving nature. The ultimately sensitive communication and collective interaction, first between molecules, then between cells, etc., that make possible evolution to greater complexity again is executed by the gentle probing action of a host of photons, real and virtual.

Also, in the case of the Tao and Shinto it is the whole manifold of keenly sensitive electrodynamic exchanges that give vitality to every rustling leaf, the petal of every flower, the mini-ecosystem of plant and animal life in a quiet pond, every bird, every squirrel, and all of us, the symbiosis of which allows us to sense the grace of enfolding nature.

Although in the thought of both Whitehead and Teilhard God can be seen in varying degrees as expressing both transcendent and immanent attributes, the principal concern in this paper is the nature of the immanent attribute. It is the immanent components of the views of the two men along with the perceptions of the Tao and Shinto that have been cited as examples here to provide supporting background for one of the hypotheses of this paper, that the EMI is to a significant extent a physical correlate for the immanence of God.

Certainly with the suffusion of electromagnetic phenomena activating all of the nature with which we usually relate as well as ourselves and our brains, the EMI constitutes at least a form of physical analogue to the immanence of God which is active on this earth. But I suggest that a stronger statement has some validity: that the pervasiveness of the EMI throughout our world can be considered as a physical correlate for God's immanence. First of all, none of the other physical forces mentioned earlier can compete as such a correlate because none covers this domain so broadly and intimately, reaching right up to the frontier of our consciousness. Without the EMI, not only would we not have the capacity to contemplate the idea of immanence, much less experience it, we could not even have evolved to be here.

The entire process of evolution on earth from the assembly of molecules to form first a bacteria cell, then the myriad of plant and animal species, and finally humans has occurred with the utilisation of the EMI. In each case the breakthrough to a greater level of complexity was carried out as the result of the incessant probing and testing by a host of force-carrying photons emanating from an assembly of molecules and/or cells restlessly, unremittingly interacting, serving as agents in the experimentation and search for a higher level of order or organisation. At virtually every such level of our natural world as it is today, from the most primitive and static to the most complex and dynamic, where the theologian, spiritualist or mystic can conceive of God's indwelling to occur, the EMI is there to provide a dynamic physical grounding. The ceaseless electrodynamic interplay of molecules or organisms at each level goes hand in hand with God's presence there, and serves in a kind of rough one-to-one correspondence as a physical correlate for that presence. Through God's grace the EMI was made to serve as a physical, admittedly incomplete reflection of God's ineffable, encompassing immanence. One interpretation of the foregoing remarks is that God may have made the EMI as a necessary condition for divine immanence in us and our earthly world, but it is of course not a sufficient condition.

ELECTROMAGNETISM'S ROLE IN DEFINING THE NATURE OF GOD'S IMMANENCE

Given the extraordinary extent to which the EMI serves as a physical correlate to the immanence of God as discussed above, it obviously must play a vital role in defining the nature of that immanence. It is true that in rigorously considering the full scope of God's immanence it is an immanence that must prevail throughout the entire universe. In principle God's indwelling is just as present on a star or in a galaxy a million light years away as it is here on Earth.

This being the case one can easily argue that in addition to the EMI the other three forces are equally powerful in demonstrating God's presence throughout the cosmos. For example, as noted earlier, the gravitational force is the fundamental mechanism by which stars and galaxies are formed. Without their formation we would not be here. The nuclear and weak forces are vital in producing the heavier elements of which we are made and in providing the solar energy by which we live here on Earth.

But here on Earth it is the EMI that plays the dominant role in our apprehension of God's immanence. It is the EMI that brings the warming radiation of the sun. It is the EMI that makes possible the incredible diversity of plant life from the lowliest patch of moss to the graceful beauty of a tulip. It is the EMI that underlies the vitality of the awesome spectrum of animal life from the smallest bacteria to the largest whale. It is the EMI that is the essential physical mechanism by which all organs of our body, especially our brains, maintain their functioning. In a word it is the EMI, more than any other force of nature that makes it possible to be aware of the immanence of God and in turn provides unifying influence in developing a viable natural theology (Fagg 1996).

Thus our sense of this immanence starts here on Earth. More specifically it starts with our own spiritual response to the wonder of our being alive, the wonder of the operations of our bodies, and the wonder of the fecundity of the natural world that enfolds us. The source of our awareness of God's immanence begins with our personal spiritual contemplation, reaches out to embrace the richness of the natural world here on Earth, and projects beyond to include the whole universe. But the fullest intensity of this immanence is localised primarily with us and our immediate environs.

One way to think of how the EMI helps to define God's immanence is to visualise this immanence as spread throughout the entire universe by the underlying physical agency of the four forces of nature. In particular the gravitational force and the electromagnetic force (with its radiation, or light) because of their great ranges serving as links helping to permeate the cosmos with this immanence. This picture can be thought of as the "horizontal" aspect or dimension of divine immanence. The dimension wherein all of the inanimate material universe is regarded as an expanse of "fertile soil" with potential to nurture the growth and flowering of this immanence in terms of life and intelligent life, such as found on this Earth. This growth and flowering I call the "vertical" aspect or dimension of God's immanence and it is the EMI that plays the vital role as the physical agent for its realisation. This "vertical" aspect in favoured localities of the universe such as the Earth finds its culmination in the consciousness of God's immanence.

It is on Earth (and possibly other planets on other stars), that the EMI is the physical agent for the evolution of life reaching upward, breaking through to full consciousness of God's immanence. And it is the EMI's ability to physically underlie the evolutionary "vertical" path culminating in the consciousness of God's indwelling presence on such "islands of life" in the cosmos that helps define that immanence.

In conclusion I hold that the EMI helps define the nature of God's immanence by showing that its most complete fulfilment is found in its "vertical" aspect characterised by life, especially conscious life. In a sense God's immanence with the agency of the EMI might be seen as radiating throughout the cosmos from localities such as Earth where intelligent life exists. Thus, because of the intimate association of the EMI with our ability to sense God's indwelling, the EMI plays a role in defining the nature of divine immanence. It defines it by making possible the fountainheads of consciousness of God's immanence which hold a favoured place in the encompassing universal firmament of God's "horizontal" immanence.

ENDNOTES

1. The words force and interaction are used interchangeably in physics.
2. A quantum effect that comes into play called the Pauli Exclusion Principle, essentially says that, depending on the characteristics of an energy state of an atom (or nucleus), only a certain maximum number of electrons (or protons and neutrons) can occupy that state, others are excluded. This means there is a limit to how tightly an atom or nucleus can be squeezed, a limit only exceeded in such astronomic bodies as neutron stars and black holes.

REFERENCES

Adey, W. Ross. 1933: "Whispering between Cells: Electromagnetic Fields and Regulatory Mechanisms in Tissue," *Frontier Perspectives: Journal of the Center for Frontier Sciences*, vol. 3, no. 2.

Chew, Geoffrey F. 1985: "Gentle Quantum Events as a Source of Explicate Order," *Zygon* vol. 20, no. 2.

Fagg, Lawrence W. 1996: "The Universality of Electromagnetic Phenomena and the Immanence of God in a Natural Theology," *Zygon*, vol. 31, no. 3.

Feynman, Richard. 1985: *QED*, Princeton, NJ: Princeton University Press.

Kaltenmark, Max. 1969: *Lao Tzu and Taoism*, Stanford, CA: Stanford University Press.

Moody, Raymond A. 1976: *Life after Life*, New York: Bantam Books.

Ono, Sokyo. 1962: Shinto: *The Kami Way*, Rutland, Vermont: Charles E. Tuttle Co., Inc.

Shapiro, James A. 1995: "The Smallest Cells Have Important Lessons to Teach," *Cosmic Beginnings and Human Ends*, eds. C. N. Matthews and R. A. Varghese. Chicago: Open Court.

Ta-Kao, Ch'u. 1982: *Tao Te Ching*, London: Unwin Paperbacks.

Teilhard de Chardin, Pierre. 1959: *The Phenomenon of Man*, trans. B. Wall. New York: Harper and Row.

Underhill, Evelyn. 1930: *Mysticism*, London: Methuen.

Welch, Holmes. 1957: *Taoism, The Parting of the Way*, Boston: Beacon Press.

Whitehead, Alfred N. 1929: *Process and Reality*, New York: Harper and Row.

THE BEGINNING OF THE WORLD
IN SCIENCE AND RELIGION:
A POSSIBILITY OF SYNTHESIS?

GREGORY BUGAJAK

(*Warsaw, Poland*)

Abstract: The beginning of the world seems to be a subject of investigations of contemporary sciences on the one hand, and a part of the religious truth on the other. Technical and scientific progress is conducive to constructing new models of the world and inspires modification or rejection of existing ones. The aim of the first part of this paper is to show some problems, among others methodological, theoretical and interpretational, that arise on account of current scientific theories. Certain basic features of a so-called scientific world view are pointed out. In the second part, the fundamental essence of the religious and theological truth of the creation is investigated. On the grounds of discussed issues, a possibility to achieve a kind of synthesis of both scientific and religious world views is considered in the third part. It is suggested that the general outlook on life could be a proper base for such a synthesis. However this solution proves to be unsatisfying, because of the mosaic, incoherent character of an outlook of life. The task to construct a more cohesive view of the world remains open. In the paper, a few lines for further investigation are drawn.
Key words: Big Bang, creation, faith, outlook on life, science, theology, world view.

I. INTRODUCTION

If we had wanted to pose the question of the beginning of the world some tens of years ago, we would have expected the answer either from theology or from philosophy. Only those two realms of human knowledge dealt with such ambitious problems. What the separate character of science consisted in, was — among others — that the greatest questions were not considered to be scientific ones. The aim of science was much more unpretentious, when scientists asked why an apple falls from the tree or what way parental characteristics are being inherited by progeny. Questions like what is the universe or how did it originate could not even come to scientific minds.

In early years of the XX century, the scientific world was shaken by some unexpected discoveries, which brought about a so-called revolution in physics. Among well known traits of this revolution was the fact, that scientists began to question the universe as a whole. That was when scientific cosmology appeared. Albert Einstein, after having formulated the equations of General Theory of Relativity, tried to apply his theory to the whole cosmos. This fundamental change in the very understanding of the aims and range of science enables us to pose the question of the beginning of the world in a wider context than solely theology or philosophy.

What science can say today about the world as a whole is expressed in the language of cosmological models. It is said that the best of them is the Big Bang model, known also as the Standard Model, which is widely confirmed by observations. Common view of the Big Bang says that several billion years ago, the universe began to expand from a state called the initial singularity. Here we come to the point, where science seems to meet the religious truth of The Beginning. But such a simple statement may satisfy only a journalist looking for sensation. Trying to look at the problem in some depth, we have to ask what the truths are which are to be met and on what grounds such a meeting can take place.

II. THE SCIENTIFIC VIEW OF THE WORLD

1. Science about the Beginning?

The reconstruction of the Standard Model is not the aim of the paper. The model is well known and its presentation can be found elsewhere (see e.g. Weinberg 1977, Novikov 1995, 152-181). Let us look instead at some of its important features, in order to see what kind of the picture of the world emerges from modern science.

A. Methodological problems.

1. The laws of science deal with practically a countless number of objects. Ohm's law, for example, refers not only to one conductor with electric current, but is applied to every such a conductor. In other words, science, when formulating its laws, deals with many events or objects of the same kind, whereas cosmology tries to establish laws governing the evolution of the whole universe, the universe, which by definition, is the only one, unique subject of cosmological investigation. It shows, that the methodological status of cosmology is quite different from the status of other sciences.

2. To enable any cosmological research one has to assume that the laws of physics are the same everywhere, in the nearest, as well as in

the farthest parts of the cosmos. In fact, if it was not the case, the science itself would be impossible. In an extreme case, one could not be sure that the outcome of an experiment in one laboratory will be the same as in the next door laboratory. This assumption is therefore basic for all scientific researches, but becomes especially important for cosmology, where we just cannot have a look at the remote region of the universe to check what the laws of physics look like there.

B. The problem of experimental confirmation. When looking at the evolution of the universe going back in time, we reach the point when unification of fundamental forces should take place. Firstly, electromagnetic and weak forces become the one interaction. The theory describing this unification has been expressed by S. Weinberg and A. Salam. It was also experimentally confirmed, therefore can be considered as well-established physical theory. The next step is so-called grand unification. It is supposed that strong interaction should join the former pair and unite with them. The problem is that it seems we have no chance to confirm the theory of grand unification, since energy required for such a process is far beyond possibilities of our laboratories.[1] Therefore this process of unification is only a supposed one, and the theory describing it is not, strictly speaking, a theory but a hypothesis.

C. Theoretical problems. When we look at the past of the universe on the basis of the Standard Model we reach the point (so-called 'Planck's era', when the cosmic clock would read $t = 10^{-44}$ s), where nothing can be said about events that were taking place before, if that before has any sense at all. We do not have a theory which would describe physical processes taking place under such extreme conditions (density: 10^{93} g/cm^3, temperature: 10^{33} K). It is supposed that to overcome this problem, we should have the theory of quantum gravity. It means a theory which would join somehow two discordant theories, i.e. the general theory of relativity and the theory of quantum mechanics. Many attempts has been made to formulate such a theory, but none of them is considered to be successful. What is more, whilst some physicists say that those attempts lead in a good direction and we will have the desired theory in a few years time, the others maintain that we have not even made the smallest step towards the solution as yet. The latter call this situation crisis in physics, which has lasted for the last few tens of years, since both great theories were formulated.

Let us note what follows, science does not say a word about initial singularity (if it ever existed). The Big Bang model is based on various physical theories that are either discordant with each other (general theory of relativity and quantum mechanics) or they have not been empirically confirmed as yet (different theories of grand unification). Some important theoretical problems have not been solved yet either (various kinds of so-called theory of supergravity). It leads to the conclusion that the view of the world which appears from the theory of the Big Bang is an incompatible mosaic and all our present knowledge of the universe does not reach the very moment of the Big Bang. Therefore, the common view of the world, which as many think, appears from the Standard Model is in fact wrong when maintaining that the world has originated at the moment of the Big Bang. Such a conclusion does not follow from the current scientific theories.

D. *Idealisations.* The construction of cosmological models is always based on various assumptions of an idealisational character. One of these assumptions is so-called cosmological principle.[2] One of its forms says that the space of the universe is homogeneous (there are no distinguished points in it) and isotropic (there are no distinguished directions). In other words, the universe looks the same from every point of space. Observations on a large scale seem to confirm homogeneity and isotropy of the universe, but on the other hand, it is obvious that the universe, as seen locally is not homogeneous nor isotropic.

Similar assumptions differ from one model to the other (there are for example anisotropic models). They just enable cosmologists to construct their models or at least make such a construction easier. So far as these models are confirmed by confrontation with observations, they can be taken as describing the real world with good approximation. What I want to stress here is the mere fact that every cosmological model has to have the assumptions of this kind.

E. *Interpretational problems.* There are two basic observational tests, which are considered to confirm the Standard Model. These are background radiation and red shift in the spectrum of remote cosmic objects. Indeed, both phenomena are predicted by the model: red shift, due to Doppler effect, is a consequence of the receding of galaxies, while background radiation is the remains of the early stages of cosmic evolution. However, beside these explanations of the phenomena in question, there may also be others.

The interpretation of red-shift in terms of Doppler effect is generally met with scepticism. For example, certain objects which seem to be close to each other have a different red-shift (Davies 1995, 152-154). Also recent estimates of the age of the universe (Pierce & others 1994) that are based on the classic interpretation of red-shift are less than the age of some stars. It could be that the oldest stars are not really as old as they appear, but as the astronomer M. Pierce says: "there is no evidence that there is a problem with our estimates of stellar ages" (quoted in: Begley 1994). Such difficulties make some scientists look for other explanations of red-shift and background radiation. The former would occur, for example, if the light from remote objects passed on its way through strong gravitational fields (so-called gravitational red-shift). The latter, in turn, may be a product of hypothetical astronomical objects that existed in quite recent epochs (Jaroszynski 1993, 217). Similar attempts raise more questions than they answer. That is why they are being rejected (cf. Novikov 1995, 127-129). The whole point is however, that although the explanations provided by the Standard Model are the best ones, they are not the only possibility.

It must be stressed, that what was said above does not mean shaking conquests of science. The Standard Model is rightly said to be one of the greatest achievements of scientists of the second part of our century.[3] The point was to show some characteristic features of the scientific view of the world. Various premises, methodological and others, that one has to assume when constructing the model of the universe, as well as theoretical and interpretational problems mentioned above force us to admit, that the picture of the world which is painted by science is surely not a composition of a realist-painter. If so, we must face the question: Does science satisfy our cognitive aspirations? Does it really provide us with the picture of the world'?

2. The aim of science

Ancient philosophers distinguished two ideals of knowledge:

scire propter scire - to know to know,
and
scire propter uti - to know to use.

Which one of them is being realised by contemporary science? When it comes to its achievements, one often indicates the great technological and civilisational progress that could be made thanks to scientific discoveries. Many devices and facilities that make our life easier or just possible exist thanks to science. Humans reign over the surrounding world better and better. Science makes our species *homo sapiens sapiens* the fittest of all species, giving us undeniable primacy in the struggle for survival (cf. Dunbar 1995, 47-56; 96). Is science anything more? The answer to this question is vital if we want to build our picture of the world on scientific theories. Let us note that certain features of this picture are of different importance, depending on which of the two ideals of knowledge is realised by science. If we want to act efficiently in the world, the problems like assumptions of theories or interpretation of experiments and observations can be considered as insignificant. But if we want to really *know*, to ask questions like what is the world or what is it like, it seems that the problems pointed out become more serious.

III. RELIGIOUS VIEW OF THE WORLD

1. The picture of the world and faith

A. Is the picture of the world the object *of faith?* One of the best known theologians of our times, K. Rahner says that faith is an answer to the revelation of God. This revelation is not just information on the intellectual sphere, but it is a call to devote in love the rest of life to the Revealing (Rahner & Vorgrimler 1963, 131-132). Faith is an answer that a man gives to a personal God. It is a dialogue between persons. Therefore, the object of faith is not a truth, nor any picture of the world in particular, but God himself.

B. Does faith suppose *a picture of the world?* The picture of the world has been changing, often drastically, for centuries. However, a member of an ancient nomadic tribe, whose world was restricted by the distance he could wander during his life-time, as well as a modern scientist looking at the most remote corners of the universe, both believed and believe in the same God. They pursue their personal dialogue with Him, independently from historic background and any language the world speaks in a given moment of history. Therefore faith does not suppose any picture of the world.

C. Does faith imply *a picture of the world?* Faith certainly implies a method that should be used to achieve this picture. It results in an admission that a picture obtained by using senses alone is incomplete and very much simplified. It forces one to admit that something exists, what no one ever saw or heard, what no one ever thought could happen (1 Cor 2:9). Something that we cannot touch by our mind or senses. But no particular picture of the world is implied by faith.

As we can see, faith has no bearing on the picture of the world. What about theology then? Does it provide such a picture?

2. The picture of the world and theology

Theology is a systematic attempt to understand and explain the revealed truth. Theology always seeks but never reaches the final answers or definite beliefs (cf. theology in O'Collins & Farrugia 1991). It leads to the conclusion that if there is any picture of the world in theology, it is — similarly as in science — incomplete and non-ultimate. What is more, if the object of theology is the revealed truth, one may ask what the essence of this truth is. J. Ratzinger, commenting on human needs to know what is on the other side of life wrote that the Bible has not been written to satisfy our curiosity. Reading it, we will not find out what is going on in the heaven, but how to get in there (Ratzinger 1978, 135). Therefore, the fundamental essence of revealed truth, which theology deals with, is the truth of loving God who saves mankind. It seems that the Revelation does not include any message about the world itself. On the other hand however, one may note, that the part of revelation is also the truth of the creation of the world. It raises an important question: What is the essence of this theological truth?

A. The act of creation in the history of the world. Let us look at the history of the world for the moment, where the act of creation should be placed. Such an attempt, although certainly tempting, will always lead to misunderstandings. The analysis of the history of the universe should be left to the sciences. God is not a hypothesis to fill up gaps in our knowledge. Where science is inadequate at present, there is reason to intensify scientific efforts, to propose brave new ideas, one of which will eventually prove to be accurate. It is certainly not a place where one may meet God.

B. God as the cause of the World. May we at least say that God is the cause of the world? Let us note that suggesting such a statement we would enter the field of philosophy, since the notion of cause is of philosophical character. But is that an essence of the truth of creation? K. Rahner and H. Vorgrimler express the idea of creation of the world as follows: "The world continues utterly and completely at each moment to be dependent on God (...) This relation between God and the world cannot be classed under a general notion of causality" (Rahner & Vorgrimler 1963, 325). From this point of view we must say that God is not the cause of the world.

C. God at the beginning of the world. One may say rightly, that God was at the beginning of the world. Here the beginning is not the first moment in a series of successive numerous and comparable moments, but the principle of the whole, which only enables its history (Rahner & Vorgrimler 1963, 20). Such a notion of beginning goes beyond the framework of sciences and philosophical notion of cause alike.

IV. CONCLUSIONS: A POSSIBILITY OF A SYNTHESIS?

If science can yield a picture of the world and if theology affords such a picture, both those visions have at least one thing in common: both are of hypothetical character, and what follows, relative and change-able. Being aware of this uncertainty and of those ifs, we may ask whether an attempt to obtain a kind of an overall view of the problem of the beginning of the world is possible. Where to find a supposed common ground for such a view?

1. Theology? Theology cannot play this role. History, with the ex-ample of Galileo, gives us the most convincing proofs of this.

2. Science? It cannot be science, because religious truths, regarding its essence, are beyond the reach of scientific method — beyond the fron-tiers of empirical reality, and God is not a useful hypothesis to fill up gaps in our knowledge.

The theory of separate character of the different planes of knowledge may be unsatisfying. Although there are many kinds of knowledge, an individual who asks the questions is one who naturally defends himself from cognitive schizophrenia. The need to construct a coherent view of the world cannot however cross out the results of reflection upon the kinds of knowledge that have been achieved in contemporary philosophy. What is left then?

3. General outlook on life. It seems that the proper base for meeting different elements of the picture of the world is an outlook on life. It is a set of convictions that everybody builds for his personal use. The char-acteristic feature of it is that it can be founded on different elements, not logically connected with each other, that come from many different sources. This mosaic character of the outlook on life, its immanent inco-herence, does not preclude however rationality. When constructing a ra-tional outlook on life, it is vital to remember the following:

a) to beware of a conviction that all valuable knowledge can be achieved in one way only, e.g. empirical.

b) do not be under the misapprehension that all kinds of knowledge are equal (common knowledge equal to science, science equal to mysti-cism, etc.).

c) each proposition, conviction which is to be taken as a part of an outlook on life, has to be accepted together with the objective estimation of its credibility. Not every proposition is of the same value, and none of them is an absolute truth.

Such a solution would not satisfy everybody, because of that independence of particular elements of outlook on life. Is there any other way?

4. The task to construct a cohesive view of the world is open. Here, only a few lines for further investigation can be drawn.

a) The character of the picture of the world that could be achieved in science on the one hand and in theology on the other, if it can be done at all, should be carefully considered. The main question is what the characteristic features of these pictures are (some of them have been pointed out above) and whether or not they are comparable.

b) All considerations at the point of contact between science and theology have to assume that God does not trifle with us. It means that a statement like: "The world was created fifteen minutes ago" cannot be rejected on the ground of empirical evidence. God could have created the world together with all fossils, red-shift, background radiation and so on. In such a case, practising science would be a nonsensical game. Therefore, similar statements have to be either rejected *a priori*, or a theological proof should be found that such a state of affairs is impossible.

c) The long-lasting controversy between adherents and advocates of the eternity of the world and its beginning will not be solved. It can be only re-formulated. The question of eternity or beginning of matter may be replaced by the question of eternity or beginning of the laws of nature. (cf. Hawking 1993, 132-133). Such a question will still be posed by philosophers, theologians and everybody who rationally builds his outlook on life.

42 G. BUGAJAK

NOTES

1. See comments on the subject in a paper by J. Horgan (Horgan 1994). The decay of a proton would be also an indirect confirmation of grand unification. Such a process, however, has not been reported as yet.
2. The epistemological status of this principle is not clear. It seems that the cosmological principle may be taken either as a methodological assumption or as idealisation of observations. In both cases however, it is a kind of more or less theoretical assumption.
3. Not everybody would share this point of view. J. Maddox maintains, that the Big Bang model does not meet Popperian requirements for scientific theory: In Popperian terms, it would be excellent if the Big Bang could be made precise enough to falsify (Maddox 1994, 13).

REFERENCES

Begley, Sharon 1994: "The Cosmic Dating Game", *Newsweek*, vol. CXXIV, no. 19, 55.

Davies, Paul 1995: *About Time. Einstein's Unfinished Revolution*, London: Viking.

Dunbar, Robin 1995: *The Trouble with Science*, London: Faber and Faber Ltd.

Hawking, Stephen 1993: *Black Holes and Baby universes and Other Essays*, New York: Bantam Books.

Horgan, John 1994: "Meta-physics of particles", *Scientific American*, vol. 270 (Feb. 1994).

Jaroszynski, Michal 1993: *Galaktyki i budowa Wszechswiata* (*Galaxies and construction of the universe* — in Polish), Warsaw: PWN.

Maddox, John 1994: "Frontiers of ignorance", *Nature*, vol. 372, 11-36.

Novikov, Igor D. 1995: *Black Holes and the universe*.

O'Collins, Gerald & Farrugia Edward G. 1991: *A Concise Dictionary of Theology*, New Jersey: Mahwah.

Pierce, Michael & others 1994: "Distance to the Virgo cluster galaxy M 100 from Hubble Space Telescope observation of Cepheids", *Nature*, vol. 371, 757-762.

Rahner, Karl & Vorgrimler, Herbert 1963: *Kleines Theologisches Wörterbuch*, Freiburg im Breisgau: Herder.

Ratzinger, Joseph 1978: *Eschatologie — Tod und ewiges Leben*, Regensburg: Friedrich Pustet.

Weinberg, Steven 1977: *The first Three Minutes: A Modern View of the Origin of the universe*, New York: Basic Books.

THE FINAL ANTHROPIC COSMOLOGY AS SEEN BY TRANSCENDENTAL PHILOSOPHY: ITS UNDERLYING THEOLOGY AND ETHICAL CONTRADICTION

ALEXEI V. NESTERUK
(*St. Petersburg, Russia*)

This article is addressed to scientists, philosophers and theologians and develops a philosophical criticism of the block of ideas of F. Tipler called "physics of eternity", "omega point theory" or "theory of Evolving God" (Tipler 1988, 1989, 1994), which emerged in the scientific media as a transcendent expansion of the Final Anthropic Principle (Final AP = FAP) (Barrow Tipler, 1986). We will call the whole block of these ideas Final Anthropic Cosmology (FAC). In comparison with some recent critical reviews of these ideas (see for example Stoeger, Ellis 1995), we will direct our criticism towards two special philosophical flaws of the FAC.

The Final Anthropic Cosmology offers an eschatological scenario for life to exist forever in the universe. This scientific utopia presupposes, in fact, a strategy of exploration of cosmic space and an attitude to the physical stuff of the universe which leads to the "cosmological crisis" (Nesteruk 1993, 1994a). But this cosmological crisis reflects, from our point of view, a misuse of scientific thought which is expressed in two philosophical mistakes: (1) the epistemological mistake of treating a theoretical notion of the ultimate future end of the universe in terms of experiential physics; (2) a scientific abuse and theological misinterpretation of the idea of human life and its values.

1. THE PHILOSOPHICAL MEANING OF THE BASIC STATEMENTS OF THE FINAL ANTHROPIC PRINCIPLE

The FAP itself appears in cosmology as an attempt to extend the validity of the *Weak* and *Strong* Anthropic propositions[1] beyond the present-day state of affairs in the universe towards the remote evolutionary future. It is done because of the fear of the possible *anti*-anthropic phase in the evolution of the physical universe either to the fireball of the Big Crunch (closed universe) or to the eternal cold (open universe).

The FAP postulates the eternity of physically understood *life* in the universe (Barrow, Tipler 1986, p. 23):

> **FAP**: Intelligent information-processing **must** *come into existence* in the universe, and, once it comes into existence, it *will* **never** *die out*.

If we treat this proposition as a *theorem* the word **must** refers to its necessary conditions and is assumed to be supported by implication of the Strong AP and/or Participatory AP. The word **never** indicates sufficient conditions, which can not be testified empirically because of natural boundaries of experience and probably can not be satisfied even in a theoretical form because of trivial *contra*-example: possible termination of humankind in a global nuclear conflict, any kind of doomsday syndrome etc. That is why the only possible way to treat the meaningful part of the FAP's proposition is to treat it in the form of an antinomy.

FAP-antinomy 1:

Thesis: Intelligent information-processing in the universe *will never die out*.

Antithesis: Intelligent information-processing in the universe *will die out*.

The appearance of antinomies in the FAP indicates that speculative cosmology started to seek an ultimate presupposition which does not presuppose anything else, namely the totality of the causal sequences of physical or cosmological phenomena. Later on we will call this totality as *underlying reality* (UR).[2] What is this UR in the concept of FAP? To make it clear we have to clarify the FAP's treatment of the notion of life.

(i) Life in FAP is treated mostly as an intelligent life which is not identified with human life. Intelligent life is associated with a computer: "a living human being is a representation of a definite program, rather than the program itself" (Ibid, p. 659). In other words "a living being" is any entity which codes "information"....Thus life is a form of information processing, and the human mind-and the human soul-is a very complex computer program" (Tipler, 1988; p.322). Life understood as an intelligent information processing could be possible not only in a human body, but also in other material structures;

(ii) In this case one can describe what it might be for life to exist: "If the laws of physics do not permit information processing in a region of space-time, then life simply cannot exist there. Conversely, if the laws of physics permit information processing in a region, then it is possible for some form of life to exist there. These limitations are analogous to those imposed by food at the biological level" (Tipler, 1989; p. 223).

(iii) Eternity of life or its existence forever presupposes that intelligent information-processing continues, along at least some future-endless time-like curve all the way to the future final temporal boundary of the universe. This requires that the universe must be closed and must contain a single final point (Omega-Point in Tipler's terms) in which the world-lines of all events in the universe will coincide and there will be no horizons. The quantity of information processed in all these curves coming to the Omega-Point (Ω) must be infinite, since "only if there are infinite number of thoughts in the future it is reasonable to say that intelligent life has existed 'forever' " (Barrow, Tipler, 1986; p. 660).

In the Ω, the world lines of all events which either have already taken place or they will take place in the future universe, will converge, i.e. Ω will be equivalent to all points of physical space-time being the result of its evolution (one can say that Ω is *immanent* to space-time). At the end of evolution the entire space-time will be incorporated in the Ω and we can say that it has the attribute of "omnipresence". The Ω contains an infinite amount of information about all events that have ever taken place in the universe, which makes it possible to attach to it an attribute of "omniscience". Since this information has been somehow produced by converting the matter into information through the total control of all forms of matter and energy by life near the Ω, we can attach an attribute of "omnipotence" to it. Finally since the Ω is the boundary point of the physical space-time, and is a completion of it, it doesn't belong to the physical space-time. It is an absolute end of space and time, i.e. beyond space and time (i.e. *transcendent* to the universe) "It is natural to say that the Omega Point is" both transcendent to and yet immanent in "every point of space-time" [2, p. 322]. Life in the Omega Point becomes "eternal" in the sense of timelessness.

The very existence of life and its "eternity" is, therefore, intimately connected with the existence of Ω, which appears to be a teleological cause for the universe to exist in the sense of being called into being by observers-participants (Participatory AP). Since the Ω immanent and transcendent to space-time, its experiential existence can not be tested (this indicates the transcending of physical understanding beyond the sphere of experience). That is why one can conclude that Ω does exist as an idea. And that is why any empirical propositions about Ω lead to antinomies. This means therefore that Ω is a specific kind of UR (understood as explained above), which is sought by Final Anthropic Cosmology through synthetic *a priori* propositions about the cause of all cosmological and physical *phenomena*. In other words the *physical concept* of the Ω becomes a *philosophical idea* about UR which forms an unconditioned unity of all possible predicates about physical world. But this idea, rigorously speaking, is not a subject of science. It is rather in a sphere of reason, i.e. philosophy. The FAP-antinomy can be reformulated now:

FAP-antinomy 2:

Thesis: There belongs to the world, Ω, whose existence is *absolutely necessary* so that intelligent information-processing in our universe will never die out;

Antithesis: There nowhere exists Ω as *necessary being* as the cause of the eternal intelligent information-processing in the universe, either in the world or out of it.

We realise now that the Ω is a kind of idea about UR, i.e. that $\Omega = UR\{FAP\}$. In our thought it is playing the role of the *absolutely necessary being*, i.e. God, and the whole complex of propositions about the Omega Point forms a *transcendental theological idea* which we denote Ω_{ur}. It is clear now, that the proper epistemological (and therefore theological) meaning of the Ω_{ur} can be revealed only by transcendental analysis.

When we speak about Ω_{ur} our rational consciousness touches, in fact, the deep inference to that of the divine, which makes us human and which constitutes our humanity. We feel this inference to God and feel at the same time of how it is difficult to express this God-manhood in words of discursive logic. Analysing scientific propositions a la FAP we discover some theological ideas which manifest our affinity with the divine.

The emergence of UR-like theological ideas in scientific thought points towards that intimate and inmost centre of our reality. If we recognise that the appearance of the notion of God in the form of Ω_{ur} is inevitable within Anthropic Cosmology, we must answer the question, what is the epistemological status of Ω_{ur}, i.e. what kind of divine reality we assign to God as Ω_{ur}, and what is our attitude to God-Ω_{ur} presented in thought. Another question which we should answer is: How does (or does not) this feeling of divine in a scientific experience affect us in earthly socio-anthropic being?

2. WHAT KIND OF THEOLOGY IS EXPRESSED IN THE IDEA OF _ur?

We discovered that there is an idea about Underlying Reality which appears in the Final Anthropic Cosmology, i.e. $UR\{FAP\} = \Omega_{ur}$.

Let us look at this idea from the point of view of the most general relations in which our representations of them can stand. *First*, there is the relation of these representations to objects as phenomena. *Secondly*, there is the relation of our representations to objects as objects of thought in general, whether phenomena or not.

In the *first* case understanding synthesises the manifold sense intuition according to the category of causal relation, each of which presupposes other causal relations. Reason postulates an ultimate presupposition, which does not presuppose anything else, namely the totality of the causal sequences of phenomena: thus there arises the idea of the *world*. The speculative physicist and cosmologist seeks to extend our knowledge of the world, as a totality of phenomena, through synthetic *a priori* propositions. But this procedure, Kant maintains, leads to antinomies of pure reason.

The Anthropic Cosmology definitely recreates the fourth Kantian antinomy, which concerns the existence of a necessary being. One can formulate a generalised FAP — Antinomy in the form similar to the Kantian antinomy (Kant 1933, p. 415):

> *Thesis*: There belongs to the world, either as its part or as its cause, something ($UR = \Omega_{ur}$) that exists as an absolutely necessary being;

> *Antithesis*: There nowhere exists any necessary being (Ω_{ur}) as the cause of the world, either in the world or out of it.

The thesis represents the point of view of dogmatic rationalist metaphysics, while the antithesis represents the empiricist point of view. The transcendental approach claims that we can avoid both the fallacies of metaphysics and the dogmatic materialism: we rise above the antinomies by limiting knowledge to its proper sphere leaving degrees of freedom for practical faith based on moral experience. The UR in description of the Anthropic universe (world of phenomena) should not be considered therefore as an independent and more fundamental entity of that world. This is rather the idea of reason, which plays some regulative role in establishing a practical attitude to our world.

In the *second* case the UR (Ω_{ur}) is sought by reason as the uncon-ditioned unity of all possible predicates. This cannot be found in the stuff of empirical perfections, but has to pass beyond the conditioned. It thus objectifies the indeterminate goal of its search as the *Ens perfectissimum*. It means that underlying reality appears here as a *theological idea*.

We can state that the Anthropic Cosmology presupposes implicitly a theology which originates from scientific belief in existence of UR {FAP} = Ω_{ur} as the *Ens perfectissimum*.

This theological trend as some kind of religious theory has a practical significance only being expressed in terms of human ethics. The choice of ethics is rooted, however in the fact of clear awareness of that episte-mological truth, that UR is merely an idea. The theology of Ens perfec-tissimum being observed through the prism of Christianity represents in some sense "the last resort and means: a unity of knowledge subserving an end which transcends all knowledge" (Lossky 1957; p. 9).

Any aspiration of scientific spirit towards the UR as the supreme end of union with God must be treated only as a kind of personal *mystical experience* of deification.

Any attempt to express this experience in "physically objective" terms, in terms of theories and strategies of exploration of the world, which takes place in FAP when the UR{FAP} = Ω_{ur} = God is qualified as a *physical* end of the universe must be treated (a) from the philosophi-cal side as an epistemological mistake (*transcendental realism* in the sense of Kant (Kant, 1933)) and (b) as a *cosmic temptation* (in the sense of Berdyaev (Berdyaev 1939)), which presupposes *desanctification of Na-ture* and *depersonalisation of man* (Nesteruk 1994; Sherrard 1987). This leads in the long run to contradiction with Christian theology.

3. THEOLOGICAL TREND OF F.J. TIPLER: ITS PHILOSOPHICAL MISTAKE AND CONTRADICTION WITH A CHRISTIAN THEOLOGY

There is a temptation, however, to treat Ω straightforwardly as a "physical object" (Ω_{ph}) i.e. as an element of reality in the sense of *tran-scendental realism* (Kant 1933, pp. 345, 439). This takes place when the uncritical physical understanding fails to realise the sphere of legitimacy of its mathematical propositions. This understanding ignores the warnings of antinomies and assigns by means of dogmatic metaphysics the content of its experiential (phenomenal) activity to the whole *Universum*. Yes, indeed, combining the geometrically understood immanent + transcendent properties of the Omega Point with three omni-attributes, this physical understanding claims that the Omega Point theory (OPT) "leads naturally to a model of an evolving God" (Tipler 1988, p. 323), i.e. to the statement, that $\Omega_{ph} \equiv$ *Evolving God*. But Ω_{ph} is understood mistakenly here as not a transcendental theological idea, but as a physical object, accessible by means of the physical theory (OPT) treated as physical theology. It means that this physical theology (OPT) is substituted for traditional theology, rejecting its mystical foundations of revelation and faith.

To achieve the Ω_{ph} as a kind of physical being (reality), life, according to Tipler, must exist forever in a physical sense of the word "existence". This kind of the existence of life, understood mostly as intelligent computer-like processing, presupposes, as we have seen before, a continuous and endless production of information in amount growing to infinity. One can ask: how could this be done in physics? Tipler's answer is straightforward: by converting all the matter stuff of the universe into bites of information. Since every bite of information produced requires some matter to annihilate, there is a deep contradiction of this scientific utopia with the initial premise of the FAP that the universe must be anthropic, i.e. human, forever. This contradiction can be formulated in the following anti-anthropic statement:

> to produce an infinite amount of information, the Anthropic (i.e. human) universe as a nature is supposed to be annihilated (*destroyed*).

One can assume that the OPT gives a mathematical prescription on how to organise intentionally the Cosmological Crisis (in analogy with the earthly ecological crisis) (Nesteruk 1993, 1994a, 1994b). This manifests the theoretical desanctification of nature by demoralised + dehumanised scientific understanding (Nesteruk 1994a). This cosmological crisis being a theoretical model of a speculative cosmologist and taken as an ideology of the global evolutionism indicates the tendency of *Homo scientificus* to dominate not only the terrestrial world, dooming it to environmental degradation, but also to dominate the whole *Universum*. One can suspect that such a scenario indicates probably a *spiritual crisis of **human** scientific thought*.

Where does the source of this spiritual crisis lie? What kind of mental flaws underlie the Final Anthropic Cosmology?

4. PHILOSOPHICAL MISTAKE OF THE *FAC*

The first flaw is a philosophical (and hence methodological) irresponsibility of the creator of the OPT, expressed in a typical layman's practice of substituting the mental models (ideas) about physical reality (Ω_{ur}) for reality itself (Ω_{ph}), leading to a kind of transcendental realism. According to Kant (Kant 1933; p. 439) "the realist in the transcendental meaning of this term treats these modifications of our sensibility [appearances, representations; AN] as self-subsistent things, that is treats *mere representations* as things-in-themselves" (Kant 1933; p. 439); "..the transcendental realist thus interprets outer appearances (their reality being taken as granted) as things-in-themselves, which exist independently of us and of our sensibility, and which are therefore outside us - the phrase 'outside us' being interpreted in conformity with pure concepts of understanding" (Kant 1933; p. 346)

The identification of Ω_{ur} with Ω_{ph}, which is done in the OPT, shows that the physical mentality which produces such theories is still bounded by pure concepts of understanding. It is far away from such special cognitive faculty as reason. This unawareness of a deep dialectical distinction between understanding and reason leads the author of the OPT to the fundamental fallacy. Such concepts about ultimate reality as eternity, infinity, omniscience, omnipresence and omnipotence, which could only be attributed to Ω_{ph} and which could only be a subject of reason, are treated straightforwardly by Tipler within the headings of physical understanding. He overlooks antinomies, which we have discussed above. Kant says that the problem of the transcendental realism is the following:

"... if we regard outer appearances as representations produced in us by their objects, and if these objects be things existing in themselves outside us, it is indeed impossible to see how we can come to know the existence of the objects *otherwise like* by inference from the effect to the cause; and this being so, it must always remain doubtful whether the cause in question be *in us or outside us*" (Kant 1933; p.347)

Instead of treating this doubt carefully using the philosophical method, Tipler prefers to stay on the grounds of pure concepts of understanding, and prefers to believe dogmatically that the cause of our representations about the Omega Point does exist in a physical sense outside us, and this cause is the Ω_{ph}.

There is an alternative, according to Kant,

"to admit that something [Ω_{ph}; AVN] may be in the transcendental sense outside us, is the cause of our outer intuitions, but this is not the object of which we are thinking in the presentations of matter and of corporeal things; for these are merely appearances, that is mere kinds of presentation which are never met with save in us, and the reality of which depends on *immediate consciousness*, just as does the consciousness of my own thoughts" (Kant 1933; p. 347-348).

This is exactly the point which shows that an advanced physics of the OPT is merely a creative power of imagination, which presents a structure of the personal mental experience of the author of the OPT, rather than anything else, which does exist as an empirical object.

5. SCIENTIFIC ABUSE OF THE IDEA OF HUMAN LIFE AND ITS THEOLOGICAL CONTRADICTION

The FAC treats people as finite state machines. Humanity as a phenomenon and the reality of people's life is displaced and with the substitution of "intelligibility". But "intelligibility" treated as computability of our thoughts does not make a distinction among variety of the human cognitive faculties which acquire the being in its totality in different ways. It is clear that there is something in us, which is completely noncomputable and irreducible to any objective expression. The *faith*, and *revelation* in response to it, *mystical experience* and various individual *feelings* and *perceptions* hardly can be reduced to any kind of objective computation and reproduced in a "program" that is run in the body as a computer. That is why the life in the FAC is not a human life at all in its entire experience. It is only a some kind of extraction that makes all individuals similar in their ability to produce thoughts. But this similarity denies the personal dimensions of human existence and completely leaves in the mist how are people associated to their individual biological bodies. Since the questions of morality are not covered at all by FAP's concept of life there is a great mystery about the values of being and the destiny of man.

In conclusion one can say that the idea about "life" which appeared in FAC is an idea about life which has nothing in common with human life as it has been understood by humankind during the whole history of its dwelling on the Earth. In fact one can state that there is a contradiction even in the very title of the Final Anthropic Cosmology because the "life" there has nothing to do with the anthropic, (i.e. human) life. This is rather a form of existence of some post-anthropic species in the same mental space, where the Ω_{ph} does exist. And that is why the horrible conclusions about the cultivation of this non-anthropic (i.e. non-human) life in the universe, which are proposed by FAC and OPT, lead inevitably to extermination of the actual human phenomenon.

The FAC's scientific abuse of the idea of human life becomes evident and explicitly contradictory when we compare it with a Christian anthropology. Christianity offers an alternative idea of divine humanity that establishes the *norm* for man. Christ, our idea about Christ, is the *perfect model* by reference to which we can answer the question about who we are. He is *the* man, "the first-born of every creature" [Col. 1:15], the *archetype* of which every man is, in terms of his potentialities, the image. The difference between Christ and us is that He is eternally God's Son, while we are God's sons because we are created in the image of Christ's divine humanity. And to be a son of God is to have the divine as the determining element of our being. Yet if God is the inmost centre of our reality, we are also examples of God-manhood. It is precisely this that makes us human and that constitutes our humanity. *To the degree to which we fail to attain a full realisation of this we fail to be human.*

If it is true that without the divine dimension the human dimension would be deprived of reality, it is equally true that without the human dimension the divine would be deprived of self-manifestation. If we allow divorce with God in thought (which exactly takes place in FAC), we, in fact, put the existence of God in big doubt, and hence the existence of ourselves. That is why when Tipler says that the "traditional God is superfluous" (Tipler, 1988, p. 314) he denies not only the existence of the Christian God, but also the existence of all those anthropic (human) individuals who are supposed to live in the universe forever in accordance with the FAP. This is an explicit logical and ethical contradiction to the initial aim of the FAC.

The physics that based on grounds containing this contradiction is sorrowful, as we have seen before. One can only add to this some words of Ph. Sherrard, who was a strong defender of the ideals of Orthodox humanity: "Having rejected the understanding that his life and activity are significant only in so far as they incarnate, reflect and radiate that transcendent spiritual reality which is the ground and centre of his own being, man is condemned to believe that he is the autocratic and omnipotent ruler of his own affairs and of the world about him, which it is his right and duty to subdue, organise, investigate and exploit to serve his profane mental curiosity or his acquisitive material appetites" (Sherrard 1987, p. 43). For although the body of man comes into existence from the underlying matter of the world and is independent in some ways of the soul, there is an indissoluble relationship between soul and body. But man has an affinity with the divine, while with his body he is linked to the material world. This is what gives him such a key position and role in the universe. He stands between God and the material world, between heaven and earth. Nothing is external to him. This is in contradistinction to that scientific view of things, which presupposes that the evolving universe is an object external to him. In this picture there is a loss of that consciousness in which nature is seen as a part of his own subjectivity and consequently there is a loss of the sense of man's decisive role in relationship to the rest of creation.

Christianity states that the destiny of the universe is in the hands of man. Because it is only through man fulfilling his role as mediator between God and the world that the world itself can fulfil its destiny and be transfigured in the light and presence of God. This is the only possible Christian theological alternative to the idea of Evolving God.

6. CONCLUSION

Our analysis of the main propositions of the FAC has proved that the majority of claims done by the OPT has no physical meaning. The OPT does not deal with physical entities as existing in reality; on the contrary it produces a mathematical model for some mental constructions based on some kind of internal and personal belief of the author of the OPT. This belief is that it is possible to catch a glimpse of ultimate reality by physical understanding. But this has nothing to do with established physics as well as with the traditional theology. In spite of the fact that the origin of this belief is rooted in natural religious predisposition to feel ourselves connected with the world of divine, the scientific community finds it sometimes irrelevant to speak about this true source of our existence, substituting, instead, some fixed ideas.[3]

It does not help the dialogue between science and theology; more than that, it can cause an impression of some kind of scientific fundamentalism in questions about human values, its ultimate reality and meaning, which can actually discredit science for one group of society and mislead other communities about real meaning of the traditional theology.

I am grateful to Prof. Lawrence W. Fagg for helping to polish the language of the paper.

NOTES

1. The *Weak* AP concentrates upon the privileged spatio-temporal location of intelligent observers in the evolutionary universe: they find themselves at a rather specific site, and at a later stage of the history of the universe. The *Strong* AP points to the specificity of the entire universe needed for the creation of human observers, at least at some stage and place within it. The physics of our world must be fine-tuned with great accuracy for that. Even tiny disturbances in the hidden harmony of the laws of nature would lead to a sterile world incapable of creating complex building units of intelligent life.

2. The ideas about Underlying Reality (UR) which appear in the Anthropic Cosmology have already been stated (Nesteruk 1995). The Strong AP introduces the idea of *many worlds* (MW), i.e. UR{SAP} = MW: The Participatory AP introduces the notion of a generalised *observer* (O), i.e. UR{PAP} = O.

54 A.V. NESTERUK

3. We find it useful to conclude with a quotation from a book that treats many of the scientific advances as a *scientific mythology*. Speaking about the Anthropic Principle M. Midgley writes: "Its authors feel the need of teleology for exactly the same reason that other people do - because they are not satisfied with unintelligible world - and are already so fully committed to this kind of faith that they see it as the only possible candidate. They disguise it heavily in scientific clothes because they think its naked form would be indecent (Midgley, 1992; p. 201)."

REFERENCES

Barrow J. D., Tipler F.J. 1986: *The Anthropic Cosmological Principle*. Clarendon Press, Oxford.

Berdyaev, N. A. 1939: *On the Slavery and the Freedom of Man*. YMKA-Press, Paris, (in Russian).

Kant I. 1933: *Critique of Pure Reason*. Translated by N. K. Smith. London (2nd edition).

Lossky V. 1957: *The Mystical Theology of the Eastern Church*. James Clarke, London.

Midgley M. 1992: *Science as Salvation: A Modern Myth and its Meaning*. Routledge, London.

Nesteruk A.V. 1993: *The Metaethical Alternative to the Idea of Eternal Life in Modern Cosmology*. DIOTIMA, v. 21, Paris: Librarie Philosophique J. Vrin, p. 70-74.

Nesteruk A.V. 1994a: "Ecological Insights on the Anthropic Reasoning in Cosmology: Ecological Imperative versus Cosmological Eschatology." Proceedings of the First International Conference Ecology and Democracy: The Challenge of the 21 Century, Ceske Budejovice, September 1994, pp. 110 — 113.

Nesteruk A.V. 1994b: "The Idea of Eternal Life in modern Cosmology: its Ultimate Reality and Metaethical Meaning". Journal of Ultimate Reality and Meaning, v. 17, no. 3, pp. 222 -231, Toronto University Press, Canada.

Nesteruk A.V. 1995: "Theological Meaning of Anthropic Cosmologies as seen by Transcendental Philosophy." Proceedings of the 7th Congress of IACP, Albi, France, July 18-24, 1995 (in press).

Sherrard Ph. 1987: *The Rape of Man and Nature*. Golgonooza Press, Suffolk.

Stoeger W.R., Ellis G.F.R. 1995: "A Response to Tipler's Omega-Point Theory". *Science and Christian Belief*, v. 7, pp. 163 — 172.

Tipler, F. J. 1988: "The Omega Point Theory: a Model of an Evolving God." *Physics, Philosophy and Theology* (Eds R.J. Russell et al), Vatican, pp. 313-331.

Tipler, F. J. 1989: "The Omega Point as Eschaton: Answers to Pannenberg's Questions for Scientists". *Zygon*, v. 24, no. 2, pp. 217-253.

Tipler, F. J. 1994: *The Physics of Eternity: Modern Cosmology, God, and the Resurrection of the Dead*, Doubleday.

COMMUNITY AND PLURALISM
IN COSMOLOGY AND THEOLOGY

DUANE H. LARSON
(Gettysburg, USA)

Abstract: An adequate description of a world-view shared by physical cosmologists is an ambitious task. Yet there are commonalities among disparate cosmologists which, when collated and summarised, may bear striking consonance to world-views intended or implied in contemporary Trinitarian theological constructions. For example, the implied ontology of quantum theory, especially as qualified by Bell's theorem, suggests that there might be a "multidimensionality" to the universe wherein our space-time dimension is a concrescence of the higher dimensionalities. In such a frame, time is embedded in eternity, rather than in opposition to it. Explicit attention to the work of Andrej Grib, Stephen Hawking, and Christopher Isham is given in the effort to discern such common ground. Resonances are then sought in the work of contemporary Trinitarian thinkers like Jürgen Moltmann, Wolfhart Pannenberg, and Colin Gunton. Their variations of Trinitarian panentheism suggest a cosmology that is consonant with that of the sciences here explored, and this appears to be the favoured mode of theological reflection on a global scale today. Its most visionary implication is that contemporary diversity is to be affirmed insofar as it contributes to community, and this diversity is grounded in the quintessential community of the triune God: Father - Son - Holy Spirit.

Key Words: Trinity, temporality, eternity, quantum physics, world-views, community, pluralism, cosmology.

The assignment for this conference was to consider the concept of world-views in theology and science. The very theme implies acknowledgement of the virtually necessary pluralism which characterises thinking, praxis and discourse in and between communities. That we do communicate is the empirical fact that denies the possibility of radical pluralism - solipsism writ large. But, clearly, that communication as a task implies that all the bio-mechanical, behavioural, psychological, cultural and existential fodder that make for human being is exceptionally complicated and nigh impossible to parse. If such is the case for human individuals, how much more so for communities.

The term "world-view" itself allows no positivistic purchase. It enjoys no consensus regarding its meaning (Osthuis 1985; Honner 1988). World-views, like words themselves, can be described at best in somewhat general terms. Theology's modes of divine description, it appears, apply in a rather critical realist fashion to all objects of reference; adequate description, while self-acknowledged as fuzzy, is still more referential than fuzzy, and it steers between - while still bumping up against - analogy and apophatism. The term "paradigm" has been used of the sciences as pertaining to world-view. But this, too, is referentially problematic. Even though Kuhn provided a rather narrow definition of paradigm as "*standard examples of scientific work* that embody a set of conceptual and methodological assumptions" (quoted in Barbour 1990, 50; emphasis mine), the term has become a popular means to identify what a community might pre-reflectively hold in common. In other words, the current use of "paradigm" accents the second half of Kuhn's definition, and so functions as an *ad hoc* synonym for "world-view."[1]

Can, then, some common coin be found with respect to world-views in theology and science? My introduction so far certainly would claim an ameliorated status of whatever world-view might be found betwixt them, if at all. But this is not at all to suggest that the effort is fruitless. Quite the contrary, precisely when one recognises the qualified character of description that pertains to both endeavours (as well as to all description of "the real"), one may enter a well buffered boat that can steer the river waters between the rocky shorelines of the analogous and the apophatic. Further, of course, there are more clearly marked reference points in the disciplines of theology and science that do more than serve as rules for language games (contra Lindbeck 1984); they serve more as pointers to the real, "where" the "real" is, and in such a way are quite necessary to a good map, with which aid our boat may be steered. It may be, then, that differing world-views find convergence when such markers are shared. Conversely, common markers, held to be far more referential than not, may well imply a convergent world-view, or, at minimum, a consonance of views. It is with this extended caveat that I propose in this paper to identify certain markers within and between natural science and Christian theology, so then to suggest what those markers might imply about a "world-view" that could be shared by, if not already operative for, the both.

Now, where might such markers be found, and how "large" ought they to be to count as significant for the theology-science conversation? Since extrapolation along inductive lines from the very small has its clear and present dangers, I suggest that larger possible fields of inquiry are the more appropriate candidates for comparison; indeed, I would suggest the largest, most speculative, field of all: ALL THAT WAS, IS, AND/OR CAN BE. I do not proffer this area of inquiry out of arbitrariness, arrogance, or even combination of same. Since world-views, systematically rendered, are coherent accountings of a totum, it would make good sense to start there. Further, science has its specific and correlative area of inquiry in cosmology, and theology its own in the perduring question of the relationship of time to eternity. If any possibilities of shared, or at least consonant, world-views - *eidoi tou kosmou* - are to be discerned, it is reasonable to suppose they would more evidently pertain to things cosmic. I shall take the terminology of "time and eternity" as the "shorthand" referring to fundamental work in cosmology, as it is certainly also a shorthand in theology for the relation of transcendent divinity to the creation. My first effort, therefore, will be to seek commonality of thought among cosmologists, a community of diversity, to be sure!, all the more diverse by the highly speculative nature of the enterprise. In section one, after exploring what would seem to be some shared themes in cosmology today, I will ask if any commonality of thought about time and eternity might be garnered from three disparate cosmologists and whether such commonality might constitute the fundaments of a world-view. In the second section, I will attend to summary themes in contemporary Trinitarian theology, posing the argument that this allegedly esoteric doctrine was initially in its own right a shorthand, as it were, meant to evince a world-view that held together "the one and the many". It should be clear by the end of that section that theology in its most speculative locus bears striking resemblance as an agenda, if not in its very view of cosmic structure (however seen in a glass darkly), to apparently shared themes in natural scientific cosmology. A brief concluding section then will explore implications of the possible consonances under the themes of community and pluralism.[2]

I. QUANTUM KNOWING AND THREE COSMOLOGISTS

It may seem an odd choice to set the stage for a discussion of cosmologists with a review of epistemological and ontological implications of quantum theory. Why speak about the small before the large? Contemporary cosmology recognises, however, the exceptional significance of quantum theory, particularly insofar as it is the physics of the very small that is at debate with respect to the initial singularity of our universe. The three cosmologists whom we shall consider, too, explicitly appropriate quantum themes, and so it may be helpful here to set the stage at least for them, noting that we have not the privilege of covering all the issues, and can but barely allude to many related ones.

And since it bears clearly on the matter of "world-view," how one might observe something and what one may observe, let us begin with

Heisenberg's Uncertainty Principle. It stands in the centre of many con-
troverted claims in physics and cosmology. According to many interpretations of quantum physics, this "observer-observed" complement is a
result of the non-local, holistic character of sub-atomic phenomena, at-
tributable particularly to the influence of Bell's Theorem. But "where",
or "how", or even "whether" reality is observed is open to controversy.
The controversy seems to centre around the "realism" claims an interpretation adopts. If the claims are poised between realism and anti-realism,
an agnostic, or positivist, instrumentalism might be posed as a practical
compromise. Interpretations rarely, however, assume an anti-realist stance.
Niels Bohr has been argued to represent the instrumentalist agnostic approach, which holds that an observer cannot ask whether an electron has
position. This view is, even so, weakly realist, not anti-realist. Heisenberg,
as another example, presumes an "ontology of indeterminism", which assumes something more of a realist epistemological stance, however critically qualified it is. Herein there is at least the possibility that one may
invoke the Aristotelian categories of formal and efficient causality, along
with reference to substantial phenomena. This "school" of interpretation
maintains that somewhere in the causal chain of observed-instrument-ob-
server the observed comes into "reality". What path or history an electron
might take, of course, could not be predicted with exactitude. The superposition of a quantum event can only be interpreted probabilistically.

We must note that Heisenberg's Principle applies with equal force
to any attempt simultaneously to measure time and energy. As with the
Heisenberg uncertainty relation with respect to momentum and position
of a particle, the uncertainty in the measurement of energy of a particle
times the uncertainty in the time it exists can never be less than Planck's
constant (Polkinghorne 1984, 50). Suppose, for example, that the energy
of a nucleus is well known. Concomitantly, the period of time over which
the nucleus might instantly decay is less known. The quantum theory
exposes an intimate relationship between energy and time. This leads us
to a most nagging question of quantum theory. Clearly, no observer can
be "objectively" detached from the observed; what is measured is nature
exposed to our way of measuring. The uncertainty is all the more radi-
calised when one acknowledges that the observer's measurements are but
themselves electrons distorting the electrons of the object observed. This
is unlike the degree of detachment which the observer may exercise in
the macroscopic world wherein a sensitive enough instrument might have
little affect on that which is measured. How then is something so unpredictable and unvisualizable "found" or "realised" in the act of measurement? How is the observed connected to the observer and how does it
finally achieve its "observability"? Where along the causal chain does the
collapse of the wavepacket occur?

One may surmise, then, the strength of an observer's "quantum knowing" falls between and includes the poles of instrumentalist agnosticism and, at the least, weak realism. How one defends one's epistemology - and, by direct implication, one's ontology - centres on the argument as to where the even is indeed knowable. Somewhere along the journey from the unobservable object to my knowledge of it the actual result of the observation is fixed. Somewhere along the line the quantum rules change; the "spread-out" superposition must somehow turn into one unique reality. The informal arguments suggest what von Neumann demonstrated more exactly with his mathematics: "if the whole world is described quantum-mechanically, in terms of proxy waves, then somewhere between the quon source and final result a 'wave function collapse' must occur" (Herbert, 151). Some physicists go so far as to say that it is the observation itself which fixes the result. Others would say that the result is fixed somewhere along the chain before the actual observation of it. The intervention of consciousness is certainly the latest point possible. And, it seems, equally possible is the realisation of the event at any prior point. With respect to describing the reification - and the knowledge thereof - of the quantum world, there are, of course, general "schools" of agnostic instrumentalism, ontology of indeterminacy and quantum logic. John Polkinghorne suggests a taxonomy of four different possibilities of interpretation (Polkinghorne 1984, 63ff.) Nick Herbert is more nuanced yet in suggesting eight (Herbert, 63-68). I will outline four options in more depth and with additional qualifications.

The first option, consonant with agnostic instrumentalism, is to suggest that it is all a matter of epistemology. The wave function is understood simply as my description of it. I am not worried so much about the "deep reality" of the matter as I am with an adequate description of what is going on. If I cannot obtain a satisfactory measurement in one way, another way might do. It is a matter of my practice, as well as overcoming my ignorance. Any real change, therefore, will be in my mind, not in the measured reality itself. The disjunction between physical reality in the quantum world and my involvement in it is precisely my problem, according to this line of interpretation. Many would argue that this position is a kind of idealism. This is partly so. I would argue more that it is after the fashion of a sterile pragmatism, concerned not so much with reality as with results. In either view, the point of physics as inquiry into an "external" world is denied and ultimate inquiry is demoted to psychology or, at best, an anti-metaphysical epistemology.

A second answer, known as the Copenhagen Interpretation, presses just a bit further than the first. Copenhagenists (after Niels Bohr) believe that the Quantum Theory does not permit the option of believing that unobserved entities possess their own attributes. In fact, they claim that such attributes prior to measurement are non-existent. In such a way the

Copenhagenists take as a central clue the Uncertainty Principle. Attributes are measurement-dependent. Therefore, whatever knowledge is establishable about any microcosmic event, it is established at the stage of measurement, once the objects "get large" under the intervention of classical measuring apparatus. The Copenhagen Interpretation cannot explain how the apparatus *chooses* one history over another; the best the Copenhagenists can say is that this simply happens. Ontologically, the implications are perhaps shocking. The use of classical instruments (which is our only choice!) divides the world into the "uncertain quantum world and the objectifying world of measuring instruments" (Polkinghorne 1984, 64). Indeed, Copenhagenists maintain, as it were, that the quantum world therefore is objective but objectless; the only "hard fact" is the measuring device itself (Herbert, 162).[3] This is the Copenhagen Interpretation at its most modest. There are, however, two interpretative positions which elaborate upon this.

A stronger Copenhagen view holds that it is not the apparatus which so defines the result as it is the observer. The end of wave-packet collapse is supposed here as the very observer who peeked into Schrödinger's cat's box. But this is also the intervention of an agency altogether different from the preceding possibilities. Proponents of this school of observer-created reality maintain that by your choice of what attributes you look for you choose what attributes a system may seem to possess. Eugene Wigner is a proponent of this view, as well as John Wheeler (though he has become a proponent of a stronger view yet). Observer-created reality may be capsulized in a maxim from Wheeler. "No elementary phenomenon is a real phenomenon until it is an observed phenomenon" (Herbert, 164).

A subset of the Strong Copenhagen interpretation, that of quantum logic, posits an objective quantum realm, which the human observer "reads into" classical measurement. Observation is something of a translation process, as it were, wherein some data indeed is lost in the translation. Where the "realist" claim in the Strong Copenhagen interpretation abides with the observed event itself, and brackets off discussion of reality theretofore, quantum logic presumes a reality that "becomes" empirical reality in the act of observation. Rather interestingly, in other words, here is an epistemological synthesis of a Bishop Berkeley with an Immanuel Kant; the act of perceiving is said to translate into this existence a *Ding an sich*, which is otherwise opaque to human knowing. If this position somehow mirrors Critical Realism, it also is a Critical Idealism. Even so, the *Ding an sich* allows a speculative lattice model which is heuristically helpful and referential. Quantum logic argues that at this "lower level" or "more primordial" existence there applies a non-distributive onto-logic. This argument holds that a particle is neither "here" nor "there" in the quantum world, but is "here" *and* "there" (or even "here and here" and "there and there"). The "lattice" of an electron's path contains options which, within its logic are non-commutable, in contrast to typical human Boolean logic wherein the event co-ordinates are commutable. The very positing of such a lattice in this style of argument can press a distinctly, though unique, realist position.[4]

The second derivation of the Strong Copenhagen interpretation shifts the weight of the epistemology - and causality - beyond the observer in the observer/observed nexus to the consciousness behind the observer. When combined with a strong form of the Anthropic Principle,[5] this observer-created reality position is stretched into a "consciousness-created reality" position, the philosophical consequences of which are even wilder. Those who maintain a consciousness-created reality stance differ from the observer-created reality folk inasmuch as an inanimate object - like a computer - rather than a sentient being may be the observer. The observer creates the reality by choosing what kinds of attributes to measure. But "consciousness- created reality" goes a step further in arguing that it is consciousness which actually decides what game to play; consciousness "creates reality" by deciding "what particular attribute shall materialise" (Herbert, 174). This position maintains that when attributes are not observed they exist as an objective but objectless superposition of possibilities which acquire definition only when consciously observed. These positions of the observer-created and the consciousness-created schools undeniably are imbued with the Berkeleyan vision, void even of the ameliorated Kantianism noted above in the Quantum Logic school. They also appear to practice a self-confident anthropocentrism. One would think that careful attention to the implications would make it an untenable position, as many have noted.[6] It is, yet, a seemingly lively position.

A final course of those interpretative positions that enjoy the most popularity today is the "many worlds interpretation" of Hugh Everett III. In this interpretation, all possibilities become actualised, though only one set within the observational act is classically perceived. Everett proposed that of every possibility in an event's superposition ALL of them are made real, though only one observed, when the observation takes place. What is attractive about Everett's proposal is that it seems to solve the measurement problem. Indeed, there are no measurements at all, but only correlations between observer and observed world and numerous unobservable parallel worlds (Herbert, 174). It also has been popularly extended in science fiction literature and television, as with *Star Trek — The Next Generation*. In summary, I have outlined the "schools" of (1) agnostic instrumentalism, (2) a "weak" Copenhagen interpretation, in which the only hard fact is the measurement itself, (3) a stronger Copenhagen interpretation which grants more responsibility to the observer and includes what I call the subsets of (3a) Quantum Logic and (3b) Consciousness Created Reality, and finally (4) the Many Worlds theory. All of these positions are open to modification and, in the terms of epistemology, move from instrumentalism through Kantian skepticism into realism and finally into thoroughgoing Idealism. Especially affecting, however, are the inescapable implications of Bell's theorem of non-locality, which suggests that every particle is connected globally to the converse situation of another in the same wave-function, even if the apparently superliminal "communication" between them contravenes the limits of local relativity (cf. Cushing and McMullin, 1989).

The question is begged therefore as to the realism of quantum measurements, a realism which Bell's theorem implies is classically and relativistically non-cognizable, and yet the measurements are meaningfully referential. On such basis, many physicists argue the undivided wholeness of all the physical order, visible and invisible, the incredible seeming discreteness of the quantum level notwithstanding; there is community in spite of evident pluralism. Others take a less challenging epistemological route and adopt a neorealism, claiming that because every experiment must be described in classical language, that reality itself is ordinary, too.[7]

Finally, others, like Heisenberg, may assume the converse of neorealism and say that unmeasured quantum attributes are just what they are, objective though unrealised possibilities. Those who would debate with Bell's theorem, however, are a minority decreasing in size. It appears to be the growing consensus that there exists down deep an objective "idiosyncratic reality", also amazingly open "within itself" (cf. Polkinghorne, 1991, 97). From the interpretations of Heisenberg's Uncertainty Principle alone it is evident all the more that the quantum world appears to be counterintuitive and taunting of Newtonian reality. The weight of preferred interpretation seems to bear more toward the side of a qualified realism, known formally as Critical Realism.

Even so, descriptions of the character of this relatively objective reality still vary when posed on the cosmological scale. The three figures whom we shall now investigate represent some of this variety. If they share any common ontological claims, we might surmise the further that their commonality is representative of a whole larger than their parts.

Andrej Grib, for example, carries forward the quantum logic position (3a) with a healthy portion of epistemological idealism. He agrees that the property of time as "becoming" is absent in classical special and general relativity. It is when we turn to the quantum world that we may describe the non-Boolean lattice of *"objectively existing" potentialities* (Grib 1993a, 103-4; 1993b, 181) as potentialities which "become" events by the translative agency of the Boolean consciousness that gives truth values to elements of the lattice. Time, therefore, is a human construct in quantum cosmology. Quantum cosmology, Grib avers, has no time inherent to it. This "physics of eternity" implies a block-universe, within which time emerges from its quantum origin into the entropical arrow of time of classical physics. Presuming a Kantian transcendental condition, and following the Strong Copenhagen Interpretation, Grib holds that the Boolean logic of human reasoning "reads out" of the non-Boolean lattice of quantum reality a temporality which is not initially there (Grib 1993b, 182). So, time is both a matter of the observer's choice (1993a, 104) and something which a Boolean mind necessarily perceives in non-Boolean structures. But if the property even of "being in time" is created by the Boolean observer, the question arises, when does this happen? In Grib's program, the conjecture is made that the choice is "now"; it is a "now" which is in eternity, and it is by this "now" that we have "becoming" (Grib 1993b, 178). The difference between the past and the future is that "the past is defined as that Boolean set of events which can't be changed in this choice of defining time, but the future is still open for choice." And what is open for choice is that "objectively existing" set of potentialities in the non-Boolean world. Grib intends a particular agenda with the term "observer". He believes that the only means by which two different observers can see the same quantum event is that there be posited the existence of some Ultimate Observer who guarantees the continuity of the created order. There finally really is "reality" to the quantum order, as well as the classical relativistic order, because there is an agent external to the whole process who, by "observing it," guarantees its coherence for those lesser observers who, like human beings, have at least a "co-creative" status (Hefner). That there would be an agency external to the quantum system also implies the need for additional dimensions. Since additional dimensions clearly cannot be material, Grib calls this ultimate observer 'spirit' (Grib 1993a, 107). In other words, Grib is an exemplar of the Quantum Logic position discussed above; if he is philosophically disposed toward Kant, he is also equally sympathetic with Berkeley.

Where Grib poses a cosmology of a "finite eternity," Stephen Hawking's is a "timeless quantum cosmology". Recognising that relativity theory can apply only to an expansionary macro-universe and is not adequate to deal with the problem of an originating singularity, Hawking includes quantum mechanics in his proposal for a cosmology. In doing so, Hawking does not disavow the thermodynamical arrow of time; he understands it as internal to the system. He does, however, conceive it as "local", while the macro-universe need not display any such correspondence. In Hawking's quantum gravity qualification of the Vilenkin model, time differs from one local region to another. Furthermore, a quantum explanation is needed because of the high density of the supposed original singularity. Such an explanation must use the concept of "imaginary time" (IT) to cover global, and not just local, effects. This is Hawking's novel move. His conclusion, as we well know, is that IT establishes a 4-dimensional space with a single three-dimensional boundary. Therefore the only boundary condition of the universe is that it has no boundaries. The combination of quantum mechanics with general relativity forms a finite four-dimensional space with no singularities (Hawking, 173-4). The universe can be accounted for in this model as one epicyclically expanding and collapsing, or simply as always existing, thus necessitating no notion of any absolute beginning to Creation (Hawking, 116).

The Hawking model, of course, is of a closed universe "type", but with no singularity. It resembles the standard Big Bang model with a finite past and finite future, except that the unboundedness variation suggests that space-time, like the universe, simply "is," and thus is uncreated. Indeed, for the universe simply to "be", as Hawking avers, yet with an acknowledged direction of real time within the "being", may suggest a consonance more with a proper definition of eternity than with infinity (Hawking, 133-141). His universe "transcends while enveloping regions of temporal passage." Displaying his deism, he also says the universe does so without God (Peters 1993, 164-5).

Christopher Isham believes the Hartle-Hawking proposal is a viable physical description. The use of imaginary time as a means to "smooth out" the conical singularity of an origination point coheres well with the phenomenological character of time. One of the most attractive features of the Hartle-Hawking scheme, he believes, is that it describes the evolution of the physical parts of the system by use of this internal/phenomenological time (Isham 1988, 400). As we "go back in time" by way of this phenomenological time, we find that the underlying equality of space and time is increasingly asserted, such that finally time is imaginary as it is associated with its non-physical features. Isham gives this a creative theological interpretation. Viewed from "the other direction", i.e., "since" the Big Bang, time as an imaginary number comes more into focus Gess imaginary) as the size of the three-dimensional surface expands. Insofar as this evolution proceeds from a formally mathematically describable region of IT, Isham shows this could provide a literal formal description for what it means for creation to have come "out of nothing" (Isham 1988, 401).

Isham regards this model positively because it is predictive, comprehensive and elegantly fruitful in resolving traditional demarcation problems between four-dimensional "paths" and three-space state functions. Above all, however, Isham favours the implication that time can be interpreted as a genuine variable only well away from the quantum region. Unidirectional, classical time may be construed as an "emergent" phenomenon; likewise with quantum probabilities. "...like the notion of classical time, probabilities may 'emerge' from the formalism and that, near the creation region [the wave function of the universe] may not have any direct physical interpretation at all!" (ibid.).

In sum, Isham proposes that a real-time universe such as ours "emerges" from a primordial imaginary-time four-dimensional sphere. What "once" was a Hawking universe without an edge may have evolved, in other words, into our universe with a quasi-edge; it is, as it were, a "pinch" in the expanding cosmic balloon. Thereby, imaginary time evolves into phenomenological time, which evolves into our real-time (Isham 1993, 74ff.). Isham indicates a preference for this model. But whether it be this or other quantum cosmological models explored by Isham, "they all agree on the idea that space and time 'emerge' in some way from a purely quantum-mechanical region which can be described in some respects as if it were a classical, imaginary-time four-space" (75). This shows convergence with Grib, as well as Hawking. Isham does not erase temporality for the sake of eternity. But he does show that there is an arena in which time has no place; in which time may even be likened to timelessness. There are those who take this to mean that the fundamental structure of the universe is, in fact, "timeless". I will comment upon this implication below. One thing is clear, however. The extra-scientific implications of Isham's work, along with those derived from the preceding cosmologists, are evocative.

Where does the discussion of quantum knowing and the brief look at three cosmologists lead us? I suggest that a consensus of perspectives culled from the three figures, then, would include the following observations. I will state them rather desultorily, and then explore each a bit more. (1) Time is emergent; (2) the future is open; (3) the role of observership is contested, but requires a critical realistic approach; (4) a critical realistic approach, combined with the recognition of the emergent character of time, requires holistic explanation; (5) this further implies the viability of a notion of an integral universe; (6) eternity is construable as an envelope of temporality. Finally, an explicitly non-scientific implication may be named, i.e., (7) transcendence and eschatology may play a role as part of the holistic and complementary explanation of eternity's relationship to temporality.

The above cosmologists agree with (1). However, proposition (2), that the future is open, may appear to be an oxymoron. How can one ascribe openness, indefiniteness or even infinity to something preceded by the substantive designation of "the"? What we are comfortable about asserting is that chance and indeterminacy play such a significant role at the microlevels of the universe that anticipation — if not hope — may spring eternal. This also means that "the future" does not exist in some sort of timeless Platonic world, though this claim may be a compromise for Grib.

As for proposition (3), though there has been little discussion above regarding critical realism, and though neither Grib nor Hawking show direct concern about this epistemological issue, certainly they refer to the real, and Grib further so in the somewhat ameliorated Kantian terms of quantum logic. Also, Isham has elsewhere questioned the instrumentalist tone of the conventional interpretation of quantum theory. He maintains that meaningful probabilistic statements affirm something with (or close to) probability one. This he aligns with a modest philosophical realism (Isham 1988, 403-404).

Proposition (4) is warranted as a general implication of Bell's theorem and the principle of complementarity, as well as being a necessary consequence of critical realism. We can also at least say that differing logics (as in Boolean and non-Boolean) may evidence the greater need for complementary explanations of phenomena pertinent to their own levels, and we see some display of this in the holding together of differing components and definitions of temporality by the three cosmologists above.

This further suggests (5) the viability of the notion of an integral universe, in which past and present events are connected and growing in their nexus as they are informed by new events of an expanding cosmos. I employ the term "integral" so as to avoid the block-universe debate (Russell et al 1994, 135-144), the very term of which nevertheless would support the inductive conclusion that cosmologists hold a world-view of diversity-in-relation, which includes predicates of temporality. The term 'integral' refers to the wholeness of the universe as it is given at any moment. It may also refer to the relationality shared by the constituents of the universe. The universe is the integral phenomenon of integral phenomena, as it were; it is a relative pluralism; it is a community. The reticence to use the language of a block universe, too, is to aver that this universe does not have a fixed future. Nor is it constituted by Parmenidean Forms or Platonic Ideals, and its possibilities, if even "objective," are infinite. Such a universe, in which space-time is part of the fixed matrix, implies a kind of "finite eternity" if the universe is closed; an "infinite eternity" if it is open and expanding.

In either case, eternity need not be synonymous with timelessness (6). In arguing the contrary, Willem Drees comments that the consonance which authors seek between a theistic view of creation and Big Bang cosmology lies not with the interpretation of "$t = 0$," but with the basic role of time as displaying a dynamic rather than static view of the universe (Drees 1993, 339). I fully agree, and hope the discussion to this point has made this clear. Following Isham's work, however, Drees argues that since the quantum, "fundamental" level of the universe shows no temporality, theistic critical realists have a fundamental conflict with cosmology, unless they were to accept a cosmological view of eternity as timelessness. He further argues for God's timelessness and the possibility that spatial dimensions over and above the physical be added to cosmological models so as to allow for such a "transcendence of timelessness".

This approach has merit and precedent. It makes it possible to imagine transcendence; God hereby may be seen in this 'supratemporal eternity' as intimate with all events without constraining God by simple temporality.

Why Drees prefers the nomenclature of platonic timelessness I am not clear, for his elaborations otherwise would be most amenable to the sketch I have drawn of an eternity of "supra-timefullness". It may also may serve as a segue to a final theological proposition (7), that transcendence and eschatology may play a role as part of the holistic and complementary explanation of eternity and temporality. In other words, an integral universe, as I have imagined it, requires much further description as to how it relates to its (or "a" or "the") future, and such descriptions may be of the sort regarding contingency that Wolfhart Pannenberg (1988) and Robert John Russell (1988) have posed and of the extra-dimensionality that is fundamental to Michael Welker's metaphysical vision (Welker 1994).

II. TRINITARIAN THEOLOGIES TODAY

The next question is whether there is anything already within Christian theology with which these propositions might resonate. My proposal is that resonances may be found in contemporary Trinitarian theology. I begin with a somewhat more personal setting of the background, and thereby would pose an answer to the still oft asked question these days of "why bother with such an arcane doctrine as that of the Trinity, anyway?".[8]

Trinitarian theologians today bloom from the recognition, re-established early in this century by Karl Barth, that the Trinity is the root of the Christian confession. God the Trinity is the origin, sustenance and eschatological promise of all life. The doctrine of the Trinity is the foundation of the three classical creeds. Their very evolution demonstrates how critically important the doctrine is to authentic Christian language. And, at its inception, this was no esoteric or ivory tower concern. Butchers, bakers and beauticians argued passionately in the marketplaces over whether the Son was begotten or created, and equally with investment over whether the Spirit was the Son's kindred or "proceeded" from the Father (LaCugna 1991).

Indeed, I argue that the Trinitarian confession was so cherished at Christianity's origins because the common person recognised, if only implicitly, that here in this doctrine was the explication of an ontology as well as a theological confession of faith. The doctrine was and is the primal explanation of the mystery as to how a transcendent God so other than the world could yet create and relate to this world. In other words, the doctrine is an inspired notation of how the eternal relates to the temporal.

Furthermore, in a non-hierarchical way, the doctrine of the Trinity is a grand resolution of the ancient problem of reconciling the one and the many. It gives an answer almost two thousand years ahead of our contemporary situation to the apparent conflict of communitarian and individualist interests. It exposes radical pluralism as an impossibility, and so would imply much for ethics and the construction of public policy. For example, it deconstructs both the socialistic utopianism of the human common denominator and the conservative fallacy that confuses unity with identity, and that usually according to an imposed norm that violently dismisses the dignity of one who is an "other". The Trinity opposes predication of pluralism as radical and the pretension that unity equals homogeneity, which is to say that the Trinity is the ground of authentic community of difference. In short, the doctrine of the Trinity - and of course the Trinity itself - is All encompassing. It is, or intends to be, for Christian theology what cosmology is to science.

Now, what of method? How does one begin to think theologically about the Trinity? Most contemporary theological reflection on the Trinity, other than Thomism, currently assumes the methodological starting point of accepting revealed "threeness" before adumbrating the unity of the Godhead. The revelation of threeness in the experience of people of faith attested in the Bible is, one must admit, a revelation "synthetically" derived. The scriptural language of one God, e.g. in Deuteronomy 6:4, so to cohere with the attested experience of God as Father, Son, and Spirit in the New Testament, came to be understood at Nicaea in the "wholistic" designation of God as one-in-three and three-in-one. This move echoes the earliest doctrinal insights of the Greek fathers, especially through the Cappadocians. Thinking on this doctrine has been reinvigorated in this century by Karl Barth and Karl Rahner, who rightly saw that the hyper-Augustinian distinction between the immanent Trinity and the economic Trinity was leading theology into mere speculation about God "in Godself," with no import on the salvific value thereof for the creation. Further, such a separation tended to gut the economic Trinity of its constitutive immanent relations. Also, a fear of tritheism collapsed the identification of God in Trinitarian theology to a divine monism, what Moltmann has, somewhat misleadingly, pejoratively labelled as monotheism (Moltmann 1981 and 1992). This western tendency toward divine monism, or unitarianism, is seen in the ready repetition of the so-called Augustinian maxim that the *opera trinitatis ad extra indivisa sunt*, to the neglect of its immanent trinity correlate that the *opera trinitatis ad intra divisa sunt*.[9] The right-headed correction this century, especially rendered by Rahner, is that the economic Trinity truly reflects the relations of the immanent, and vice-versa. The triune God is revealed in salvation history, and salvation history does refer to the "real" Triune God, though not exhaustively so. Reference to the ground of reality here in theology is as critically realistically meaningful as it would be in other - say, scientific - discourse. This "Rahner's rule" is shared as a basic assumption almost globally today. Formal constraints allow only a summary of such Trinitarian thinking hereafter.

Because the economy of the Trinity is of primary import *pro nobis*, the starting point for theological reflection on the Trinity is, so to speak, empirical, insofar as the primary Christian experience of the presence of divinity is historically given in Christian scriptural revelation and worship. In this neo-Thomism and neo-orthodoxy agree (Barth 1975; Rahner 1970), though both were open to the critique of maintaining modalistic tendencies (Moltmann 1981, 139-148; Pannenberg 1991, 296).[10] The *oikonomia* of salvation reveals God as the Trinity. This revelation of God in history is not as a unity, but as three identities, the recognition of which leads epistemologically to the positing of a necessary internal relatedness in God (Jenson 1982). Moltmann and Pannenberg are much more "social" in their interpretations of the persons of the Trinity "ad extra," with Pannenberg even characterising them as three "living realisations of separate centres of action" (Moltmann 1985; Pannenberg 1991, 319). This internal relatedness itself is the ontological condition for the derivative realisation of the external relatedness of the triune persons both to each other and to the creation. The relations constitute, in others words, richly in-formed persons who are ever more person-al even as they together are ever more intimately one. Such dynamic relationality, what Christianity means by the love of God, intentionally drives beyond "itself" into causing the emergence of the creation, caring for the creation's own modes of causality, and co-ordinating that creation's future through redeeming and sanctifying activities of ongoing creation.

"Relatedness" is far more profound than a mere connection of external agents (divine persons). Theology has long affirmed that a person is constituted by relationships, the Augustinian and Boethian emphasis on "an individual substance of a rational nature" notwithstanding. Contrary to the Augustinian/Boethian synthesis, which in western culture has tended to emphasise individualistic autonomy at the expense of corporate responsibility,[11] God the Trinity, as the consummate and unbounded relatedness of the divine persons, is the ontological ground and epistemological basis for a proper Christian understanding of personhood and of the intended divine natural order. This view is shared today by many otherwise disparate theologians (cf. Torrance 1993; Schwöbel 1994; Zizioulas 1985; Suchocki 1989; Kaufmann 1993).

The common - and I think original - Trinitarian insight (cf. Gunton 1993) is that, while constituted by relationship with the "whole," creaturely "parts" still have their individual integrity. An ecosystem is necessarily defined by its diverse and plural constituents, and vice-versa. Theology holds here, too, that something like a principle of complementarity must be employed theologically so as to avoid both an oppressive communitarianism and self-defeating individualism. Indeed, Walter Kasper's insight about the christological paradox - that simultaneous with the constitution of individuality by the "other" in relationship there occurs a more profound identity of "others;" indeed, that a healthy pluralism includes concomitant growth in communality - finds its basis in a Trinitarian ontology (Kasper, 289 & 305). This community is of a plural rather than monistic character precisely because the unity of the Trinitarian persons is perichoretic rather than con-fused. Threeness precedes and establishes oneness; oneness does not precede and administer itself into threeness. The contemporary theological consensus opts more for the Cappadocian preference that contributed to the construction of the Nicene Creed, rather than Augustine's interpretation of it. Gunton's perspective, which I quote liberally here, captures the insight well.

What becomes conceivable as a result of such a development is an understanding of particularity which guards against the pressure to homogeneity that is implied in modern [cultural] relativism and pluralism. Both cosmologically and socially, we may say, there is need to give priority either to the one nor to the many. Being is diversity within unity. By making it possible to show that there is a continuity and analogy between the universe as a framework and the human life that takes shape within it, christological and pneumatological emphases together enable us to understand the world as the context within which free personality and open society may develop. The human is like the non-human in being spatio-temporally particular, while it is also continuous with it in being bound up perichoretically with all of being. Thus can be found a framework which liberates rather than imprisons human life on earth, and which enables a rather symbiotic conception of the relation of man [sic] and nature, of a kind of community which makes us neither wholly active and dominant nor wholly passive and receptive in relation to the rest of creation. (Gunton, 213)

Again, the source of this pluralism-in-community is the Trinity itself, wherein the divine persons are not merely related, but are constituted by each other in the relations. "Father, Son, and Spirit are eternally what they are by virtue of what they are from and to one another. Being and

relation can be distinguished in thought, but in no way separated ontologically; they are rather part of the one ontological dynamic" (Gunton,
214). God's Trinitarian character is one of sociality, therefore, distinct
from the tri-theism of a "social model" of the Trinity (cf. Boff 1988),
which many fear inheres in the social model (cf. Peters 1993, 110-114).
The biblical term for this sociality is *koinonia* or communion.[12] Humans
believed to be created in the "image of God," I would argue - and as
representatives of the creation in which we are ecologically related and
share being - bear the *imago dei trinitatis*.

The complementarity of particular and whole, given a dialectical
frame by Gunton, is seen by Pannenberg as rather similar to the concept
of field in physics (Pannenberg 1994, 105ff.). Further, that there is yet
freedom and transcendence in the divine persons means that the future
enjoys priority. It is the future, not the past, which bestows upon the past
and present their promise-filled qualities to be cherished, because the future is also always open. Of the future, there is "always more." Even
when all is reconciled at the eschaton, the priority of "the more," even
the terms of temporality, will abide, because there shall always be the
surplus of transcendence-freedom-future in the Trinity (Moltmann 1985,
214). Thus the doctrine of the Trinity alludes to the ultimate vision of
pluralism in community, established by and intended toward a sublime
pluralism-in-community which is God the Trinity itself.

III. A SHARED WORLD-VIEW?

This last affirmation marks the point where Christian theology di-
verges from any scientific world-view *per se*, simply because at this juncture the vision is enhanced by Christian faith and hope. But much
consonance transpires before the divergence. For example, what I have
proposed to be named an "integral universe" in section II above appears
to be similar to the Trinitarian panentheism I have just described. Indeed,
to put it in highly synthesised terms, this Trinitarian panentheism is a
metaphysical principle that undergirds every other assertion in many theological programs. As I already observed, Pannenberg, for example, understands Trinitarian divine interrelatedness to be the ground for the
Spirit's activity as the field of force holding together the components of
creation (Pannenberg 1994, 79ff.). Welker does the same, with a focus
on the Spirit as the concretization of divine higher dimensionalities. As
Reconciler, the Spirit is analogous to (if not the definer off) the physical
principle of non-locality (Welker 1994). Nevertheless, within such an ex-
quisite web of universal relatedness, creatures great and small enjoy integrity and freedom. Thus Polkinghorne writes of the "butterfly effect"

(Polkinghorne 1994, 76-77) and Peacocke of chance in an open system as intended by God (Peacocke 1993, 156), such that creaturely agency, natural law (including the algorithmic randomness of evolutionary processes; cf. Dennett 1995), and divine providence are not necessarily mutually exclusive. Zizioulas has persuasively shown how this freedom-within-relatedness has been the reality statement of Trinitarian theology (Zizioulas 1985). This insight is currently common to feminist theologies (McFague, 1993) and to post-modernity's discovery of the "other" (Sponheim 1993).

And while all is related, which is to say there can be *no* such thing as *radical* pluralism, the relationality extends vertically as well as horizontally. Science and theology perceive emergent structures that are hierarchically ordered in multiple levels and are both upwardly and downwardly causal or implicative. Theology would formally differ from science here with the assertion that God exercises agency on these structures and does so as the Power of the Future (Peters 1992); I understand the terminology of "the Power of the Future" to connote how God's being in dimensionalities higher than our space-time dimension becomes our future as the higher dimensions are concretised - kenotically, so to speak - in our dimension (Larson 1995, 181). There is difference in particularity, spatiality, temporality and yet all is related, there can be more, and time may march on. ALL THAT WAS, IS, AND/OR CAN BE happens *within* a complex of dimensionalities. Like a Russian painted egg, dimensionalities that embrace dimensionalities are embraced ultimately by the triune godhead. If any world-view be shared by theology and the sciences, perhaps it is describable with such predicates as above, less the egg's ultimate shell.

In the end, I here neither seek to lay a Trinitarian pattern upon a physical world-view, nor to force a scientific template upon a dispirited theological corpus. But I might be so bold as to ask whether something *like* the relational terms of reinvigorated Trinitarian theology might be behind the retina of the basic scientific world-view. Perhaps this possibility might emerge into my strongest claim yet, in the tradition of Tillich and Schleiermacher: that a Trinitarian ground may be inferred from existence, characterised as existence is by pluralism (in its usual tragic mode of fracture) intent on community without loss of self. In the quest for understanding, which itself is a drive toward unity of the All without loss of particulars, there may be far more consonance between theologians and scientists in a post-modern world than we have heretofore imagined. Scattered ruminations on time may lead one to this vista. If such happens, after it happens, perhaps the discoverer will be impelled to exclaim that we can settle for no less a vision than time's embeddedness in the womb of eternity and that we should settle for nothing less than good stewardship of such promise-filled life.

NOTES

1. Many philosophers of science now criticise Kuhn severely; so many definitions have been tendered for "paradigm" that it itself bears little meaningful referentiality. Cf. McMullin 1970, 61-63; and, particularly, Barbour 1974, 108ff.

2. Much of the following is a reframing and synthesis of chapters V and VII of (Larson 1995).

3. Herbert provides the helpful example of a rainbow as something that is objective but not an object. The rainbow appears in a different place for each observer; each sees a slightly different rainbow. Yet it can be photographed. It is an objective phenomenon. An electron's attributes are said to be a similar illusion ... until it is "photographed." In other words, "an electron's attributes do not belong to the electron itself but are a kind of illusion produced by the electron plus 'the entire experimental arrangement.'"

4. A lattice is a hypothetical complex nexus that provides a map for "where" an event might "go" and where from it derives. It models a quantum logic which is quite distinct from the more familiar distributive logic we know as Boolean (after the algebra of George Boole, 1815-1864) wherein, for example, 'a(b+c) = ab+ac' and 'a×bc = (a×b)(a×c)'. By extension, one might first think that 'a∧(b∨c) = (a∧b)∨(a∧c)', where ∧ = 'and', and ∨ = 'or'. However, in quantum logic, where we are concerned with, for example, a polarisation attribute, there can result only two states (cf. Herbert, 177-182). The result of our supposed extension is the additional clauses of '= 0 **and** = 1.' That is, in this non-distributive logic, something can both be and not-be. As Paul Davies notes, quantum logic presumes that physical systems can exist in superpositions of alternative states (Davies 1992). Thus the distributive law of our Boolean example above is compromised; combination attributes will not behave like the sum of the parts. A most helpful diagram of the lattice model is found in (Grib 1993, appendix).

5. The so-called strong form of the Anthropic Principle (SAP) is the scientific agreement that large-scale number coincidences within but micro-seconds of the Big Bang could eventuate into only this kind of self-cognizing universe viz a vis humankind. There are numerous resources available with reference to the Anthropic Principle. The magisterial primary source, of course, is Barrow and Tipler, 1986.

6. Polkinghorne writes with characteristic forthrightness. "Are we to suppose that in the thousands of millions of years before conscious life emerged in the world - and still today in those extensive parts of the universe where no conscious life has yet developed - no wavepacket has ever collapsed, no atom for certain decayed? That quantum mechanics as we know it is a biologically induced phenomenon? That photographic plates stored away uninspected at the end of an experiment only acquire a definite image when someone opens the drawer to have a look at them? It takes a bit of swallowing" (1984, 66).

7. Such is the attempt, though he clearly swims against the current, of G. Cavalleri of Italy, who claims that all relative motion and quantum phenomena can be adequately described in classical terms. Unpublished paper, ECST IV, Rome, 1992.

8. Such an arcane doctrine is, of course, no more arcane than the vocabulary of quantum mechanics. For theology the problem is exacerbated, however, by its own, as many theologians openly question its meaningfulness and pertinence today. Cf. John Cobb 1984.

9. One will not find this "Principle" exactly quoted so in Augustine. I believe it is a post-Augustine synthesis of his thinking in de Trinitate.

10. Modalism is the teaching that God in Godself is above time and that the distinctions of Father, Son and Spirit appear only serially in these roles to create, redeem and sanctify. This had been standard theory since AD 190 up until the mid-4th century in Rome. It was a direct attempt to keep God timeless. Its result is that none of the three is understood as God himself. Subordinationism, on the other hand, seems at least to identify "Father with God; it also provided the hierarchical ranking so desired by Greek thought, made paradigmatic in Origin and Athanasius. In such a scheme Christ could easily come to be seen as merely the "halfway house" to heaven.

11. The western tendency, again, to reduce a Trinitarian doctrine of God to a unitarian modalism, combined with the Boethian definition of personhood ends in the antipoetic imagination that every man is an island; it provides the theological justification for a culture of narcissism and right wing libertarianism, as in the United States with its "freemen" movements, "possecomitatis" militias and so forth.

12. The term koinonia itself, and its wide usage today, indicates how embracing this Christian world-view indeed is. It is the dominant theme for ecumenism, ecclesiology and theological anthropology, as well as for Trinitarian thinking. cf. (Best and Gassmann 1994).

REFERENCES

Barbour, Ian 1974: *Myths, Models and Paradigms*, New York.

Barbour 1990: *Religion In An Age of Science*, San Francisco.

Barth, Karl 1975: *Church Dogmatics*, I. 1, trans. G. W. Bromiley, Edinburgh.

Best, Thomas J. and Gassmann, Günther 1994: *On the Way to Fuller Koinonia*, Geneva.

Boff, Leonardo 1988: *Trinity and Society*, trans. Paul Bums, Maryknoll

Cobb, John 1984: "Reply to Moltmann's 'The Unity of the Triune God,'" *St. Vladimir's Theological Quarterly*, (28:3).

Cushing, James T. and McMullin, Ernan (eds.)1989: *Philosophical Consequences of Quantum Theory*, Notre Dame

Davies, Paul 1992: *The Mind of God, The Scientific Basis For a Rational World*, New York.

Dennett, Dennis 1995: *Darwin's Dangerous Idea*, Cambridge.

Drees, Willem 1993: "A Case Against Temporal Realism?," *Quantum Cosmology and the Laws of Nature: Scientific Perspectives on Divine Action*, eds. Russell et al. Vatican City, 331-366.

Grib, Andrej A. 1993a: "Time and Eternity in Modern Relativistic Cosmology," in Coyne, et al (eds.) *Studies in Science & Theology, 1. origins, time & complexity*, Geneva, 93-113.

Grib 1993b: "Quantum Cosmology, The Role of Observer, Quantum Logics," in Russell et al (eds), *Quantum Cosmology and the Laws of Nature*, Vatican City, 163-184.

Gunton, Colin 1993: *The One, The Three, and the Many*, Cambridge, UK

Hawking, Stephen 1987: *A Brief History of Time, From the Big Bang to Black Holes*, New York.

Hefner, Philip 1993: *The Human Factor, Evolution, Culture and Religion*, Minneapolis.

Herbert, Nick 1987: *Quantum Reality, Beyond the New Physics*, Garden City.

Honner, John 1988: "Not Meddling with Divinity: Theological World-views and Contemporary Physics," *Pacifica* (I:Oct.) 251-272.

Isham, Christopher J. 1993: "Quantum Theories of the Creation of the universe," *Quantum Cosmology and the Laws of Nature*, eds. Russell et al., Vatican City, 49-90.

Isham 1988: "Creation As a Quantum Process," *Physics, Philosophy, and Theology, A Common Quest for Understanding*, eds. Russell et al. Rome, 375-408.

Kasper, Walter 1992: *The God of Jesus Christ*, New York.

Kaufman, Gordon D. 1993: *In Face Of Mystery, A Constructive Theology*, Cambridge.

LaCugna, Catherine Mowry 1991: *God For Us, The Trinity and Christian Life*, San Francisco.

Larson, Duane H. 1995: *Times of the Trinity*, New York.

Lindbeck, George 1984: *The Nature of Doctrine*, Philadelphia.

McFague, Sallie 1993: *The Body of God, An Ecological Theology*, Minneapolis.

McMullin, Ernan 1970: "The History and Philosophy of Science: A Taxonomy," in Steuer (ed.) *Historical and Philosophical Perspectives of Science*, New York, 12-67.

Moltmann, Jiirgen 1981: *The Trinity and the Kingdom*, trans. Margaret Kohl, New York.

Moltmann 1985: *God in Creation*, trans. Margaret Kohl, San Francisco.

Moltmann 1992: *History and the Triune God, Contributions to Trinitarian Theology*, trans. John Bowden, New York.

Osthuis, James H. 1985: "On World-views," *Christian Scholar's Review* (14:2) 153-164.

Pannenberg, Wolfhart 1991: *Systematic Theology*, v. 1, trans. Geoffrey Bromiley, Grand Rapids.

Pannenberg 1994: *Systematic Theology*, v.2, trans. Geoffrey Bromiley, Grand Rapids.

Pannenberg 1988: "The Doctrine of Creation and Modern Science," *Zygon: Journal of Religion and Science* (23:1) 3-21.

Pannenberg 1993: *Toward A Theology of Nature, Essays on Science and Faith*, ed. Ted Peters, Louisville.

Peacocke, Arthur 1993: *Theology for a Scientific Age*, Minneapolis.

Peters, Ted 1993: *God As Trinity, Relationality and Temporality in Divine Life*, Louisville.

Peters 1992: *God — The World's Future*, Minneapolis.

Polkinghorne, John 1994: *The Faith of a Physicist*, Princeton.

Polkinghorne, 1991: *Reason and Reality, The Relationship Between Science and Theology*, Philadelphia.

Polkinghorne 1984: *The Quantum World*, Princeton.

Russell, Robert John 1988: "Contingency in Physics and Cosmology: A Critique of the Theology of W. Pannenberg," *Zygon: Journal of Religion and Science* (23:1) 23-43.

Russell et al (eds.) 1988: *Physics, Philosophy and Theology, A Common Quest for Understanding*, Vatican City State.

Russell et al (eds.) 1993: *Quantum Cosmology and the Laws of Nature, Scientific Perspectives on Divine Action*, Vatican City State.

Schwöbel, Christoph (ed.) 1995: *Trinitarian Theology Today, Essays on Divine Being and Act*, Edinburgh.

Sponheim, Paul 1993: *Faith and the Other*, Minneapolis.

Suchocki, Majorie Hewitt 1989: *God, Christ, Church, A Practical Guide to Process Theology*, New York.

Torrance, T. F. 1993: *The Trinitarian Faith*, Edinburgh.

Welker, Michael 1994: *God the Spirit*, trans. John Frohmeyer, Minneapolis.

Zizioulas, John 1985: *Being As Communion*, Crestwood.

WHAT IF THERE WERE
OTHER INHABITED WORLDS?

CHRISTOPHER J. CORBALLY, S.J.
(Vatican Observatory)

Abstract: In astronomy, though not shared so convincingly in biology, there is increasing evidence for life-bearing planets around other stars. Here we consider some historical positions and the current data for the existence of other intelligent beings in the universe. This analysis clarifies the dominant principles underlying positions for and against the many worlds hypothesis, and so it allows us to project the impact of extraterrestrials by understanding our response to any unknown and our relationship to a revealing God.
Keywords: many worlds debate, interdisciplinary relationships, extraterrestrial life, exploration, revelation, the Christ-event

I. THE QUESTION IN HISTORY

Popular culture shows that people are currently fascinated with the possibility of other inhabited worlds (Dick 1996, Consolmagno 1996). Yet, we are far from being the first or the last to wonder about extraterrestrials. Indeed, the whole question of their existence, far from being frivolous, has a solid and long intellectual history, one woven into each era's science, philosophy, and theology. That would be why Albertus Magnus, the teacher of Thomas Aquinas, said that the concept of a plurality of worlds was "one of the most wondrous and noble questions in nature" (in Dick 1982, 37). While the "what if" question is not new, each advance in scientific understanding gives a new platform from which to view it. To begin, a highly-selective review of its history can lead us in the right directions for our own response to the question. My sources in this review are mainly Steven Dick (1982) and Michael Crowe (1986).

The two camps, pro- and anti-other worlds, were set up by ancient Greek philosophers, particularly in the fourth century B.C.:

There are infinite worlds both like and unlike this world of ours.
For the atoms being infinite in number, as was already proved,

are borne on far out into space. For those atoms which are of such nature that a world could be created by them or made by them, have not been used up either on one world or a limited number of worlds .... So that there nowhere exists an obstacle to the infinite number of worlds. (Epicurus, in Bailey 1926, 25)

Either, therefore, the initial assumptions must be rejected, or there must be one centre and one circumference; and given this latter fact, it follows from the same evidence and by the same compulsion, that the world must be unique. There cannot be several worlds. (Aristotle, in Guthrie 1953)

Epicurus's philosophy of atomism (all matter is made up of microscopic atoms) leads to a plurality of worlds; Aristotle's philosophy of absolute natural place (each element moves towards its natural place) leads to a uniqueness of the known world. So, two philosophical understandings of the nature of matter lead to opposing perspectives on the universe. When Aristotle's thought was rediscovered in the Middle Ages, and particularly his rejection of many worlds in *De caelo*, his arguments were not accepted uncritically, even though these were not for the most part contrasted with the atomists' standpoint. The concepts of centre, of void, and of natural motion became the objects of debate. Thomas Aquinas (1224-1274) approached the debate from the Aristotelian perspective, but his main concern seemed to be to show that a single world would not compromise God's omnipotence and that indeed, since perfection was to be found in unity, a single world would be more in accordance with God's perfection (Aquinas 1952). For a time then, perfection rather than plenitude dominated scholastic thinking about God and the world.

That thinking changed radically in the sixteenth century, under the influence of such as Copernicus's *De revolutionibus* and of Giordano Bruno's *De l'infinito universo e mondi*. Under this revolution in both physical and philosophical thinking, the *kosmos* was believed to consist of many worlds, each like our solar system, and the possibility even of many kosmoi could be considered. So, in Bruno the Atomists' concept of plurality returned, and he even found it possible to reconcile the properties of the four natural elements in each "world" with an appeal to an "ultimate unity" that would harmonise the whole cosmos (Singer 1950, 374). A notable inheritor of this expanded concept of the cosmos (but fortunately not of Bruno's fiery fate) was John Herschel (1792-1871). This sole son of the famous British astronomer, William Herschel, had the finest of scientific educations available and brought this to bear on his observations and on his writings. So, it was curious that in his two major books he endorsed his father's claims that the sun and the moon had inhabitants, even though his science made inhabitation of the broiling sun and the airless moon increasingly problematic.

For all of John Herschel's scientific achievements it was clear, but not to him, that his "belief in extraterrestrial life rested largely on metaphysical and religious assumptions concerning the plans and purposes of the Creator ..." (Crowe 1986, 217). Herschel's underlying assumption was that, if the universe existed for the purpose of life, that purpose could not be adequately filled by one, tiny earth. So, it was his scientific perspective that led him to go beyond that perspective and invoke a teleology, without realising he was doing so.

A truly fascinating person in the debate is William Whewell, a contemporary of John Herschel and likewise a prominent Cambridge scholar. Whewell, for many years a proponent of the plurality of worlds, changed his mind and attacked it in 1853. What seems to have happened, according to Michael Crowe (1986, 265ff), is that Whewell came to appreciate the full significance of the Copernican revolution that took humans from their place in the centre of the universe and threw them out among the billions of stars. For Whewell, that change of perspective was an oppressive, desolate and dark thought indeed. Further, it was a thought that raised the theological problem of reconciling these many worlds with the fact that God had intervened in human history in a special way, through the incarnation and redemption of Christ. Whewell was living in the days before current science had shown how finely tuned must the universe be to allow life and how even its vastness is needed for any life to appear.

Such fine-tuning is the basis of the Anthropic Principle which, in a theological context, can restore us to the centre of God's scheme.[1] (In deference to possible aliens and to avoid chauvinism, perhaps we should now call this the Sapientic Principle.) An astronomer who was not at all perturbed by the Copernican change in perspective was Angelo Secchi (1818-78), a Jesuit and a director of the Roman College Observatory. In 1856 he wrote: "it is with a sweet sentiment that man thinks of these worlds without number, where each star is a sun which, as minister of the divine bounty, distributes life and goodness to the other innumerable beings, blessed by the hand of the Omnipotent." (Secchi 1856, 158) Secchi conceded that these worlds may not be accessible to his telescopes, but by analogy with the earth and the solar system he was well persuaded that the universe is a wonderful organism, filled with life. So, even if Secchi's science failed him in proof, it fuelled his sense of the limitless wonders of the universe. This open enthusiasm for plurality was remarkable in one so close to a usually cautious Vatican, but it will strike a chord in those of us who have enjoyed the myriads of stars on a dark night.

II. PRINCIPLES AND CLARITY

These examples from history illustrate what might influence one's position in the many worlds debate. These underlying principles may be categorised under the three disciplines: philosophy, theology, and science. Now, there is nothing wrong with having such principles: what is unfortunate is not recognising them as such. Further, in the many worlds debate, principles from one discipline have influenced those from another. Let us consider some in more detail.

For Thomas Aquinas, we have indicated that his main theological principle was that of *perfection*, which included the ideas of *unity* and of *order* (a hierarchy of relations) whenever God acts in creation. I think that there is little question among theists about God having these attributes; the question comes in the definitions and implications of doctrines. George Schner (Regis College, Toronto) and others refer to theological doctrines and propositions as "rules for theological discourse," since they set the parameters and context for theological explanations. For some Christians, the rules of the fall of humanity and its redemption through an incarnate God, when coupled with the perfection of God, imply that this programme could only have happened once and so that humanity is unique in the universe. If Christ is not the absolute communication of God, then God has deceived us, which is a contradiction. This is the argument that Whewell followed, in the tradition of Aquinas, but only when he was confronted by science with a vast universe. For others, the perfection of God, which was exhibited in the redemption of humanity, must be balanced against God's *omnipotence*. So we find in 1277 AD, only three years after Aquinas died, the very blunt condemnation by the bishop of Paris, Etienne Tempier, against a belief "that the First Cause cannot make many worlds." (The whole 219 condemned articles are listed in translation by Fortrin and O'Neill [1963, 337-54].) Clearly, the argument is not going to be solved by the swapping of "anathema sit" among those who would condemn the other side, but by resolving just what these principles mean and so what might be their harmonisation.

In case the scientists among us feel a bit smug over the quarrels of the philosophers and theologians, I should point out that Herschel's stretching of the scientific evidence about the sun and the moon to accommodate his solarians and lunarians on these bodies is but one example of mixing a philosophical principle, *teleology*, into a scientific discussion. It was Roger Joseph Boscovich (1711-87), a Jesuit scientist, philosopher and poet, who brought scientific clarity back into the discussion of lunarians by analysing occultations of objects by the moon and concluding that the moon possessed too thin an atmosphere, if any, for supporting life. With that clarity established, Boscovich could allow himself to speculate on possibilities, based on what he knew of the physical world. He imagined beings insensitive to fire, and multiple universes, and so he entertained the idea of many worlds, or at least of many universes. We also saw that Secchi's theology of *plenitude* coloured his scientific appreciation of the boundless nature of the universe. Again, there is nothing wrong in this, but one must preserve clarity between the three disciplines.

How might we attain that clarity? A first "clarifier" is to recognise and preserve the limits of discourse within each discipline. For instance, science cannot address the reason why something exists rather than does not exist. Its methodology brings out processes among material things, not purpose and meaning. So, the words "creation of the universe" when applied in scientific cosmology and when used in theology have to mean two different things: we should be clear whether we are talking about physical interactions or about the work of a non-physical, Prime Mover.

A second and related clarifier is to find the right relationship between the disciplines. In a previous discussion of faith and science, I wrote that

> (faith) *cannot* be used to support or dictate the correctness of a scientific theory: e.g., the Big Bang model of the universe or natural selection in biological evolution do not find authentication through the first chapter of Genesis. Neither can a scientific theory support a theological concept: e.g., the Big Bang does not ground, of itself, an absolute beginning in time of creation. The two need a weaker logical relation, such as Ernan McMullin's suggestion of "consonant with" (McMullin 1981): thus, God's ordering in the Genesis account is consonant with the order science finds in the cosmos. People are still debating the right "c" word to use (congruence, consonance, concord ...), but it must be one that preserves the rightful autonomy of each kind of knowledge while allowing for some proper interaction. (Corbally 1994)

Much has been written on the correct relationship between science and theology (e.g., Barbour 1990[2]), but the above will suffice regarding the many worlds question. Now that we are alert to some of the influences and principles that affect us, we can look with increased clarity at the evidence for extraterrestrial life.

III. THE EVIDENCE

The scientific evidence for life beyond the Earth is tantalising. Unlike Herschel, who had to invent ways that solarians could live on the burning Sun or survive on an apparently airless moon, we can probe much further out, even beyond our Solar System to find out whether there may be other habitable planets. We do already know some intriguing things: when stars form, most do so with surplus gas and dust particles surrounding them which can be detected in the infrared and which can be the source-material for planets; three massive, Jupiter-like planets are the best way to explain the variations in the period of their host-star, now a pulsar, PSR B1257+12; Michel Mayor and Didier Queloz (1995) have claimed that a near Jupiter-mass planet is orbiting the solar-like star, 51 Pegasi, only 42 light years away from us, and this claim was recently upheld by Geoffrey Marcy and Paul Butler, who added evidence for Jupiter-like planets round 70 Virginis and 47 Ursae Majoris. The prospects of finding more evidence for planets around nearby stars, and even for a planetary environment modified by life, are very good as telescopes and their instrumentation improves (Angel and Woolf 1996).

So, in grant proposals for such technical improvements the appeal to the popular, planet-search theme is justified. We live in exciting times, astronomically-speaking. It is as potentially exciting on the biological side of the scientific question. However, while the first condition for other life, namely the existence of habitable planets around other stars is widely believed (but not yet indisputable), the second condition, the exact process of how life appears is not established. We do know a vast amount more than we did a few decades ago about the building blocks of life, and that the first blocks were more likely to be RNA (ribonucleic acid) than DNA (deoxyribonucleic acid). The quest is now to find out how the RNA strings of genetic coding arose in the first place (Orgel 1994). Producing amino acids from laboratory-simulated, primitive atmospheres, which was pioneered in 1953 by Stanley Miller and Harold Urey, is just the beginning of the story. The crucial step is the one from chemistry to life, but at least we can say that the "chemistry for life" is abundant in the Solar System and in the Galaxy. Still, the answer to whether there are other life-bearing planets is still just beyond our scientific reach.

With the hope of extending that reach, the various Search for Extra-terrestrial Intelligence projects (SETIs) were started. In the tradition of Frank Drake's first search in 1960, these use large radio telescopes, sophisticated receivers, and modern data analysis to look for signals coming from an intelligent origin beyond our solar system. A promising boost to SETI was the funding through NASA of the first large-scale, systematic search in 1992. When the US Congress cancelled that project a year later, it re-arose as the privately-funded Project Phoenix, whose first technically successful run took place early in 1995. I heard a report of that first run from the project director, Jill Tartar, and I was impressed by the team's technical sophistication and enthusiasm. For all that expertise and effort, and even though radio searches hold the best promise for finding other intelligent life, there has been no detection yet, only good reasons to continue; so they keep looking and hoping.

The situation seems no better on the theological side. We can swap "proof texts" from scripture, such as John 1:10 ("He was in the world [i.e., singular] that had its being through him ...") or Ephesians 1:10 ("... he would bring everything together under Christ, as head, everything in the heavens and everything on earth"); but the historical debate over the many worlds question has not provided any theologically compelling evidence that traditional religions should uphold or deny many worlds and their extraterrestrials. If there had been any such evidence, the debate would have ceased (as would have the scientific debate, given any concrete scientific evidence). What we do have, following Ashkenazi (1991) and Peters (1995), is the indifference shown to the question by Hinduism and Buddhism, the inevitability of other intelligent life for the Mormons, the possibility of the prophet being replicated elsewhere for Muslims, the accommodation by Jewish theology, and the lack of official pronunciation by the Christian religions (except perhaps that of the Bishop of Paris, Tempier, if his condemnation is taken as an affirmation).

The same lack of conclusion is shown by philosophy. We have become aware that there are principles underlying people's positions. Any of these *a priori* principles have to be tested, in the end, by their coherence with the experienced, though not purely physical, universe. For example, Steven Dick (1982, 188) points out how the concept of extraterrestrial life became a serious concern just as scientific theory drew a better picture of the universe. With respect to aliens, philosophy can only look at the possibilities, not at actualities, until the evidence is forthcoming. Where philosophy can help is in our understanding of self-conscious, rational life. This matter-to-mind step may be an even bigger one than from chemicals to life, and one comparable with the discontinuity of the Big Bang that seems to have begun our present universe; but standing on that step opens up an expanse of study too large to explore here.

IV. THE ORIGINAL QUESTION

At this point I am tempted to say with Mark Twain, "First gather the facts, then you can distort them at your leisure." The facts are that aliens are an astronomical probability (in view of the probability of other planets suitable for bearing life), a bio-chemical possibility (since the exact origin of life is still not understood), and a theological and philosophical wait-and-see. The distortions come from our own prejudices that dictate whether we believe in aliens or not(note the word "believe"). Although I have shown that we cannot say whether there is other intelligent life in the universe, is it even worth addressing the original question of impact, "What if there were other inhabited worlds?"

Certainly, since I find the key both to the worth of answering and to finding an actual answer in the idea of *exploration*. That idea is vital to progress in the physical sciences, for without curiosity in how things work there would have been no understanding of planets and stars and galaxies, and further, no significant progress in technology. Exploration is also needed in the "sciences" of theology and philosophy, so that the same urge to push back the boundaries of knowledge can bring new insights into traditional doctrines and questions. Even though we may be alone in the universe, considering the question about extraterrestrials will extend our understanding, at least of ourselves and the known universe; we can explore our principles and the known data.

But if popular hopes, and fears, are indeed realised and we do encounter another inhabited world, how would I go about assessing its impact? I would try to "explore" the phenomenon, both scientifically and theologically.

This exploration is what I do daily in my scientific research with the spectrum, or rainbow, of a star. That spectrum has more than a band of colours: there are places of relative darkness where part of a colour is missing, and these features characterise the star's physical conditions. When I look at a particular star's spectrum, I look at it as a specimen: I try to let that star *be what it is*, without forcing it into a classification category. It may end up being classified easily, and 95 per cent of stars fall readily into the Morgan-Keenan classification system (Osterbrock 1994), but I would loose potential insights if I jumped too readily to a classification for that spectrum. I find my preferred way of doing science is synthetic, starting with observations, rather than analytic, starting with theory. So, scientifically, I would try to explore the alien by letting "it" be what it is, without rushing for a classification category, not even presuming two genders.

Similarly, I would want to let the alien be what it is theologically, without rushing for the baptismal water. Perhaps it is better to speak of letting the alien "reveal" what it is, since Christians speak of the essence of the Christ-event as the concentrated point of God's "self-revelation" to human kind (Peacocke 1993, 315). We find the Gospel of St. John appropriately using "Word," *Logos* in the Greek, to describe this divine self-communication. But while Christ is the First and the Last Word (the Alpha and the Omega) spoken to humanity, he is not necessarily the *only* word spoken to the universe.

I can amplify that openness of revelation in two ways, one more from the alien's religious perspective, the other more from our own receiving of the Word. Firstly, the central meaning of the Christ-event is outlined by Peacocke (1993, 330ff), drawing on P. Fiddes's interpretation of the atonement in Abelard, as "the power of the divine love to *create or generate love within human beings.*" While Peacocke restricts his discussion to humanity, his refusal to use the word "Christ" as anything resembling a surname, preferring instead "Jesus the Christ", indicates that he leaves open the cosmic possibilities of the Christ-event. For, the Word spoken to us does not seem to exclude an equivalent "Word" spoken to aliens. They, too, could have had their "Logos-event". Whatever that event might have been, it does not have to be a repeated death-and-resurrection, if we allow God more imagination than some religious thinkers seem to have had. For God, as omnipotent, is not restricted to one form of language, the human. That lack of restriction is a clear message after Christ's resurrection, when the human boundaries of room walls are no obstacle to the Risen Christ's appearances and when the Ascension allows the resurrection to extend beyond Palestine's boundaries. However, while the "language" of that Logos-event would be different, its content would be the same: the power of divine love to create that same love in creatures made in God's image.

Secondly, while the concentrated point of God's revelation to humanity is in the death-and-resurrection of Christ, that revelation is deepened daily for each Christian through the experiences of his or her life. Revelation, in that daily sense, is mediated to me also through my science and discoveries. We just have to think of the Copernican universe, the evolution of biological species, or the discovery of the Americas, to see the difference these have made for the context in which the Word of God is spoken to each generation. We understand revelation slightly differently, though not more fully, by living in a different world than the first century AD of the New Testament. If the third millennium were to bring us significant dialogue with aliens living on, say, a planet of 70 Virginis, the models by which we express the Logos-event would undoubtedly be expanded, though exactly "how" should properly await the encounter.

So, my final answer to the question of impact is "I don't know," at least not without first letting the alien be, as a specimen and as a revelation.

V. ENDING VISION

Given the fascinating possibilities in the question of aliens, this answer is bound to be superficially unsatisfactory. Yet, it hopefully now reflects what will be our response both to any created unknown and to the ultimate unknown, God. I suggest that this response should be guided, even driven, by an openness to the phenomenon. That openness tries to be aware of its assumptions. It becomes informed by past experience and a structured knowledge. So, it is not a New Age openness, but it brings a really deeper understanding to what has already been revealed and to what is to come. It is from such a *grounded openness* that we can appreciate the vision Alice Meynell (1923) expressed in the last four verses of her "Christ in the universe."

No planet knows that this
Our wayside planet, carrying land and wave,
Love and life multiplied, and pain and bliss,
Bears, as chief treasure, one forsaken grave.

Nor, in our little day,
May His devices with the heavens be guessed,
His pilgrimage to tread the Milky Way,
Or His bestowals there be manifest.

But, in the eternities,
Doubtless we shall compare together, hear
A million alien Gospels, in what guise
He trod the Pleiades, the Lyre, the Bear.

O, be prepared, my soul!
To read the inconceivable, to scan
The million forms of God those stars unroll
When, in our turn, we show to them a Man.

ACKNOWLEDGEMENTS

Critical reading of an early version by Susan Ashbourne and input from those in Workshop 4 of the Sixth European Conference on Science and Theology have proved very helpful to the author.

NOTES

1. A simple discussion will be found in John Polkinghorne, Serious Talk (1995), p.68-72, while a fuller discussion and references are given by G.F.R. Ellis, "The Theology of the Anthropic Principle," in *Quantum Cosmology and the Laws of Nature*, Vatican (1993), p.367-405.
2. Ian Barbour's work is discussed extensively in Zygon 31, No.1, 1996.

REFERENCES

Angel, Roger P., and Woolf, Neville J. 1996: "Searching for Life on Other Planets", *Scientific American*, 274, No.4, 60-66.

Aquinas, Thomas, edition of 1952: In *Aristotelis libros de caelo et mundo, generatione et corruptione, meteorologicorum expositio*, Rome, Lectio XIX, 94.

Ashkenazi, Michael 1991: "Not the Sons of Adam: Religious Responses to ETI", a talk at *42nd Congress of the International Astronautical Federation*, Montreal.

Bailey, Cyril, ed. and trans. 1926: *Epicurus: the Extant Remains*, Oxford.

Barbour, Ian G. 1990: *Religion in an Age of Science*, London: SCM.

Consolmagno, Guy J. 1996: "Astronomy, Science Fiction and Popular Culture: 1277 to 2001 (and Beyond)", *Leonardo*, 29, No.2, 127-132.

Corbally, Christopher J. 1994: "Science and Faith: An Astronomer's Perspective", *America*, 170, No.12, 22-25.

Crowe, Michael J. 1986: *The Extraterrestrial Life Debate 1750-1900*, Cambridge: CUP.

Dick, Steven J. 1982: *Plurality of Worlds*, Cambridge: CUP.

Dick, Steven J. 1996: "Other Worlds: The Cultural Significance of the Extraterrestrial Life Debate", *Leonardo*, 29, No.2, 133-137.

Fortrin, L. and O'Neill, Peter D. 1963: *Medieval Political Philosophy: A Source Book*, New York.

Guthrie, W.K.C., trans., 1953, of Aristotle's: *On the Heavens*, Cambridge, Mass.: Loeb Classical Library, bk 1, ch 8, 277a, lines 11-13.

Mayor, Michel, and Queloz, Didier 1995: "A Jupiter-mass companion to a solar-type star", *Nature*, vol. 378, 355-359.

McMullin, Ernan 1981: "How Should Cosmology Relate to Theology", *The Sciences and Theology in the Twentieth Century*, Notre Dame, 30.

Meynell, Alice 1923: *The Poems of Alice Meynell*, New York.

Orgel, Leslie E. 1994: 'The Origin of Life on the Earth', *Scientific American*, 271, No.4, 77-83.

Osterbrock, Donald E. 1994: 'Fifty Years Ago: Astronomy; Yerkes Observatory; Morgan, Keenan, Kellman', *The MK Process at 50 Years: ...*, San Francisco: A.S.P., 199-214.

Peacocke, Arthur 1993: *Theology for a Scientific Age: Being and Becoming Natural, Divine, and Human*, Minneapolis: Fortress.

Peters, Ted 1995: 'Exo-Theology: Speculations on Extra-Terrestrial Life', a talk at *IRAS Star Island Conference*, Portsmouth, N.H.

Secchi, Angelo 1856: *Descrizione del nuovo osservatorio del collegio romano*, Rome.

Singer, Dorothea W. 1950: *Giordano Bruno: His Life and Thought, with annotated translation of his work On the Infinite universe and Worlds*, New York.

Section 2

Biology and Theology

EVOLUTIONARY CONTINGENCY
AND COSMIC PURPOSE

Templeton Lecture delivered by
ERNAN MCMULLIN
(*Notre Dame, Indiana, USA*)

Does the contingency of the evolutionary account of origins, particularly of human origins, make it more difficult to see the universe as the work of a Creator? Does it, effectively, rule out purpose at the cosmic level and leave us in a world from which religious meaning has departed? Some would answer yes to both questions. It has always been clear that chance played an important part in the Darwinian theory. But it seems easier, somehow, to construe evolution as God's mode of bringing about the Divine ends when evolution itself is understood as a process whose general shape could be anticipated in advance, and could thus be relied on in the carrying out of the Divine plan. The emphasis on the contingency of evolutionary outcomes on the part of writers like Monod and Gould could easily suggest that ours is a universe on whose processes purpose *could* not be imposed, not even by a Creator.

In this essay, I first want to outline two very different understandings of evolution. According to one, evolution is, in broad outline at least, predictable, given the right conditions; natural selection works in a more or less law-like way to bring about increasing complexity. According to the other view, evolution is in no way predictable; contingency limits the operations of selection so heavily that outcomes simply cannot be anticipated, even in the most general way. One way in which the contingency of the evolutionary account of human origins might be countered from the theistic point of view would be to suppose that God "intervened", in one sense or another of that inadequate term, to bring about the appearance of humanity. But there is another alternative. In the final section of the essay, I recall the traditional theological doctrine of God's eternity in order to decide whether, according to this account, the contingency of

evolutionary processes need have the negative import often claimed for
it in regard to cosmic purpose. If the Creator is understood to escape the
limits imposed by temporality, would radical contingency still render evolutionary outcomes impervious to the Creator's purposes?*

1. PREDICTING EVOLUTION

The reader may not be familiar with the "extraterrestrial civilisation
equation" which was first formulated by radio-astronomer, Frank Drake,
back in the 1960s. Drake and some of his colleagues were convinced that
the powerful new technology of the radio telescope ought to be utilised
in a systematic effort to discover whether radio messages were being
beamed in our direction by extraterrestrial civilisations sufficiently advanced to generate such signals. To justify devoting precious time on
these expensive instruments to such a quest it was crucial to estimate
how likely it was that such civilisations existed, and if so, in what numbers. How likely would it be that one lay within, say, twenty light years
of us? Even with one as close as that, the forty-year interval between
message and response would make for slow dialogue!

At a conference on extraterrestrial intelligence sponsored by the National Academy of Sciences in 1961, Drake proposed the following equation:

$$N = R \; F_p \; N_e \; F_l \; F_i \; F_c \; L$$

N is the number of civilisations in our galaxy with both the capacity and
the interest for interstellar communication. R is the mean rate per year
of star formation averaged over the lifetime of the galaxy; F_p is the fraction of stars with planetary systems; N_e is the mean number of planets
in such systems with environments favourable for the origin of life; F_l is
the fraction of such planets on which life does develop; F_i is the fraction
of these planets on which intelligent life with manipulative abilities arises
during the lifetime of the local sun; F_c is the fraction of these latter planets
that give rise to an advanced technical civilisation; and L is the mean
lifetime of such a civilisation.[1]

It might seem as though this does not get us far towards calculating
the value of N, given that there are seven unknown quantities on the other
side of the equation. But Drake, and following him Carl Sagan, were not
daunted by this challenge and proceeded to give a rough estimate for
each of the seven. Sagan's figures for these are: 10, 1, 1, 1, 10^{-1}, 10^{-1},
for the first six. L gave him more trouble. Would a technical civilisation
quickly destroy itself so that its mean lifetime might be no more than
100 years? Or would it control its impulses to violence and settle into a
stable mode of existence that could last as long as the planet does (10^8

years)? The first value of L would imply that N would be of the order of only 10, the second that N would be 10^7. As a compromise, Sagan settled on 106 as a reasonable estimate of the number of advanced technical civilisations in our galaxy. And this figure thereupon attained a certain status in the ETI literature.[2]

There is obviously much that one could say about this rather carefree calculation.[3] But my interest here lies in Sagan's understanding of biological evolution as a process that, given the right environment, will necessarily occur and in the course of time necessarily give rise to intelligence. Without some such assumption, a value for N could not be estimated, not even in the roughest way. This way of understanding the operation of natural selection has, indeed, been a fairly common one. Textbook presentations of Darwinian theory often make it seem like a simple consequence of natural selection in operation: heritable variations that favour differential survival of descendants will tend to spread in the population. There may be additional complications involving geographical isolation, environmental change and the like, but the impression is of a gradual but steady drift towards greater complexity. Organic structures become more complex as new organs develop and old ones find new uses. Intelligence itself, with the enormous advantage it confers in terms of survival and propagation, may then seem an almost inevitable development, if the time-scale be generous enough.

This "upward and onward" view of the action of evolution finds some support in the text of *The Origin of Species* itself:

> Natural selection acts, as we have seen, exclusively by the presentation and accumulation of variations which are beneficial under the organic and inorganic conditions of life to which each creature is at each successive period exposed. The ultimate result will be that each creature will tend to become more and more improved in relation to its conditions of life. This improvement will, I think, inevitably lead to the gradual advancement of the organisation of the greater number of living beings throughout the world.[4]

One recent strong supporter of the inevitability of the evolutionary development of life is Nobel prize-biochemist, Christian de Duve. In his book, *Vital Dust* (1995), he argues that as we have come to understand the complex processes of the living cell, we have been able to give a more and more satisfactory account of the developments that could have led up to the appearance of the first cell. He maintains that: "Most of the steps involved must have had a very high likelihood of taking place under the prevailing conditions."[5] The universe, he concludes, "is pregnant with life":

In this organic cloud, which pervades the universe, life is almost bound to arise, in a molecular form not very different from its form on Earth, wherever physical conditions are similar to those that prevailed on our planet some four billion years ago. This conclusion seems to me inescapable. Those who claim that life is a highly improbable event, possibly unique, have not looked closely enough at the chemical realities underlying the origin of life. Life is either a reproducible, almost commonplace manifestation of matter, given certain conditions, or a miracle. Too many steps are involved to allow for something in between.[6]

And he extends this argument from the development of the first cell to the appearance on earth of intelligence; he "sees at work throughout animal evolution a strong selective pressure favouring the creation of neuronal networks of increasing complexity."[7] And again: "The drive toward larger brains and, therefore, toward more consciousness, intelligence, and communication ability dominates the animal limb of the tree of life on earth."[8] His conclusion is directed specifically against Stephen Gould: "The history of life on earth allows less leeway to contingency and unpredictability than current fashion claims."[9]

But it was among philosophers, perhaps, that the progressivist view of the development of life found the warmest welcome originally, especially among those who generally regarded evolution as the key to their cosmology and to their philosophy. Herbert Spencer formulated a "law" of evolution that would, he believed, hold not only for living things but for the physical world in general. Organic structure, he claimed, tends to become more and more differentiated over time, with new forms of integration constantly appearing. Following Lamarck, he maintained that the use or disuse of an organ could lead to hereditable changes of function. Later philosophers like Lloyd Morgan, Samuel Alexander and Henri Bergson, proposed theories of evolution that departed even more from the Darwinian norm than did Spencer's, while agreeing that evolution is a relatively steady and progressive process.

It is notable that those philosophers who have represented evolution in strongly progressivist terms have as a rule (Spencer would be an obvious exception) seen evolution as God's mode of action in the world. This conjunction finds its most striking expression, perhaps, in the work of Pierre Teilhard de Chardin. He sought an explanation for the steady "complexification" he found in the fossil record of life in a "psychic" or "radial" energy that operated directively, unlike the "tangential" energies treated in physics and chemistry. Though he allows for a degree of "groping" along the way, evolution is for him "a grand orthogenesis of everything living toward a higher degree of immanent spontaneity," "a spiral which springs upwards as it turns. From one zoological layer to another, *something is carried over: it grows, jerkily, but ceaselessly and in a constant direction.*"[10] So steady, indeed, in his view has the upward curve been that he felt entitled to extend it into the far future to an Omega Point where consciousness will finally be fully realised, a Final Cause in which an explanation will be found for the entire course of evolution that inexorably led in its direction.

Few other evolutionary philosophers were quite so confidently orthogenetic in their understanding of the evolutionary process. But philosophers, like the physicists and earth scientists who compute the likelihood of intelligent life elsewhere in the universe, have been on the whole more likely than biologists to see the operation of evolution in terms of *law*, of a force analogous to Newtonian gravity that relentlessly alters the composition of the gene-pool to create more and more complex organisms. In this understanding, evolutionary theory becomes a predictive resource and not just an explanation for the radiation of living forms in times past.

2. THE CONTINGENCY OF EVOLUTION

Those who shaped the "new synthesis" in evolutionary biology over the past half century were never comfortable with the predictive uses of evolutionary theory by exobiologists and others, and were flatly opposed to orthogenesis in any shape or form. Ernst Mayr and Theodosius Dobzhansky were among those who expressed their scepticism about this way of understanding evolutionary modes of explanation. The most outspoken critic was, perhaps, George Gaylord Simpson who in *This View of Life* developed an extended polemic against the assumptions underlying the predictivist account. He emphasised, in particular, the fundamental differences between such non-historical natural sciences as physics and chemistry and the historical sciences: geology, paleontology and evolutionary biology. The latter deal with unique events for which the notions of law applicable in physics simply do not work. The complexity of the interactions between environment and gene-change is so great that any attempt to abstract "trends" or "tendencies" is bound to fail. "There is direction, but it wavers, and apparently random effects also occur."[11]

In *Chance and Necessity* (1971), Jacques Monod celebrated the decisive role of chance in evolution. Since mutations in DNA:

> constitute the *only* possible source of modifications in the genetic text, itself, the *sole* repository of the organism's hereditary structures, it necessarily follows that chance *alone* is at the source of every innovation, of all creation in the biosphere. Pure chance, absolutely free but blind, at the very root of the stupendous edi-

fice of evolution: this central concept of modern biology is no longer one among other possible or even conceivable hypotheses. It is today the *sole* conceivable hypothesis.[12]

Mutations are "chance" events for him in two different senses. First, they represent the convergence of previously unrelated causal chains: second, they are quantum events and hence essentially unpredictable. The course of evolution is thus itself unpredictable in detail. Yet despite the far-reaching consequences that Monod draws from the primacy of chance in the story of evolution (losing our "necessary place in nature's scheme" condemns us to "a frozen universe of solitude"[13]), he is still willing to allow that evolution follows a "generally progressive course", that its general direction is "upward", that an initial commitment in particular groups to a certain kind of behaviour "commits the species irrevocably in the direction of a continuous perfecting of the structures and performances this behaviour needs for its support".[14] So the operation of natural selection seems to restore a fair degree of directionality, and even of progress, to the course of evolution after all.

Stephen Jay Gould takes a much stronger line regarding the contingency of evolutionary change. He will have no truck with "upward courses" or "trends", or with predictability of even the most modest kind. And his emphasis is not on the randomness either of the mutations that afford the material for natural selection nor of the genetic drift in founder populations. Rather, it is on the lack, in general, of connection between the multiple lines of causality that affect singular historical events, such as changes in the gene-composition of a population.

In his popular essays, he returns over and again to the flexibility of the evolutionary process that makes it something other than simple selectionist accounts would lead one to expect. In the title essay of *Eight Little Piggies*, he argues that the pentadactyl limb we share with so many other mammalian species "just happens to be". It ought not necessarily be taken to testify to some intrinsic adaptive advantage of five, as against some other number, of digits; the earliest tetrapods, in fact, had seven or eight digits. Rather, the number may derive from:

> the complex, unrepeatable, and unpredictable events of history. We are trained to think that the "hard science" models of quantification, experimentation, and replication are inherently superior and exclusively canonical, so that any other set of techniques can pale by comparison. But historical science proceeds by reconstructing a set of contingent events, explaining in retrospect what could not have been predicted beforehand.... Contingency is rich and fascinating; it embodies an exquisite tension between the power of individuals to modify history and the intelligible

limits set by laws of nature. The details of individual and species's lives are not mere frills, without power to shape the large-
scale course of events, but particulars that can alter entire futures,
profoundly and forever.[15]

The nature of history and of historical science is the theme around
which *Wonderful Life*, his lively account of the successive and conflicting
interpretations of the Cambrian fauna found in the Burgess shale, is organised. He has long been a critic of the gradualism of the traditional
Darwinian account of the operation of natural selection, urging instead a
"punctuated equilibrium" in which long periods of stasis, when species
remain more or less unchanged, are interspersed with moments of relatively sudden speciation.[16] In this ambitious work, he reconstructs the
extraordinary original flowering of the major phyla of nearly all modern
animal groups within a geologically (and biologically) brief interval of a
few million years during the Cambrian period, beginning around 570 million years ago. What excites Gould most about the "Cambrian explosion",
as it has been called, is not just the fact that the phyla appeared over
such a relatively brief time nor that no new phyla have appeared since,
but that the vast majority of the arthropod "ground-plans" found in the
Burgess shale have no modern representatives. Put in another way, of the
twenty-five or so diverse anatomical designs found in the shale, any one
of which *could*, in Gould's view, have served as ancestor for a distinct
phylum, only four survived the Cambrian period and gave rise to the
modern animal phyla. It is this decimation of phylum-candidates, this
"lottery" as he terms it, that Gould sees as testimony to the effects of
historical contingency. The conventional response, of course, would be
that the four surviving phyla were in some way better adapted for changing environmental conditions. Gould regards this as implausible. But even
if this were to have been the case, under a different environmental scenario the list of survivors (he claims) would have been quite different.
And everything that came later would then have taken a quite different
direction.

Gould's emphasis on extinctions, particularly the great extinctions of
life that marked the end of the Permian period, when up to 96% of marine
species died off, and of the Cretaceous, when the dinosaurs vanished, is
in some ways reminiscent of the catastrophism that enlivened geological
debate two centuries ago. His claim is that in such episodes natural selection of the usual sort would cease to operate; it would in large measure
be a matter of luck which among all the existing species would survive
to propagate themselves in a depopulated world.

Furthermore, the causes of such massive extinctions are a matter of
chance, relative to the prior history of the affected populations. And so
he concludes:

Since dinosaurs were not moving toward markedly larger brains, and since such a prospect may lie outside the capabilities of reptilian design, we must assume that consciousness would not have evolved on our planet if a cosmic catastrophe had not claimed the dinosaurs as victims.[17]

The strength of Gould's case lies in his insistence on the importance of the web of necessary conditions in any explanation of a complex historical event, conditions, that is, in whose absence the outcome would have been different, perhaps altogether different. One specific source of contingency to which he often returns is the constraint set on possible adaptive lines of development in a particular population by the availability in some corner of that population, for quite other reasons, of the appropriate anatomical framework for that development. Thus, one obscure group (lungfish/coelocanth) belonging to the vast domain of fish species in the Devonian period happened to have the sort of skeleton that would permit the development of limbs, thus allowing locomotion on land. Had those species not been present, as they might well not have been, Gould remarks, amphibians could not have invaded the land, which in that event might still be inhabited by insects only.[18]

Few have pushed the theme of contingency as far as Gould has; others have found his emphasis much overdone.[19] He is, of course, right about the overall contingency of the evolutionary path actually followed. But "contingency" is ambiguous in this context: it may refer to the chance character of the *particular* outcome, or to the unlikelihood of an outcome of this general sort. Accepting the first by no means commits one to the second. The question remains: how does one know what would have happened if life *had* taken a different fork along the way? Or more exactly: how likely was it that life on land would not have developed if lungfish had not been around at the right time? Or that consciousness would *not* have developed if an asteroid had not hit or if climate change had covered Africa in forest three or four million years ago? The massive evidence for parallel evolution of such organs as the eye or of physiologically very similar species ought to give one pause in making such claims of unlikelihood. It seems as though contingency has in many instances been overridden by strong selective advantage.

There appears, then, to be a considerable risk involved in adopting either of the extremes above, the appeal to laws or tendencies that would allow one to assert that life on land or the advent of consciousness would assuredly have come about anyway, or the emphasis on radical contingency that allows Gould to conclude that *Homo sapiens* is a "tiny twig on an improbable branch of a contingent limb on a fortunate tree." "Replay the tape a million times from a Burgess beginning," he remarks," and I doubt that anything like *Homo sapiens* would ever evolve again."[20]

How *can* we be so sure either of the inevitability or the improbability of the advent of consciousness?

Most evolutionary biologists and philosophers of biology seem to adopt a middle course somewhere between these extremes, but this still allows for a lot of latitude. Dobzhansky, for example, disagrees with what he regards as an overemphasis on chance on the part of Monod. On the contrary, he remarks: "Viewing evolution of the living world as a whole, from the hypothetical primeval self-reproducing substance to higher plants, animals, and man, one cannot avoid the recognition that progress or advancement, or rise, or ennoblement, has occurred."[21] Though chance predominates in mutation and recombination, he goes on, natural selection serves to counterbalance this as an "anti-chance" factor. Thus, though the course of evolution cannot be predicted, "it does not follow that the human species arose by a lucky throw of some evolutionary or celestial dice."[22] In a recent assessment of the issue, Elliott Sober is more cautious. He is sceptical of the suggestion that the evolutionary process has in the past displayed progress or even direction. Though there may have been directional trends within specific lineages, all that the theory of natural selection allows one to conclude is that such trends are *possible*. It does not, however, allow one to anticipate them in advance; the multiple sources of contingency exclude this.[23]

What may we conclude from this rapid survey? Macro-evolution is an irregular process, admitting of breaks, reversals, large-scale extinctions. Its course can, in principle at least, be explained *after* the fact, but we cannot anticipate this course. The last billion years has seen an enormous growth in the variety and number of species. There has been a concomitant growth in the complexity of organisms that, (according to some) can be construed as a form of progress; it has, however, proved difficult in practice to find an agreed definition of what "complexity" and "progress" should be taken to mean in this context.[24] Nevertheless, as the palaeontological and geological records come under closer scrutiny and genetic mechanisms come to be better understood, the fragile character of the causal skein leading up to the first appearance of humans becomes ever more evident.

The contingency of this appearance may be enormously increased, according to a recent argument, if one moves from biology to cosmology, specifically to the newest versions of Big Bang theory. In their joint work, *Theism, Atheism, and Big Bang Cosmology*, Quentin Smith and William Craig debate the consequences of the new cosmology for belief in God. Smith claims that Big Bang cosmology effectively disproves the existence of a Creator. One of the arguments he uses is of special interest because it carries further the implication that contingency and Divine purpose at the cosmic level are radically opposed. The argument runs like this. According to Big Bang theory, the universe began from a singularity. Such singularities are *inherently* chaotic and unpredictable. No physical laws connect them to later states; in fact, the form taken by later physical laws, the relative magnitude of the four fundamental forces, for instance, is not determined by the initial singularity and is, in principle therefore, a random outcome. Thus, "God has no basis on which to compute what will emerge from the singularity."[25] God cannot, then, have had as purpose that the created universe should contain animate creatures, since a universe in which such creatures could never appear could equally well have developed from the initial singularity (indeed, according to recent "anthropic" arguments would have been far more likely to do so). This, therefore, according to Smith, constitutes an argument against the sort of Creator that religious people normally believe in, namely one whose purposes in creating the universe included the bringing to be of the human race.[26]

What are the theological implications of this, emphasis on contingency, whether at the evolutionary or the cosmological levels? Belief in a Creator has usually gone hand in hand with a conviction that the human race has a special role to play in the story of the Creation: fashioned in the Creator's image, the only creatures so far known to us that are able freely to offer or to deny the Creator their love. Jews, Christians and Moslems would be at one in supposing that insofar as we can speak of God's plans at all, we can assume that humans have a significant part in at least one corner of them. It would seem to follow, then, that the appearance of the human species would not, as it were, have been left to chance. If it was part of the Creator's purpose that humans should eventually make their entrance on planet Earth after a fifteen-billion year preparation, can the story of that long prelude be as shot through with contingency as it seems to be? Conversely, if the contingency thesis be accepted, even if not in as radical a form as Gould or Smith propose, does this not cast doubt on the belief that the Creator intended the cosmos to bring forth human beings? And if it does, would it not also call in question the whole notion of an omnipotent Creator whose purposes give meaning to a universe that would otherwise be pointless?

The frank anthropocentrism of the line of inquiry these questions open up runs counter, of course, to the instincts of scientists who sometimes call on a "Copernican principle" to justify their refusal to grant any form of privilege to humans. But Western theology is of its nature anthropocentric; it is concerned centrally with human destiny. When theologians hurdle the eons of evolutionary time in order to concentrate on the relationship between human beings and God, the form their inquiry takes will necessarily appear alien to scientists who look on humans as one node, admittedly a particularly intricate node, in a vast network of living kinds. But if scientists ought to be careful not to rush too rapidly to judgement when their theological colleagues focus on human destiny, theologians have to take seriously what the sciences have to say about how human beings came to be here in the first place.

3. PURPOSE AND CONTINGENCY

How *are* purpose and contingency to be related at the cosmic level? Popular writers on evolution, as we have seen, tend to see them as antithetical.[27] But not all evolutionary biologists are so quick to judgement. Simpson, for example, remarks:

> Adaptation is real, and it is achieved by a progressive and directed process. The process is wholly natural in its operation. This natural process achieves the aspect of purpose without the intervention of a purposer; and it has produced a vast plan without the concurrent action of a planner. It may be that the initiation of the process and the physical laws under which it functions had a purpose, and that this mechanistic way of achieving a plan is the instrument of a Planner - of this still deeper problem the scientist, as scientist, cannot speak.[28]

He speaks of "long and continued trends" that are "kept going by natural selection," where "creative natural selection" is "the directive, pseudo-purposive factor back of adaptation;" he notes, however, that it is "not always the decisive factor in evolution and it never acts alone."[29] The trends can thus be interrupted, hence his insistence (as we have seen) that the course of evolution cannot be predicted in advance. Even though evolution is "a deterministic process to a high degree," the factors that have determined the appearance of human beings are so intricate and so special that though "human origins were indeed inevitable under the precise conditions of our actual history, that makes the more nearly impossible such an occurrence anywhere else."[30] Inevitable in one sense as it may have been, then, no finality could have been involved: "If evolution is God's plan of creation - a proposition that a scientist as such should neither affirm nor deny - then God is not a finalist."[31] A plan, somehow, but without "finality."

Gould would object to this talk of trends and plans, and would place the emphasis on the fragility of the line leading to the human, a theme on which he and Simpson could agree. His own sympathies, he tells us, lie with the tentative solution Darwin once offered, in his correspondence with Asa Gray, of the dilemma of how God could permit the suffering that is everywhere to be found in non-human nature: perhaps one could hold that the *details* of the operation of nature are a matter not of law but of chance. The implication is that God is responsible for lawlikeness, with its overtone for purpose, but not for chance outcomes. The advent of *Homo sapiens* is "a wildly improbable evolutionary event," Gould remarks. It is a "contingent detail" of cosmic history, something that very well might not have happened, something that in consequence (Gould implies) cannot be attributed to purpose. Nevertheless, we "may yet hope for purpose, or at least neutrality, from the universe in general."[32] The rather half-hearted suggestion on the part of both authors is, then, that there may be enough lawlikeness in the universe, despite the prevalence of contingency, to sustain some sort of claim for purpose at the cosmic level. But how? For one possible answer we might return to an objection posed by the Aristotelian Simplicio to Salviati, Galileo's spokesman, in the great *Dialogue Concerning Two Chief World Systems* (1632). If Copernicus were right about the earth's motion round the sun, a parallax shift ought to be noticeable in the relative positions of the stars. Yet none is seen. The alternative is that the stars are at an enormous distance from us. But then, to what purpose are these great spaces? Are they not "superfluous and vain"? To which Salviati replies that God may well have other plans in mind besides the care of the human race. And in any event: "it is brash for our feebleness to attempt to judge the reasons for God's actions."[33] Good advice still!

But suppose we put this objection again today. Our universe, we now know, is far, far greater than Copernicus could ever have dreamed; space and time stretch out to the limits of human imagination. Does this not greatly enhance the difficulty for the theist? Perhaps not. Might it not be said that such great spaces populated by billions of galaxies that have developed over billions of years may have been needed in order that, in a natural way, the cosmos might give birth somewhere within it to human life one or maybe a multiplicity of times? The contingency of the single evolutionary line might thus be overcome by the immensity of the cosmic scale. Evolutionary biologists are divided, as we have seen, as to whether, on general evolutionary grounds, life of a broadly human type would be *bound* to originate somewhere in all those myriad planetary systems. But assuming for the moment a positive answer to this question, the enormous space of evolutionary possibilities would then make it possible to maintain that there could be a cosmic purpose at work here on the part of a Creator, a purpose that the contingency of particular evolutionary lines would not defeat.

If God be conceived as a time-bound Creator whose knowledge of the future depends on a knowledge of the present, this way of swamping contingency in order to achieve a distant end would be appropriate. It does presuppose, of course, that human life would inevitably appear in a universe of this general sort, if it be large enough and long-lived enough. And this, some theists would object, we do not really know. There might very well be steps in the process that would require some sort of "special" action on God's part to enable them to occur. In a recent essay, the philosopher of religion Peter van Inwagen observes:

> Since the actual physical world seems in fact, to be indeterministic, it is plausible to suppose that there are a great many states of affairs that are not part of God's plan and which, moreover, cannot be traced to the free decisions of created beings. I very much doubt that when the universe was (say) 10^{-45} seconds old, it was then physically inevitable that the earth, or even the Milky Way Galaxy, should exist. Thus, these objects, so important from the human point of view, are no part of God's plan—or at least not unless their creation was due to God's miraculous intervention into the course of development of the physical world at a relatively late stage. I see no reason as a theist, or as a Christian, to believe that the existence of human beings is a part of God's plan.[34]

Realising that this last suggestion is likely to shock the average Christian, van Inwagen adds a significant qualifier: "I am sure that the existence of animals made in God's image - that is, rational animals having free-will and capable of love - *is* a part of God's plan." Though he sees "no reason to believe," on theological grounds, that God planned this *particular* race of human beings, he is sure, on these same grounds, that *some* human-like race is part of God's plan.[35] Like those evolutionary biologists who regard the contingency of the human line as an obstacle to describing the appearance of humanity as an outcome of purpose, van Inwagen takes contingency very seriously as a negative sign when attributing some feature of the universe to God's plan. (Note the 'thus' in the middle of the passage quoted.) But he suggests a way in which such contingency can be, as it were, transcended, one that does not depend on cosmic scale. God may intervene miraculously in the causal process to ensure a particular outcome, in which case that outcome, despite the appearance of contingency from the scientific standpoint, would still be the result of plan, God's plan.[36] Here, then, is a second way in which the contingency of the evolutionary process leading to the human could be reconciled with the claim that the appearance of the human on earth is, nevertheless, is part of God's plan for the cosmos.

Van Inwagen does not develop this suggestion of a "special" action of some sort on the Creator's part at crucial steps in the development of life on earth. But a good many others have done so, and from a variety of widely different points of view. The most radical claim would be that of the defenders of so-called "creation science" who defend a more or less literal interpretation of the *Genesis* account of human origins.[37] A much more nuanced view would be that of Alvin Plantinga who argues for the insufficiency of current evolutionary theory to account for various stages in the development of life, beginning with the appearance of the first living cell, and the consequent greater likelihood, from the Christian standpoint, of a "special creation" on God's part at crucial steps along the way.[38] And a very different approach again would be that of John Polkinghorne who finds in chaos theory and quantum theory warrant for a causal "looseness" in physical process that would have been excluded in the Newtonian world-view. This leads him to suggest that God can operate in the ontological "gaps" thus opened up, communicating information without altering energy. God might in this way accomplish the ends of Providence without miracle, in the sense of an observable departure from the normal order of nature.[39]

These three accounts of Divine action within cosmic process disagree fundamentally, particularly regarding the role to be played by natural science in illuminating the course of that process. But they implicitly agree in linking purpose at the cosmic level to a "special" action of some sort on the Creator's part within cosmic process. I am not going to discuss the merits and demerits of these views here. Instead, I propose to examine an alternative way of dealing with the challenge that contingency offers to our irremediably earthbound notions of a Creator as a Being whose action is guided by "purposes" and who "makes plans". Might not chance be one way for God to get things done? Does contingency hinder plan on the part of an agent who does not have to rely on a knowledge of the present in order to plan future outcomes?

4. ETERNITY AND TELEOLOGY

In our discussions so far, we have made some simple, and on the face of it, plausible assumptions about the relationship between time and teleology. But what if these were to be challenged? What if the Creator be supposed to stand outside of temporal process entirely? This, after all, has been the dominant view of the Creation within the Christian tradition from Augustine's day onwards. It is true that it has been challenged in recent times, but it retains strong support among Christian theologians. Would such a view make any difference to our assessment of the significance of the evolutionary sequence? First, a quick outline of the view itself.[40]

Augustine saw God not as a Demiurge shaping an independently existing matter nor as a First Mover responsible for the motions of a world whose natures were not of the Mover's fashioning, but as a Creator in the fullest sense, a Being from whom the existence of all things derives. Such a Being cannot be operating under constraints, as the God of Greek philosophers did. Temporality is the first and most obvious constraint of the created world, a mark of its dependent status. A temporal being exists only in the present moment, without secure access either to its past or its future. Its past is no longer; its future is not yet. So even though both past and future are somehow constitutive of what "it" is, in a real sense, they do not exist. Such a being is evidently lacking, incomplete.

The Creator on whom the universe depends for its existence cannot be limited in this way. Time is a condition of the creature, a sign of dependence. It is created *with* the creature; by bringing a changing world to be, God brings time, the condition of change, to be. The act of creation is a single one, in which what is past, present or future from the perspective of the creature issues as a single whole from the Creator.[41] God is not part of the temporal sequence that the act of creation brings to be; God is not one more temporal thing among other things. The Creator is "outside" time created, though the metaphor is an imperfect one. Calling God "eternal" is not a way of saying that God is without beginning or end, like Aristotle's universe.[42] "Eternal" does not mean unending duration; it means that temporal notions simply do not apply to the Creator as Creator. Nor does it mean "static", as nineteenth-century critics charged. In a famous formula, Boethius expressed it in lapidary terms: "Eternity is the whole, simultaneous and perfect possession of boundless life."[43] God's life transcends the sort of dispersal that is the first characteristic of the creature; it is not subject to the kind of division that time-marking would require.

Creation and conservation blend together in this view, as do transcendence and immanence. Creation was not just a moment of cosmic origination a long time in the past, though we often speak of it that way since the first moment seems to call in a special way for a transcendent cause. Creation continues at every moment, and each moment has the same relation of dependency on the Creator. God transcends the world; the Divine Being in no way depends on the world for existence nor requires it as complement. Yet the Creator is also immanent in every existent at every moment, sustaining it in being. God knows the world in the act of creating it, and thus knows the cosmic past, present and future in a single unmediated grasp.[44] God knows the past and the future of each creature, not by memory or by foretelling, then, as another creature might, but in the same direct way that God knows the creature's present. When we speak of God's "foreknowledge", the temporal "fore" has reference to our created reference-frame, within which the distinctions between past, present and future are *real*. From God's side, however, there is only knowledge, the knowledge proper to a maker who is not bound by these distinctions.

This is familiar, of course. It is all very conceptual, as philosophers' talk of God inevitably is. It is no more than an exploration of an initial postulate concerning the act of creation, when that act is understood as a bringing into existence and a holding in existence, both entirely outside the range of our experience. How would such an account be supported? How does it meet the two major objections that Augustine already anticipated: Can this way of construing the work of creation be made compatible with the reality of human freedom? Does it not saddle the Creator with responsibility for all of the manifest evils of cosmic history? I am leaving these familiar and troubling questions aside in order to focus oñ a limited but perhaps more tractable issue: How does the apparent defeasibility of the evolutionary line leading to the emergence of *Homo sapiens* fit with the view that the act of creation is a single atemporal action on the part of God?

What I want to argue is that both Christian evolutionists who have assumed that the purposes of the Creator can be realised only through law-like, and more or less predictable, processes as well as those who on the contrary infer from the contingency of the evolutionary process to the lack of purpose and meaning in the universe generally, are mistaken from the perspective of the traditional doctrine of God's eternality. Our notions of teleology, of purpose, of plan are conditioned by the temporality of our world, in which plans gradually unfold and processes regularly come to term. In such a world, purpose depends on foreknowledge, and foreknowledge in turn depends on the predictability of the processes involved. Lacking such predictability, there cannot be reliable foreknowledge, and without foreknowledge purpose is ineffective. But a Creator who brings everything to be in a single action from which the entirety of temporal process issues, does not rely on the regularity of process to know the future condition of the creature or to attain ends. The notion of "purpose" must itself be reinterpreted in such a case. God's knowledge of how a situation will develop over time is not discursive; God does not infer from a prior knowledge of how situations of the sort ordinarily work out. It makes no difference, therefore, whether the appearance of *Homo sapiens* is the inevitable result of a steady process of complexification stretching over billions of years, or whether on the contrary it comes about through a series of coincidences that would have made it entirely unpredictable from the (causal) human standpoint. Either way, the outcome is of God's making, and from the Biblical standpoint may appear as part of God's plan.

Terms like "plan" and "purpose" obviously shift meaning when the element of time is absent. For God to plan is for the outcome to occur. There is no interval between decision and completion. Thus the character of the process which, from our perspective, separates initiation and accomplishment is of no relevance to whether or not a plan or purpose on the part of the Creator is involved. Reference to "cosmic purpose" in the evolutionary context need not, however, involve design in the traditional sense. That is, it does not point to features of the process or the outcome that specifically require the intervention of mind and that would, therefore, allow one to infer to the agency of a cosmic Planner. There is nothing about the evolutionary process in itself that would lead one to recognise in it the deliberate action of such a Planner. It does not look like the kind of process human designers would use to accomplish their ends. When critics of the Christian understanding of cosmic history conclude in consequence that we live in a universe lacking in purpose, they are pointing to the lack of independently *recognisable* design in evolutionary change. But the Creator may not be a designer in this time-bound sense.

The type of contingency we have been discussing bears on the outcome of a process, the evolutionary process, so it involves time in an essential way. But contingency can take other forms, and at least one of these does not involve time directly. Discussions of the so-called anthropic principle begin from the claim that the application of general relativity theory to the first moments of the cosmic expansion postulated in the Big Bang cosmological model shows how extraordinarily contingent the initial conditions were that permitted a universe in which heavy elements, planets and ultimately complex life, could develop. It had been assumed in cosmological discussions from Descartes' time onwards that no special setting of the initial conditions would be needed in order for a universe of the kind we know should come to be.[45] The shock of discovering that this was apparently not the case led to various attempts in the 1970's to explain how such an "unlikely" universe might have originated.

Two types of "anthropic" explanation were proposed. Collins and Hawking suggested that if there were a vast number of independent universes than we would naturally find ourselves in one where human life could evolve, so there would be nothing surprising about the fact that the universe seems "fine-tuned" for life. A very different sort of explanation was theological in inspiration: the universe is the work of a Creator whose purposes in creating included humanity. God simply chose the initial energy-density and the laws of force that would allow that purpose to be realised. In the evolutionary context that we have been discussing, contingency has been seen as a *challenge* to the possibility of cosmic purpose. In the cosmological case, on the contrary, contingency is regarded as a sign of cosmic purpose.[46]

The attribution of cosmic purpose in the two cases must be carefully distinguished. Proponents of the anthropic argument claim to find recognisable signs of design in the initial cosmic configuration, so that the cosmological evidence is urged as independent evidence of cosmic purpose and even of the existence of a Designer.[47] Whereas in the evolutionary context, the claim that the advent of human life displays purpose, despite the contingency of the process leading to it, is based not on the scientific evidence but on considerations that are either theological or metaphysical in nature.

We have concluded that the contingency or otherwise of the evolutionary sequence does not bear on whether the created universe embodies purpose or not. Asserting the reality of cosmic purpose in this context takes for granted that we already believe that the universe depends for its existence on an omniscient Creator whose action is sufficiently like ours to allow us to call it purposive, in an admittedly analogical sense. It does not mean that we are privy to that purpose, though the traditions of the Torah, the Bible, the Koran, would imply a recognition of at least a part of it. Only to the extent that such a recognition were possible could one allow cosmic purpose to constitute a form of teleology (recalling that "teleology" refers to specific modes of explanation). When in the *Confessions* Augustine looks back over his life and finally recognises a Providence at work through all the contingency, it is to teleology of this sort that he is appealing.

Linking plan to Providence in this way gives rise to many other questions, of course. One would need, in particular, to be allowed to distinguish between God's intending and permitting something to occur.[48] But the answers to those questions, important, indeed crucial, though they are, do not affect the contention of this essay: that if one maintains the age-old doctrine of God's eternality, the contingency of the evolutionary process leading to the appearance of *Homo sapiens* makes no difference to the Christian belief in a special destiny for humankind.

* An earlier version of this essay has appeared in Finding God in All Things, edited by Michael Himes and Stephen Pope, New York: Crossroad Press, 1996.

NOTES

1. See I.S. Shklovskii and Carl Sagan, *Intelligent Life in the universe*, San Francisco: Holden-Day, 1966, chap. 29. One further factor, at least, would have to be considered: the likelihood that a technically advanced civilisation would, in fact, devote (and continue to devote) its resources to interstellar communication. The original point of Drake's formulation was simply to separate out the independent factors whose magnitudes would have to be calculated, at least roughly, if an estimate of the value of N were to be arrived at. As such, the "equation" is quite instructive.

2. Commenting on the ETC equation, Christian de Duve remarks: "Although quantitative estimates vary widely, the consensus is that the history of the earth is probably not unique. The figure of about one million 'habitable' planets per galaxy is considered not unreasonable." *Vital Dust: The Origin and Evolution of Life on Earth*, New York: Basic Books, 1995, p. 121). In *Persons: A Study of Possible Moral Agents in the universe* (New York: Herder and Herder, 1969), Roland Puccetti makes use of Sagan's analysis to conclude that "a correct analysis of the person-concept, combined with the not unreasonable belief in extraterrestrial natural persons, actually undermines the Christian belief in God" (p. 143). His argument is that since the total number of communities of persons in *all* the galaxies could be as many as 1,018, and since God could not be simultaneously incarnate in more than one person, there would be no way for God to become incarnate in all these communities within the life-span of the universe, as Christian belief would seem to require. The argument is fascinating but exceedingly porous. See McMullin, "Persons in the universe", *Zygon* 15, 1980, 69-89.

3. See McMullin, "Estimating the Probabilities of Extraterrestrial Life", *Icarus*, 14, 1971, 291-4.

4. *The Origin of Species*, Philadelphia: University of Pennsylvania Press, 1959, p. 221.

5. Christian de Duve, *Vital Dust*, New York: Basic Books, 1995, p. 9. See also his "The Birth of Complex Cells", *Scientific American*, 174 (4), 1996, 50-57.

6. *Vital Dust*, p.292. This last inference seems to risk begging the question.

7. *Vital Dust*, p. 285.

8. *Vital Dust*, p. 297.

9. *Vital Dust*, p. 296. What strikes the reader, besides the ingenuity of the tentative reconstructions de Duve offers of the biochemical pathways that could have led from one stage to the next, is the exceedingly tentative character, by his own admission, of some of those reconstructions, and hence the real difficulty in specifying the probabilities involved in a step of the particular sort. There is a temptation to say that if the time actually taken between one major biochemical development and the next was in fact T, then T is "the time it takes" for a transition of this kind to occur.

10. Pierre Teilhard de Chardin, *The Phenomenon of Man*, New York: Harper, 1965, pp. 151, 149. Emphasis in the original.

11. *This View of Life*, New York: Harcourt, Brace and World, 1964, p.189.

12. Jacques Monod, *Chance and Necessity*, New York, Knopf, 1971, pp. 112-3. Emphasis his.

13. *Ibid.*, pp. 169-170.

14. *Ibid.*, pp. 119, 124, 127.

15. *Eight Little Piggies*, New York: Penguin, 1993, p. 77.

16. Ernst Mayr, a leading exponent of the synthetic theory, claims that an apparently discontinuous sequence of this sort can easily be incorporated into a broadly Darwinian account of evolutionary change; he recalls, indeed, that he had already indicated the need for such a modification in some of his own early work (*Toward a New Philosophy of Biology*, Cambridge MA: Harvard University Press, 1988, chap. 26: "Speciational evolution through punctuated equilibrium").

17. *Wonderful Life*, Cambridge MA: Harvard University Press, 1989, p. 318.

18. *Wonderful Life*, p. 318.

19. See, for example, the extended polemic in Daniel Dennett, *Darwin's Dangerous Idea*, New York; Simon and Schuster, 1995, chap. 10.

20. *Wonderful Life*, pp. 291, 289.

21. Theodosius Dobzhansky, "Chance and Creativity in Evolution", in *Studies in the Philosophy of Biology*, ed. F.J. Ayala and T. Dobzhansky, London: Macmillan, 1974, 307-338; pp.309, 311.

22. "Chance and Creativity", pp. 318, 329.

23. Elliott R. Sober, "Progress and Direction in Evolution", in *Creative Evolution?*, ed. J.H. Campbell and J.W. Schopf, Boston: Jones and Bartlett, 1994, 19-33.

24. Francisco Ayala, "The Concept of Biological Progress", in *Studies in the Philosophy of Biology*, 339-356.

25 Quentin Smith in Wilham Lane Craig and Quentin Smith, *Theism, Atheism, and Big Bang Cosmology*, Oxford: Clarendon Press, 1993, p. 212.

26. Smith makes the argument even more sweeping by arguing (1) that a universe brought to be by a benevolent Creator would have to have as one of its purposes the coming to be of animate creatures, and (2) that a theist cannot fall back on God's knowledge of counterfactuals because the needed counterfactual in this case "is inconsistent with the semantic properties of counterfactuals" (p. 213).

27. Critics like Dennett and Dawkins are not primarily thinking of the contingency issue when they reject any appeal to a Creator as a means of anchoring cosmic purpose. Their argument, rather, is that the Creator is an "idle wheel", that the neo-Darwinian argument, allied with standard astrophysical argument in cosmology, needs no further supplementation, no "skyhooks", in Dennett's metaphor. See Daniel Dennett, *Darwin's Dangerous Idea*; Richard Dawkins, *The Blind Watchmaker*, New York: Norton, 1987.

28. *This View of Life*, p. 212.

29. *This View of Life*, p. 210.

30. *This View of Life*, p. 268.

31. *This View of Life*, p. 265.

32. *Wonderful Life*, p. 291.

33. *Dialogue Concerning Two Chief World Systems*, transl. Stillman Drake, Berkeley: University of California Press, 1953, 367-8.

34. Peter van Inwagen, "The Place of Chance in a World Sustained by God", in *Divine and Human Actioni*, ed. T.V. Morris, Ithaca: Cornell University Press, 1988, 211-235; p. 225.

35. At first sight, it might seem that the distinction van Inwagen draws here is the same as the one just discussed: the contingency of the particular evolutionary line leading to humanity is contrasted with the inevitability of finding human-like beings *somewhere* in a universe so vast. But, in fact, this is not the ground of

the distinction he has in mind. Indeed, he rejects the suggestion that in a universe so large human-like beings would be bound to appear. Instead, he implies that it is sufficient for God to aim at the general end of bringing life to be somewhere in the universe, whereas the appearance of this particular race, not being "physically inevitable", need not be regarded as part of God's plan.

36. Van Inwagen is using the term 'miraculous' in a broader sense than the usual one to cover, for example, physical sequences that could be imperceptible to us. And he warns against taking the term 'intervene' to imply that God is in any sense external to the process; we simply do not have a word to convey a "special" action on God's part to bring about an outcome outside the ordinary run of nature. (I am grateful to Professor van Inwagen for our discussion of the ramifications of his essay.) If God were to "intervene" in a causal sequence, it would, of course, have to be in a *particular* sequence. So if (as van Inwagen supposes; see his "Doubts about Darwinism", in *Darwinism: Science or Philosophy*, ed. J. Buell and V. Hearne, Richardson, TX: Foundation for Thought and Ethics, 1996, 177-191) there is reason to believe that God intervened to supplement the evolutionary process leading to the appearance of the human race on earth, there would also be reason to believe that the existence of human beings on earth is a part of God's plan.

37. See, for example, Henry Morris, *Scientific Creationism*, San Diego: Creation-Life Publishers, 1974.

38. See Alvin Plantinga, "When Faith and Reason Clash: Evolution and the Bible", *Christian Scholar's Review*, 21, 1991, 8-32. Two critical responses to his essay appear in the same journal issue: Howard J. Van Till, "When Faith and Reason Co-operate", 33-45; Ernan McMullin, "Plantinga's Defense of Special Creation", 55-79. Plantinga replies to them in turn: "Evolution, Neutrality, and Antecedent Probability", 80-109. A further comment: Ernan McMullin, "Evolution and Special Creation", Zygon, 28, 1993, 299-335.

39. See John Polkinghorne, *Science and Providence: God's Interaction with the World*, Boston: Shambhala, 1989. For a critical evaluation of this proposal, see Steven Crain, *Divine Action and Indeterminism: On Models of Divine Agency that Exploit the New Physics*, Ph.D. dissertation, Ann Arbor: Ann Arbor Microfilms, 1993.

40. See, for example, Alan G. Padgett, *God, Eternity, and the Nature of Time*, New York: St. Martin's Press, 1992, chap. 3: "The Doctrine of Divine Timelessness: A Historical Sketch". I am grateful to David Burrell and Fred Freddoso for our discussions of the issues arising in this section.

41. How to relate the temporality of the creature with the eternality of the Creator without either making temporality unreal (by assuming that the future already exists) or making God quasi-temporal, has vexed philosophers from Aquinas's day to our own. See Eleanor Stump and Norman Kretzman, "Eternity", *Journal of Philosophy*, 78, 1981, 429-459.

42. See G.D. Yarnold, "Everlasting or Eternal?", chap. 9 in *The Moving Image*, London: Allen and Unwin, 1966, 139-152; Brian Davies, "A Timeless God?", *New Blackfriars*, 64, 1983, 218-224; Julie Gowan, "God and Timelessness: Everlasting or Eternal?", *Sophia*, 26, 1987, 15-29.

43. *The Consolation of Philosophy*, 5.6.

44. Aquinas enters a formal defence of the thesis that God knows future contingent things (*Summa Theologica*, I, q. 14, a.13). Such things are contingent relative to their antecedent physical causes, which is why temporal creatures like us, whose assessments of the future depend on a knowledge of such prior causes, can only

conjecture about their contingent outcomes. But God knows these outcomes directly in their presentness as their Creator; the act of bringing them to be has no temporal divisions within it. Some of the analogies Aquinas draws on here need careful construal: "He who sees the whole road from a height sees at once all those travelling on it" (a.13, ad 3); "His gaze is carried from eternity over all things as they are in their presentness" (a.13, c.). Such analogies might suggest that our inability to predict a contingent outcome is simply due to our lack of proper vantage-point: the various events taking place at this moment on the road just happen to be out of our sight. This in turn might be taken to imply that the future is already set, that it is only our powers of knowing that are unequal to the task of grasping it. But contingency is *real*, as Aquinas elsewhere makes clear. God knows contingent things that are future to us, not as a viewer would features of a landscape already determinate, but rather as a maker might, a unique sort of a maker who respects contingency in the cross-causal connections between the things made.

Debate about the manner of God's knowledge of future contingents intensified after Aquinas's day, particularly about how it was to be reconciled with the reality of human free choice. It came to a head between the Dominican supporters of Banez and the Jesuit followers of Molina at the end of the sixteenth century in the famous controversy "*de auxiliis*". For an account of the subtleties to which this protracted discussion gave rise, see William L. Craig, *The Problem of Divine Foreknowledge and Future Contingents from Aristotle to Suarez*, Leiden: Brill, 1988.

45. See E. McMullin, "Indifference Principle and Anthropic Principle in Cosmology", *Studies in the History and Philosophy of Science*, 24, 1993, 359-389.

46. The anthropic argument, it should be emphasised, is a vulnerable one in a number of respects. See E. McMullin, "Fine-tuning the universe?", in *Science, Technology, and Religious Ideas*, ed. M. Shale and G. Shields, Lanham MD: University Press of America, 1994, 97-125.

47. See, for example, M.A. Corey, *God and the New Cosmology: The Anthropic Design Argument*, Lanham MD: Rowman and Littlefield, 1993.

48. Following once again a traditional path, it seems consistent to maintain that sinful actions on the part of free agents or natural evils like the AIDS epidemic need not be intended by the Creator but are permitted because they are consequences of something that *is* intended. I am inclined to think that this is the only way one *might* meet the objection that has troubled so many since Darwin first proposed the hypothesis of natural selection: how can a good God allow suffering on the cosmic scale that selection appears to require?

SEARCHING FOR BEATITUDE IN
AN HIERARCHICALLY STRUCTURED UNIVERSE

TERENCE KENNEDY
(*Rome, Italy*)

Abstract: This essay takes the manner in which the difficulties raised by teleology in nature have influenced ethics as its starting-point. Etienne Gilson criticised Aristotle's conception of teleology for "reading into" nature purposes not discoverable there. Teleology is a concept that belongs to the philosophy of nature and should not be used to determine method in the natural sciences. Contemporary scientists have found successful ways of describing nature's functioning as a hierarchical structure. Michael Polanyi invoked Einstein's principle of boundary conditions to demonstrate how dual control operates at each level in this hierarchy. He identifies levels of achievement in nature and its evolution with different fields of teleology. Now the highest form of teleology occurs where the human person searches for fulfilment. St. Thomas Aquinas argues that God fulfils this desire through grace because the human person has a openness to transcendence, i.e., there is a teleology toward God as beatitude. At this level we recognise that the teleologies inherent to the universe are fulfilled in the beatitude promised in the Scriptures. Beatitude is therefore consistent with a dynamic, evolutionary image of the universe.
Keywords: Aristotle, beatitude, ethics, fulfilment, hierarchy, science, teleology.

The conflict between scientific and theological world views has nowhere been so intense as over the issue of teleology. The word "teleology" was an eighteenth century invention in philosophy and denotes the study of final causes in nature. Today it is understood as purposive or goal directed activity. Its invention did in fact mark the parting of the ways between the old *telos*-directed Aristotelian physics and the new experimental sciences based on accurate observation and mathematical measurement. This conflict of methods was resolved when Aristotle's authority was overthrown by excluding *telos* from the empirical and experimental explanations of the natural world. This essay seeks to explore the reasons why *telos* was rejected, its weaknesses and what some scholars see as still valid and useful in it today. It is in no way an apology for the Aristotelian view since it presupposes science's findings on, for example, the creation and the origin of the universe as well as the question of its end or finish as more recently raised by cosmologists whose enquiries have opened up the possibility of relating eschatology to cosmology. It focuses on a kindred concern seemingly suppressed because of the methodological expulsion of *telos* from modern physics, namely, how does our view of the universe relate to human destiny, conceived as beatitude in classical and Christian tradition. Teleology is probably the most difficult and perhaps most intractable question to be faced in the dialogue between faith and science. And teleology in its highest realisation is called beatitude. The present essay will, therefore, be restricted to developing three points: 1) the enigma of purpose i.e., how purpose has again become a topic of discussion in science and in ethics, 2) towards breaking the impasse i.e., what is valid in the idea of teleology? 3) beatitude in a hierarchically structured universe i.e. how beatitude as the highest form of teleology fits into a hierarchical image of the universe.

I. THE ENIGMA OF PURPOSE

The question of beatitude has come back into consideration because the former understanding of nature without *telos* has become uncertain and in many ways enigmatic. Several events witness to a new interplay between a scientific view of an open universe and a vision on purposefulness. The first difficulty arose with Alasdair MacIntyre's call in *After Virtue* for a renewal of ethical thinking by a return to Aristotle (MacIntyre 1981, 111). He argued that ethics has been fragmented into mutually irreconcilable systems precisely because it had forgotten the *telos* of human action. This move reintroduced, as he forcefully asserted, the whole discussion of happiness or beatitude as the end of ethics. It resulted in a tension between ethics and the scientific world view. "Although this account of the virtues is teleological, it does not require the identification of any teleology in nature, and hence it does not require any allegiance to Aristotle's metaphysical biology" (MacIntyre 1981, 182). This stance is unsatisfactory since happiness depends on having a right or appropriate environment, on one's real position in the world, especially on the friendship of others. Aristotle's view of felicity can only be explained when the moral agent is well integrated into the *polis* in a physical ambient where it can survive. MacIntyre has long held the view that the social sciences study human realities and what is normal in human behaviour. They thus treat of human intentions that must ultimately come under the *telos* of human action. His later books, *Whose Justice? Which Rationality?* and *Three Rival Visions of Moral Enquiry* have dropped the mention of Aristotle's biologism, moving closer to the traditional doctrine of a purposeful universe where human action seeks beatitude. However I have not found a full account of this conviction in his writings.

A dramatic testimony to the dilemmas raised for a scientist by purpose in the universe is Michael Polanyi's concluding statement in *Personal Knowledge*. "We may envisage then a cosmic field which called forth all these centres by offering them a short-lived, limited, hazardous opportunity for making some progress of their own towards an unthinkable consummation. And that is also, I believe, how a Christian is placed when worshipping God" (Polanyi 1958, 405). He clearly asserts that purpose in the universe cannot be proven from the evolution of complex organisms in nature. But he then seems to almost contradict himself by claiming just such finality. This would not be credible, he says, "had I not before me the rise of human personhood, which manifestly demands the assumption of finalistic principles of evolution" (Polanyi 1958, 402). All of the problems are concentrated here. Can the drive toward purpose and meaning rooted in a cosmic field of evolutionary forces indicate or even prove the active presence and existence of God? It seems not for Polanyi. But the wonder of it all arouses feelings of Christian worship. Polanyi seems to sway between discovering purpose in the universe and submitting to a divine providence anathema to the Enlightenment because it would predetermined natural processes and so the results of science. The above statements occasioned the Richard Gelwick — Harry Prosch debate about Polanyi's attitude to religion. Even though science recognises fields of forces progressively organising different levels of complexity, does this really reveal a personal *telos* embracing the entire universe?

II. TOWARD BREAKING THE IMPASSE

Etienne Gilson in *From Aristotle to Darwin and Back Again* (Gilson 1971) attempted a philosophical assessment of the impasse between science as we know it and Aristotelian purpose in nature with special reference to evolution. Here are some of his conclusions regarding the validity of Aristotle's philosophical conception of teleology:

1) *Telos* for Aristotle primarily refers to the human person as its subject. In other words we recognise purpose because of our experience of intention toward an end in human action. We experience purpose working in ourselves i.e., the physical serves the vegetative, the vegetative the sensitive and the sensitive the rational in the make-up of human nature. *Telos* in nature is then recognised by translating the changes (i.e., movement for Aristotle) in inanimate things and life forms below the human

into the language of human purposeful intention. Aristotle invokes this type of anthropomorphism and its implied biologism precisely because of our experience. The being in nature that I know the best is myself and this through my being conscious of myself. Aristotle maintains that we recognise the purposefulness of lower forms of life and of inanimate matter in ourselves and so assess them by the standards of human conscious intention. The word *telos* refers to a real goal-seeking activity in nature named by analogy with human intention.

2) All natural forms whether living or non-living are therefore permeated with mind and rationality. The form of a naturally occurring species is precisely its intelligibility. It reveals a designing mind that fitted the plurality of organs together to fashion one living entity. The plurality of organs and functions is understood in terms of the living being, which is their *telos*, by establishing order among them as their reason for being. The idea of order in nature is therefore essentially predicated on a *telos* intrinsic to nature. This type of purpose is not accessible to a mechanistic conception of the universe. *Telos* cannot be broken down into its constitutive units to be numbered, measured and calculated. It involves a way of thinking that transcends calculation since these are rendered intelligible by the *telos* without reduction to atomistic units.

3) Aristotle recognised that inanimate nature was not conscious and that life forms below the human did not enjoy reason or have rational souls e.g., a colony of ants betrays intelligence in the way its behaviour is instinctively co-ordinated. This pointing to intelligence does not mean that the ants themselves are intelligent or conscious of that intelligence. Yet they are all permeated by rationality, purpose and design. To explain this enigma Aristotle has recourse to the analogy of an artist producing a work of art. In the artist's mind all his materials and the parts that compose the finished work are integrated into one conception that guides all his activity till it is fully realised. An artist has to consciously strive to achieve his desired effect. Nature, however, is not conscious of itself, and yet without this type of striving spontaneously produces its marvels. By contemplating the ordered beauty he perceived in nature Aristotle came to think of it as a unconscious, spontaneous artist whom the professional human artist could but imitate in painting, sculpture and even in the theatre. Art is then the imitation of nature, and the arts representing the human are but the mirror reflection of human nature.

4) The tragedy of Aristotle's view of natural science, according to Gilson, was that his view of nature as artistry led many of his followers to "read in" purposes and teleologies not really to be found there. Aristotle

himself says that we do not know the nature of the animate and inanimate beings below the human. Thus we cannot deduce properties from their definitions since we do not know the essential terms in those definitions. The only essential quality in which they all agree is that they are material beings that change and so there is a certain hierarchy among them from the inanimate, to the sentient and the rationally conscious. This furnishes the basis for a philosophy of nature but not for an experimental science that uses mathematical measurement as its interpretive tool.

5) Gilson concludes that scientists can indeed recognise limited areas of purpose, but these do not reach beyond what is observed in the functioning of the entities in nature. The argument from teleology is limited by the goal-seeking qualities intrinsic to such entities. It follows that Paley's proof for the existence of God by means of an extrinsic teleology is an invalid extrapolation. Any such type of overall universal purpose transcending the limits of the universe itself cannot be discerned by science, and so cannot be founded on science. In this sense the rebellion against Aristotelianism in the sixteenth and seventeenth centuries was utterly justified. The recognition of limited purposes in nature acts as a background to the work of scientists and furnishes presuppositions that show how their endeavours are inherently rational. It is not necessary to explicitly invoke a philosophy of *telos* in science in order to make it practicable or intelligible. There are real purposes in nature but these cannot simply be "read off" from essences as so many Aristotelians pretended.

6) Scientists feared that Christianity would impose interpretations on science beginning with, for example, the fixity of species in the Genesis account of creation. Their fears were largely realised in the debate about whether evolution was a fact or not. Again, the premise seems to be that what constituted a perfect species could be "read off" from our experience of the animal kingdom. These ideas were then thought to be confirmed and justified by Scripture. This implies a serious misunderstanding of Scripture and the doctrine of creation based on it. Creation is a free decision of God to bring the universe into being *ex nihilo*. The details of his plan and design for nature are something to which we humans do not have direct access. The universe he created is contingent and therefore the characteristics God gave it must be discovered through the long hard work of observation, research and interpretation. The same applies to God's will and intention for nature's functioning. His salvific message is direct and clear but its ramifications for science only appear gradually through investigating faith's meaning. We may summarise the position of Aristotle on finality in relation to modern experimental science under three headings:

1) His schema of a hierarchy of ends in nature prevented the growth of a mechanistic view of the universe and so of a reductionist methodology in science (Gilson 1971, 17-31). These took over as the predominant philosophy of science in Western culture only after *telos* had been discredited. Aristotle's thought can still provide points of valid criticism of mechanistic and reductionist philosophies of science.

2) The association of purpose in nature with human intention is the basis for the accusation of anthropocentrism and biologism against his thought. Aristotle said that motion and hence *telos* ran through nature as "a sort of life" (Owens 1996, 192). As a result teleology ceased to be a term of reference in science because it lead to the personalising of nature as a unitary organismic entity.

3) Teleology does not determine the methods of the experimental sciences. Joseph Owens, a contemporary expert on Aristotle, notes how the attempt to form a research programme for science on the basis of Aristotelian teleology had been a tragic disaster. "It is as though one had insight into the forms of natural things in the way one can read the blueprint of a house, and reason from the plan to the details in actual reality" (Owens 1996, 196). To know that the eye is meant for seeing does not provide the means for analysing the organ's basic structure and form. From the regular motion of the heavenly bodies it is not possible to deduce that they are composed of incorruptible matter. Owens notes that, "Aristotelian natural philosophy has no means of entering into any part of the field of experimental science" (Owens 1996, 198). Its insight into purpose in nature has a validity limited and circumscribed by the intrinsic goal-seeking characteristics of the entities in nature. To show its relevance to science, it has to rely on and reflect upon the independently and autonomously established findings of science. Teleology does not define the shape of scientific method: but science may indicate new directions for philosophical and theological research to follow.

III. BEATITUDE IN AN HIERARCHICALLY STRUCTURED UNIVERSE

What can be learnt from Aristotle is that the limited purposes perceived in the functioning of nature helps make the universe intelligible to us. Scientists have discovered that nature may often be analysed as having a hierarchical structure. This means that beings in nature have a many levelled structure and that they can be studied by a variety of disciplines that reflect a hierarchy of understanding in the sciences. Hierarchy is a useful principle because it respects the autonomy of each level of achievement as having a meaning or purpose unique to itself while it is at the same time related to all the other levels of functioning and achievement within nature. This implies that the meaning of one level cannot be read off from another so that, e.g., lower levels could not be flattened into the highest denominator. Rather than such a projection upward, one level is integrated with and into the wider purpose of that above it. A lower level can be said to contribute elements or constitutives to a higher one whose functioning now gives it new direction and scope.

Michael Polanyi described *telos* in terms of achievement and constructed a hierarchy of achievement on the basis of Einstein's idea of "boundary conditions" that set up dual levels of control. A machine, for instance, can be described in terms of its physical and chemical composition. To understand its functioning we have to grasp the engineering principle according to which it is designed. The engineering principle sets the boundary conditions for the operation of its physical and chemical components. By applying the logic of boundary conditions to the emergence of living beings Polanyi discovered a hierarchy of levels within the living being. The first level is that of being itself i.e., typical shapes or taxonomy or morphology, from which we move to growth and generation i.e., morphogenesis and embryology. The third level is that of the healthy functioning of the various organs of the body. We then go to the actively perceiving individual who makes correct or mistaken "decisions" about its learning of perception. At a still higher level we can speak of "conviviality" as the typical participation of living beings in each other's lives (Polanyi 1958, 327-405). We see dual control at work on each level.

The vegative system which sustains life at rest leaves open the possibility of bodily movement by means of muscular action. This level leaves open the possibility of integration into innate patterns of behaviour. This leaves open the sharing of intelligence (Polanyi 1966, 41). The highest level of achievement is for Polanyi to be open to transcendent values which characterises the human person as such. Although he could not name it, this is the level where humans strive for happiness. Breakdowns and failures in achievement are caused by misfunctionings of goal-directed activities within this hierarchy. Teleology does not cease but is active in the chaos surrounding the process of natural selection. Ian Barbour points out how science has recognised many forms of hierarchy in complex systems in which there is an two-way flow of information. Our image of a hierarchical universe has developed in a dynamic and evolutionary way that Aristotle could never imagine. Evolution can be understood as a process of emergence in time whereby species arise and disappear to give way to others. This is a world of death, pain, the struggle for survival and the effort by each species to preserve and extend its genetic pool. The evolutionary tree shows a groping toward further achievement through the succession of forms in nature. Edward T. Oakes

makes the remarkable observation that the cosmological anthropic principle, "is by far the most resolutely teleological theory of the origins of the
universe since Aristotle" (Oakes 1992, 540).

Ian Barbour maintains that there are basically two forms of hierarchy:
1) genealogical as in a gene, an organism and a species, and 2) organisational, as in an atom, molecule, cell, organ, organism, population and
ecosystem (Barbour 1990, 165). Subsystems that have emerged in the
course of time are constrained by the boundary conditions set up by higher
level systems. The principle of dual control may also be invoked to relate
knowledge through faith with our understanding of a hierarchically structured universe. Although working within an Aristotelian image of the
world, St. Thomas Aquinas was aware of the possibilities of an idea of
human nature open to the transcendent God as this citation from the
Summa Theologiae, II-II, q.2, a.3 illustrates.

> We discover everywhere that where there is an ordered pattern
> of natures two factors concur in the full development of those
> lower in the pattern: one on the basis of their own operation;
> the other on the basis of the operation of a higher nature... Only
> the rational creature has an immediate order to God... For this
> reason the full development of the rational creature consists not
> only in what is proper to it in keeping with its own nature, but
> also in what can be ascribed to it by reason of a certain super-
> natural share in the divine good... man's ultimate beatitude con-
> sists in a certain vision of God that surpasses the natural... No
> one can attain to this vision of God except by being a learner
> with God as his teacher (St. Thomas Aquinas 1974, 72-73).

It is a curious fact that Polanyi and others who theorised about hierarchy
in nature did not recognise in dual control a principle useful for relating
scientific knowledge of the universe with the Christian vision of creation.
This vision of the universe as God's creation also opened up the possibility of integrating the Aristotelian conception of felicity with the Christian idea of the Beatitudes in Mt 5:1-12. I shall not recount the long
history of this assimilation except to note that without the support of a
conception of the universe as purposeful through a hierarchy of ends in
nature Christian theology could not have made human fulfilment as final
union with God himself intelligible (Pinckaers 1995, 11-12, 134-167). St.
Thomas completed this assimilation by using Aristotle's logic to explore
the meaning of Scriptural beatitude as presented by St. Augustine. Here
faith exercised its priority over reason (Staley 1995, 311-322) in a vision
of fulfilment for which as St. Paul claims the universe itself as it were
unconsciously strives. "For the creation waits with eager longing for the
revealing of the children of God" (Rm 8:19). St. Thomas reflects the
principle of dual control in his specifying a double condition for beatitude.

First, the limited teleologies of creatures below the human strive upwards towards transcendence. They cannot, however, left to themselves alone provide a proof of God's existence nor reach him even though they may point toward him. It is only in the human person that they are enabled to arrive at God as their ultimate purpose. This opens up for us the second condition of beatitude, the deliberate grace-filled choice that directs our whole being to God as our freely chosen ultimate fulfilment. This existential choice is conditioned by the image of the universe we espouse. The theology of creation is the precondition of the doctrine of beatitude in Christian ethics (Schockenhoff 1987, 97). These two conditions are based on the truth of revelation that God speaks his word about himself as our saving beatitude and about the way whereby we are to reach him. Today, just as we cannot reasonably speak of creation without reference to contemporary cosmology, so we cannot really feel the attraction our destiny exercises upon us without relating it to the place the human species occupies in an evolving universe. The contemporary dynamic image of the universe in science is radically consistent with a conception of beatitude as future fulfilment for humanity in a "new heaven and a new earth" (Rev 21:1).

In summary, there are at least four clearly distinct meanings for *telos* which, as a concept to be predicated analogously, can define the following areas of application: 1) Purpose as encountered in inanimate creation, 2) purpose as perceived in living beings below the human, 3) intention which opens human beings to transcendent achievements thus giving meaning to human action as directed to beatitude, 4) divine intentions manifested to us through revelation as recorded in the Scriptures. And so we come to know God's intentions and recognise his providence as informing creation, redemption and final *parousia*. John Polkinghorne understands purpose as beginning in God and as always God-directed. "God's providence is then seen as a kind of teleological insight into general physical process" (Polkinghorne 1989, 40). He also highlights its significance for process theology. "The God of process is to be thought of as the one who is achieving his purpose through the evolution of the world he maintains in being" (Polkinghorne 1989, 64). Human intention and divine providence should not be projected into the subject matter of the natural sciences nor into the workings of nature in such a way as to rob them of their "short-lived, limited, hazardous opportunity" of achieving their own finite goals. Each type of teleology should retain its own intrinsic value. On that condition teleology in all its senses can be integrated, first by intention into the project of human destiny, and then by providence into God himself as its fulfilment. All teleology points to "an unthinkable consummation" that can only be grasped vaguely by faith.

The idea of beatitude implies an hierarchical integration of all the above four levels of the meaning of purpose. It has not been possible to give an adequate account of the Scriptural doctrine of beatitude nor of how the universe sings its praise in adoration of its Lord. Nor have I discussed the scandal of evil that Voltaire saw in the Lisbon earthquake of 1755, for example. I have instead concentrated on the difficulties raised by Aristotle's conception of teleology. The conclusion of this essay is at once modest and simple. Catholic theology has been so interwoven with Aristotelianism (Heller 1996, 60) that when modern science exploded his conception of teleology the idea of beatitude went into crisis with the traditional world view. Since then the history of ethics has been a search for a starting-point or foundation apart from God as beatitude. But it is not possible to think about the God of revelation without being drawn to his joy and happiness, the very beatitude he wants to share with us. This is not something that science as such evidences. But it is Christian theology that is challenged to present human destiny in a way consistent with our scientific image of a dynamic, evolving universe and with the demands of revelation. Such a universe points to God in whom faith recognises its meaning, its fullness and its joy.

REFERENCES

Barbour, Ian G. 1990: *Religion in an Age of Science*, London: SCM.

Gilson, Etienne 1984: *From Aristotle to Darwin and Back Again*, London: Sheed and Ward.

Heller, Michael 1996: *The New Physics and a New Theology*, Vatican City State: Vatican Observatory Publications.

MacIntyre, Alasdair 1981: *After Virtue*, Notre Dame, Indiana: University of Notre Dame Press.

Oakes, Edward T. 1992: "Final Causality: A Response," *Theological Studies*, 53 (1992) 3, 534-544.

Owens, Joseph 1996: *Some Philosophical Issues in Moral Matters*, edited by Dennis J. Billy and Terence Kennedy, Rome: EDACALF.

Pinckaers, Servais 1995: *The Sources of Christian Ethics*, Edinburgh: T & T Clark.

Polanyi, Michael 1958: *Personal Knowledge*, London: Routledge and Kegan Paul.

Polanyi, Michael 1966: *The Tacit Dimension*, New York: Doubleday.

Polkinghorne, John 1989: *Science and Creation. The Search for Understanding*, London: SPCK.

Polkinghorne, John 1989: *Science and Providence. God's Interaction with the World*, London: SPCK.

Schockenhoff, Eberhard 1987: *Bonum Hominis: Die anthropologischen und theologischen Grundlagen der Tugendethik des Thomas von Aquin*, Mainz: Grünewald.

Staley, Kevin M.: "Aristotle, Augustine, and Aquinas on the Good and the Human Good," *The Modern Schoolman*, LXXII (1995) 2, 311-322.

Thomas Aquinas, St., 1974: *Summa Theologiae*, Faith, Vol. 31., translated by T. C. O'Brien, London: Eyre and Spottiswoode.

TEILHARD DE CHARDIN,
THEORETICAL BIOLOGY AND THEOLOGY

LODOVICO GALLENI

(*Pisa, Italy*)

The discovery of the evolution of living beings is changing our global vision of life. Actually evolution and the change in time of natural events are the present days tools for our understanding of the universe: we are living in a universe whose mechanisms and modalities of evolution are described by natural sciences.

Time as a factor introducing changes in natural events and introducing history in nature, is an intellectual conquest which is due to geology and biology and which was then recovered also by physics, for instance with the Big Bang theory and universe expansion.

According to this vision, life is a result of evolution and comes out thanks to a process of auto-organisation of non-living molecules; it is itself evolving. Origin of life, of species, of mankind are the results of evolutionary biology and are studied by the different branches of biology which found in evolution their unifying background. As a matter of fact the discovery of the evolution of living beings is changing our global vision of life and throwing new light onto the intersections between biology and theology.

The traditional vision derived from the Bible of a well ordered universe together with that of the fixity of species is actually related to the fusion of different traditions. The first stages of science, still based on the observation of nature, suggested the stability of species. Ernst Mayr, one of the biologists who contributed to the revision of Darwinism called "the modern synthesis," spent some months in a stone age culture in New Guinea. He was impressed by the fact that they described and gave a name to 136 different species of birds, when he was able to recognise (according to the taxonomic science of the twentieth century) and describe and give a name to 137 different species. The stone age culture and the modern biologist's culture obtained nearly the same result while describing the discontinuity in a peculiar class of living objects and giving them a name. To recognise discontinuities in animal diversity and to give them a name is the first result of the sciences of nature and this result is that reported in the older compilation of the book of Genesis. In the more recent compilation, written in contact with the more advanced scientific culture of Babylonians, the concept of species is more complex and scientifically more detailed. The term of species is used, as well as the concept of reproduction: each species is created with its own seed. The idea is that the characteristics of each species are maintained and transmitted thanks to reproduction. Actually this more recent and complex concept of species could be derived by a second level of scientific approach toward nature: that of common experience. From the observation of nature the presence of discontinuity among living beings allowed the first concept of species. From the common experience this concept is further enriched: the characteristics that are typical of this or that species and allowed the observer to give to the species its name are maintained and transmitted from one generation to the following generation thanks to reproduction. This second concept of species, which involves the maintenance of specific characteristics thanks to reproduction, are those reported in the more recent compilation written in contact with the advanced scientific culture of Babylonians.[1]

The conclusions are that the concepts of species reported in the first chapters of the book of Genesis had no theological value at all, but they are reported directly by the science of the time. Other concepts came out of Greek philosophy. The ordered universe as the direct result of creation from a provident demiurge and the concept of a world of ideas characterised by stability and perfection was derived from Plato's philosophy, while from Aristotelian philosophy came the great chain of beings and the finality of complex structures. All these concepts merged with the theological concepts of Bible and originated in the strong paradigm of a well ordered universe: a universe which came out directly from God's hands and is perfectly constructed. It is to be remembered that the provident God (or, anyway the provident Demiurge) is typical first of all of the Greek and Roman tradition and was used as a metaphysical background for true scientific research program by scientists of the classical Roman and Greek tradition such as Galeno.[2] From this vision came the provident God of the natural theologists that characterised natural science in Europe until the development of evolutionary hypothesis.

The Darwinian interpretation of evolution by means of natural selection asked for a big change: before Darwin the misery of mankind, so perfectly depicted by many authors (among them T.R. Malthus),[3] was a consequence of original sin: the well constructed universe showed by natural theologists was ruined by the sin of the free, thinking creature. This contraposition between a perfectly ordered nature and the suffering status of mankind was presented many times in Christian apologetic, see for instance a book that was widespread in the nineteenth century: "La genie du Cristianisme" written by R. de Chateaubriand.[4]

Darwin, extending to all the evolution of life the malthusian interpretation of the struggle of life and the concept of misery, removed this optimistic vision. Our vision of creation was dramatically chanced and the Darwinian universe was an universe where the absence of finality, the presence of the struggle for life and of the various degrees of pain was not a consequence of sin, but part of the stuff of the universe. The provident God who created a well structured universe gives way to the God of change and selection, to the great breeder who, thanks to the struggle for life and the survival of the fittest is not the guarantee of the path toward mankind, but merely reflects the blind path of chance. Actually it is the blind watchmaker described by Hawking. Anyway, this interpretation forced theology to confront Darwinian mechanisms and this confrontation was in some ways useful. St. George Mivart, in the section of his book: "On the genesis of species"[5] dedicated to theology and evolution, among others, wrote:

"The teaching which the Author has received is, that God is indeed inscrutable and incomprehensible to us from the infinity of His attributes so that our minds can, as it were, only take in, in a most fragmentary and indistinct manner (as through a glass darkly), dim conceptions of infinitesimal portions of His inconceivable perfection. In this way the partial glimpse obtained by us in different modes differ from each other; not that God is anything but the most perfect unity, but that apparently conflicting views arise from our inability to apprehend Him, except in this imperfect manner, *i.e.* by successive slight approximations along different lines of approach."[6]

And also the last sentences of Mivart's book are worthy of quotation:

"The aim has been to support the doctrine that these species have been evolved by ordinary *natural laws* (for the most part unknown) controlled by the *subordinate* action of "Natural Selection" and at the same time to remind some that there is and can be absolutely nothing in physical science which forbids them to regard those natural laws as acting with the Divine concurrence and in obedience to a creative fiat originally imposed on the primeval Cosmos, "in the beginning" by its Creator, its Upholder, and its Lord".[7]

Mivart's approach is one of the few that opened the path toward an acceptance on the side of roman catholic theology of evolution and natural selection, but, unlucky, he was not allowed to develop his research.[8] These fragmentary views were slowly recovered in a larger landscape thank to the writings of Teilhard de Chardin. He was, for instance, aware of Darwinian mechanisms and he actually wrote that life does not advance except when it is groping among the effects of large numbers and the game of chance and that life appears from its very beginning with its instincts, passions, sufferings and death.[9]

Actually the brutal laws of the survival of the fittest and of rough mutations have negative aspects, but from here the vision of a universe where life appears and evolves thank to the large spaces of freedom allowed by these mechanisms is emerging and is underlined by many authors.

But now we have to remember that also some among the many scientific criticisms of St. George Mivart to Darwin's proposal of natural selection are of great actuality. Mivart stated that natural selection has a subordinate action in respect to other mechanisms, which are presently under investigation: thanks to the works published in many fields of theoretical biology, a more complex approach is now emerging.

Teilhard de Chardin, among others, underlined the problem of the presence, in science, of the three infinites. One of them, the immeasurable complex is object of study of biology. For this reason Teilhard de Chardin can be considered one of the first scientists to present biology as the science devoted to the study of complexity.[10] He proposed a tool to accomplish this task: he founded in Beijing a new science: Geobiology, proposed as the science whose task was to study evolutive biology not only on the side of this or that organism, of this or that species or of this or that ecosystem, but taking into consideration the biosphere as a whole evolving object.[11] In the same period many other proposals were made in order to study interactions among species (the Lotka Volterra equations)[12] and the correlation between objects (the general theory of systems of von Bertallanfy).[13] Finally with Waddington and the theoretical biology group theoretical biology reached its present status.[14]

One of the tasks of theoretical biology is that of applying to biology the methods of analysis of complexity that had developed quickly thanks to the mathematics of chaos, the mathematics of catastrophes and the non-linear dynamic.

Now we apply these new tools to the general concept of a whole evolving biosphere according to the intellectual and experimental paths proposed by Teilhard de Chardin: a whole evolving biosphere is a complex system of interrelated objects that presents phenomena of canalisation and directionality, threshold effects and catastrophic events.

Many aspects of the recent discoveries derived from the studies of complexity applied to theoretical biology show a different picture from that derived from Darwinian mechanisms. Together with the struggle for life and natural selection we also find co-operation; a species survives thanks to diversity and not to uniformity obtained with the diffusion of the fittest; auto-organisation phenomena are present which are conditioning evolution (see the books of Maturana and Varela,[15] Goodwin[16] and Kauffman[17]).

Moreover the concept of system recovers also the Aristotelian idea of a task that is referred in our contest to the mechanisms of homeostasis proposed by Lovelock: the system biosphere evolving as a whole has a task: to maintain its stability. Stability is maintained thanks to a process of diversification and complexification.[18] So far the trends toward complexity described by Teilhard de Chardin is not a superimposed interpretation or simply a description of events, but is a consequence of the task related to biosphere evolution.

A possible interpretation is that we are living in a more ordered universe where finality is present thank to the tendency toward stability. But the single individual is not taken into consideration: we have a well constructed universe where the individual has no value.

Some examples could be useful. The predator-prey relationship, for instance, is of course a violent event which, at least in mammals, is a dramatic source of suffering, but it is also a way for the prey population to maintain stability and to avoid a population explosion which could be extremely dangerous for the prey itself. Predation is a totally natural event and it is strictly related to the way life is organised and maintains its stability. In more general terms we can refer to the different models that characterise the reproductive strategies of animal species. Actually every species invests about the same percent of energy in reproduction. The strategies vary between two extremes:

> *"r" strategy:* in this case a species produces many, many eggs with a low investment of energy per egg. Actually in this case the loss of many eggs is not a problem, while the loss of an adult during the reproductive season is a problem. For this reason this species will have predators directed toward the juvenile stages.

> *"k" strategy:* in this case a species produces few eggs with a high investment of energy per egg. In this case the eggs and the juvenile forms need to be protected and the control of the population through predation is oriented toward the older specimens.[19]

Different reproductive strategies imply different ways of predation in order to maintain the stability of the prey population. The event of a lion eating a gazelle is a natural event, useful not only for the lion species but also for the gazelle species, but it takes place as a source of violent pain to that single gazelle, which is killed by that single lion.

Another example is taken directly from human genetics. A genetic disease that affects haemoglobin is diffused in the Mediterranean regions where malaria was present. Children bringing both the variant genes for the non-working haemoglobin died in the first years, while, on the contrary those bringing one functional gene and one non-working gene were healthy and were not affected by malaria. This dramatic event which meant the death of many children every generation, was very useful on the side of species fitness because it allowed to colonise very extreme habitats, such as marshland. Diversity was useful but asked for the sacrifice of many human children.[20]

As we can see the picture is emerging of a more ordered universe than that of the great breeder Darwin, where only the fittest has room, but a universe where the single individual loses his own value compared to that of his population or of his species.

It seems that a different strategy is present from the God of creation, who cares for the creation as a whole, but not for the single creature, and the God of revelation, who cares for every individual and is the reference of the Alliance with every thinking creature.

From this point of view we can underline the theological value of the different days of creation, developing the proposal of Moltmann.[21] The six days are those of the evolution of the universe and life, but with mankind's appearance God's relationship with creation changes on the seventh day. God's action stopped and is substituted by the free action of the free creature.

To the free creature, to every free creature but also to mankind in its biological, cultural and spiritual unity, God manifested his/her care thanks to the proposal of the alliance. But the alliance needs to be freely accepted.

Here we can discuss the many spaces for freedom that are present in our evolving universe: they are the space for the freedom of the thinking creature, but they are also the room for indetermination, for mechanism of change and errors, for the mechanisms that are the very causes of many aspects of mankind's suffering. There is a linkage between consciousness, freedom and suffering that was underlined by many authors and a fact that is not any more avoidable by the present day theological investigations.[22]

Actually an evolving universe cannot be a universe that develops in a strictly deterministic way if it has to be the universe that is able to give rise to the free thinking creature: a universe that is characterised by a process of complexification and by the not preventable emergence of new properties such as life or thought has to leave room for non-deterministic events, chance and errors. There is no room for constructing if everything is ordered by its very beginning or is, anyway, determined by the very beginning thanks to an unalterable program. Constructing needs raw material to be organised. And the many examples of auto-organisation and of emergence of properties suggest that a new ontological value characterises this universe: not only the ontological value of evolution but also that of construction of novelties by the side of nature: the nature that is auto-organising during evolution. This suggests the presence of a task also for the thinking creature: that of the construction of the Earth. And also this aspect is present in the works of Pierre Teilhard de Chardin.[23]

In these perspectives other aspects of the book of Genesis acquire new theological values. The original couple is the representation of the unity of mankind, unity confirmed by science thanks to the total interfecondity among human populations. To this entity is proposed the alliance, in order to build an earth that God can take delight in on the seventh day, according to Moltmann's formulations.[24]

The value of constructing the earth is also a way to maintain the freedom of the thinking creature, but to remove many of the natural mechanisms which, while they have to be considered the warranty of the freedom in the universe, are also the main source of pain in the universe. But something went wrong and the alliance did not start from the very beginning of mankind. A proposal could be that when the book of Genesis was written, the biblical authors reported the lack of alliance that they suffered looking at the misery of mankind, as a consequence of so-called original sin, and the earth which could be built thanks to the alliance as the garden of Eden.

So a new interpretation can be proposed following the path opened by Pierre Teilhard de Chardin: the space for evil is related to a universe to be built. In a universe in evolution and in a progressive organisation the order is not created at the beginning but it is the final result to be achieved. The Noosphere comes out in a universe where there is room for the free action of the thinking creature. In order for there to be freedom the individual is correlated to a space of non-determinism, which is also the space for imperfection. Again pain, freedom and consciousness are strictly related. But, of course, the lack of the alliance gave rise to a new and dramatic source of pain: that induced in a thinking creature by another thinking creature.

The necessity of a constructing universe could be found following also a more theological path. Jan Barbour in his "Religion in an Age of Science"[25] made a distinction between Natural Theology and Theology of Nature. Natural Theology finds its starting point in the ontological proof of God's existence. In this approach "arguments for the existence of God are based entirely on human reason rather than on historical revelation or religious experience."[26] On the contrary Theology of Nature "starts from a religious tradition based on religious experience and historical revelation."[27] Nature and its various aspects looked for by science is a way to bring new light into divine revelation. Here we are in the great tradition of the relationships between science and religion, where every rational investigation about God as Creator needs to be confronted with the vision of Creation suggested by science. In this way Theology of Nature can be considered a theology which, from the inside, throws new insights into creation and the Creator's will.

But a new interpretation is emerging from the side of theology. Accordingly something similar to a Copernican revolution was proposed also for theology. According to this new paradigm the present based on experience is the horizon of theology, but critically based on the Christian message.[28] This is an interesting path because at the present time, the shift from the fixist paradigm to the evolutionary one needs also a new paradigm from the side of theology.

The Christian message is not anymore the horizon of theology through which the experience was taken into consideration but, on the contrary, is the horizon of the present experience, which is the starting point, and it is the way through which theologians are able to take into consideration the Christian message.

The horizon of the present experience is that of evolution and of an Earth to be constructed. According to this new aspect perhaps a different approach could be suggested giving a different value to the "of" connection between Theology and Nature. A Theology "of" Nature, according to Jan Barbour, "starts from a religious tradition" and takes into consideration nature as the object of his inquiries. On the contrary we can think of nature not only as the passive object of theology but, thank to its more evolved sphere, the Noosphere, as the subject that makes theology: in this case is nature herself, thanks to the thinking creature now recognising itself as a part of nature, which is making inquiries about its past, its present and its future, and is building a different way of making theology. This method is similar to that proposed by liberation theology and feminist theology, where there is an inversion of the traditional theological approach to the horizon of experience. The first step is, in the new paradigm, that of the horizon of experience (to be a member of a dominated people or of a dominated sex) and then, as a second step, there is the relationship with the horizon of revelation.

A similar passage could be true also for theology of nature.

The horizon of theology is that of mankind which is actually discovering herself as a part of the evolving biosphere. In order to develop this new approach we have to come back to Teilhard de Chardin's ideas of the biosphere as a whole evolving complex and that of the task of such a complex system as biosphere. According to Lovelock's Gaia hypothesis the task of the system is to maintain stability thanks to diversity and complexity.

Actually we obtained from our scientific observations of nature that the general law of the universe is evolution and when life arises, evolution of such a complex object as a biosphere has a task, that of maintain homeostasis and stability.

The free action of mankind, which could be possible thanks to the alliance with God the Creator, needs to be inserted into the mechanisms of stability, which are discovered by the sciences of complex systems applied, thanks to theoretical biology, to the biosphere. Stability and diversity are correlated and this is a suggestion of great importance also to theology. In this case we have mankind which, thinking about its own evolution, its changing is vision of nature and of the alliance with the Creator. As we previously wrote, a new paradigm is used, for instance, by theologians both related to theology of liberation and feminist theology, who are presently making enquiries also in order to find connection between their own theological approach and that of nature conservation. They are presenting a different way of building the Earth in order to save creation and to save mankind's diversity. They can be a fruitful path in order to develop a paradigm based on the presence of evolution and Teilhard de Chardin's ideas of building an earth that is evolving thanks to the rules of complexity and to propose a new task for the action of the creature in the world.

Actually the new intellectual path that can be proposed, suggested by our present day knowledge of the science of evolution, is that in Nature there is room for the free action of the thinking creature: as a part of nature the Noosphere has the task to constructing the earth, but in the respect of the mechanisms and the tasks that the evolving biosphere developed in time. An earth has to be constructed, an earth that can be a source of delight for the Creator.

NOTES

1. This first part of this paper is widely discussed in: L. Galleni, *Da Darwin a Teilhard de Chardin — Interventi sull'evoluzione (1983-1995)* SEU, Pisa, 1996 pp.:75-92.

2. See R.J. Hankinson, Galen Explains the Elephant, in M. Matthen and B. Linsky Edtrs. *Philosophy and Biology*, Canadian Journal of Philosophy suppl. V. 14 (1988) pp.: 135-157.

3. T.R. Malthus, *An Essay on the Principle of Population*, Oxford University Press, Oxford, 1993.

4. R. de Chateaubriand, *Le génie du Christianisme*, A. Mame, Tours 1874 pp.: 47-48.

5. St. George Mivart, *On the Genesis of Species*, Macmillan and Co. London, 1871.

6. St. George Mivart, *op. cit.* p. 267.

7. St. George Mivart, *op. cit.* p.: 288.

8. The final events that brought to Mivart excommunication are reported in: D.G. Schultenover, S.J., *A view from Rome — On the Eve of the Modernist Crisis*, Fordham University Press, New York, 1993 pp.: 131-133.

9. L. Galleni, Relationships between Scientific Analysis and the World View of Pierre Teilhard de Chardin. *Zygon* 27: 153-166. (1992).

10. P. Teilhard de Chardin, *La place de l'homme dans la Nature — Le groupe zoologique humain*, Albin Michel, Paris, 1996.

11. L. Galleni, How does the Teilhardian Vision of Evolution Compare with Contemporary Theories? *Zygon* 30: 25-45 (1995).

12. See V. Volterra, Lecons sur la théorie mathématique de la lutte pour la vie. *Cahiers Scientifique 7*: Gauthier-Villars, Paris.

13. L. Von Bertalanffy, *General System Theory*, George Braziller, New York 1968.

14. C.H. Waddington, *Tools for Thought* 1977.

15. H.R. Maturana and F.J. Varela, *Autopoiesis and Cognition. The Realization of the Living*, D. Reidel P.C. Dordrecht, 1980.

16. B. Goodwin, *How the Leopard Changed its Spots*, Weidenfeld and Nicolson, London, 1994.

17. S.A. Kauffman, *The Origins of Order* Oxford U.P. New York, 1993.

18. J. Lovelock, *The Ages of Gaia*, W.W. Norton and Co. 1988.

19. See: L. Galleni, Biologia evoluzionistica e problema del male in: G. Colzani Edtr. *Creazione e male del cosmo* Edizioni Messagg.

20. See L. Galleni, *Da Darwin a Teilhard de Chardin op. cit.* p.:7.-

21. J. Moltmann, *Gott in der Schöpfungslehre*, Chr. Kaiser Verlag, München, 1985.

22. See as a reference: A. Peacocke, *Theology for a Scientific Age*, SCM Press, London 1993, pp.: 62-69.

23. P. Teilhard de Chardin, *Le Milieu Divin*, Seuil, Paris, 1957, pp.: 31-67.

24. J. Moltmann, *Gott in der Schöpfung op. cit.*

25. J. Barbour, *Religion in an Age of Science*, SCM Press, London 1990.

26. J. Barbour, *Religion in an Age of Science* op. cit, p.: 24.

27. J. Barbour, *Religion in an Age of Science* op. cit. p.: 26.

28. See, for instance, R. Gibellini, *La teologia del XX secolo* Queriniana Brescia, 1992 pp.: 540-544.

THE EVOLUTION OF INTENTIONALITY AS AN ISSUE FOR THE INTERDISCIPLINARY DIALOGUE BETWEEN BIOLOGY AND THEOLOGY

HUBERT HENDRICHS

(Bielefeld, Germany)

It is accepted practice to use intentional terms in naming a wide variety of different processes. In some cases - such as the movements of non-living objects - their use is obviously metaphorical, not implying any mental contributions. In other cases - such as the goal-directed behaviour of animals - their use often is only partly metaphorical, as mental processes can, to varying extents, contribute to orienting and directing action. Animals can aim at goals distant in space and time, and can, neglecting their actual situation, endure stress and strain, hardship and suffering, to achieve these goals. In higher mammals even individually developed mental representations can influence the orientation and direction of their behaviour (cf. H. Hendrichs 1994, 1996). While human conscientious orientations and decisions are of a fundamentally different quality, it still remains an important open question, to what extent natural mental qualities, as evolved in various steps already in pre-human mammals, may be involved in human mentality (cf. A. Haas 1961, 1964; G. Bateson 1972; J. König 1994).

The question to be addressed in this paper concerns the emergence in evolution of new mental - perceptive, cognitive and intentional - qualities in higher organised animals and in the transition from pre-human animals to humans. In these processes of emergence, the developing units outgrow their old context of organisation and gain access to a new context of organisation. Concerning such processes of emergence, or "fulguration" (K. Lorenz 1973) or "self-transcendence" (K. Rahner 1961), the following question arises: To what extent can such a development be described and understood as "pushed" or "driven out" by mechanisms of its old context of organisation, and to what extent as "pulled" or "drawn out" by qualities of its old context of organisation? An analogous example, illustrating the question, is the ontogenetic development of mentality and morality in a human being: to what extent are these qualities produced, "pushed out", by physiological processes inside the organism, and to what extent "pulled out" by the social and cultural world outside the organism? This may at first sight appear to be a simple and naive question, but may nevertheless be useful for initiating a serious discussion between biologists and theologians. In order to succeed, an interdisciplinary approach needs to start with a simple common language. The evolutionary development of mentality (including intentionality and suffering) is still not well understood in all disciplines, from neurobiology to cognitive psychology, and from artificial intelligence to synergetics. Discussions continue to be highly controversial, especially between the more reductionistic and the more holistic approaches, with different categorisations sometimes being used in the same discipline. Important and impressive holistic views, such as Whiteheadian organismic process theology and Teilhardian cosmology of consciousness appear to remain unconnected with each other and with modern biological concepts of evolution. The simple questions proposed for discussion by this paper are meant as a first approach from the perspective of biology. The proposed conceptualisation uses metaphorical terms derived from empirical biological studies on the ecology and the behaviour of mammals. This conceptualisation is not in total agreement with recent "sociobiological" concepts.

At first a specification is required of some of the differentiations used. The "levels" or "dimensions" of sociobiological processes include:

- the physicochemical domain,

- the anatomical-physiological domain (with neural, endocrine and immunological reactions),

- the ecological domain (with utilisation of abiotic, biotic and social resources and with the conditions provided by populations dynamics),

- the ethological domain (with behavioural, motivational and psychosocial processes).

One important component of the latter domain is the orientation of the organism in its surroundings when regulating its activations and guiding its actions. This capacity relies on the integration of processes of perception and motivation, of memory and cognition. The mentality of the organism can include various degrees of awareness and of intentionality, and, in evolution, can reach new dimensions of orientation. Especially

and most obviously with the emergence of conscious - and, in consequence, conscientious - intentionality, a new dimension has been added
to previous components of mental orientation. The question is whether a
new dimension of orientation, which is emerging in the evolutionary process of mental development, is produced by this process or, whether this
dimension is reached by the process as it gains access to an older component of reality - that was already active before this stage of the developing process.

Concerning phylogenetic changes in the organisation of organisms,
the following three types of processes can be distinguished:

a) Darwinian evolution: undirectedly produced ("accidental")
variability turned into an adaptive direction by natural selection,
and possibly, in intraspecific competition, generating excessive
developments by sexual selection,

b) constructive developments extending, completing and combining existing structures and organisations, including processes
of maturation and self-organisation,

c) the emergence of new qualities in structural and functional
organisation, generating new levels and dimensions of activation
and orientation.

These three types of processes do not exclude each other, but are usually
combined. They differ in their structural, causal and functional conditions.

To speak of the emergence of a new mental dimension - as that of
conscious intentionality and of morality - does not imply that there are
no previous traces of this quality manifest in the process of its realisation.
It is sufficient that a previously less relevant component of orientation
gains importance in contributing to the orientation and decision processes
of organisms. In cosmological pre-biological evolution, physical dimensions - as energy, gravidity, electromagnetism - were not created from
zero by the cosmological process, but existing possibilities of these domains were used in building up the (observable) abiotic material world,
establishing specific (measurable) fields - gravitational, magnetic - influ-
encing the processes in the observable world of material systems. The
different levels in the organisation of sociobiological processes - from
physical and physiological to motivational and mental - were not created
by Darwinian evolution in the competition for fitness, but potential
mechanisms in the different domains were used in the evolutionary development, providing constraints and possibilities for emergent properties
and capacities. One example is the multidimensional reaction of mammals
in social stress (cf. H. Hendrichs 1992). The chemical and microbiological
processes involved as well as some general behavioural and ecological

functions of this reaction are much older than the mammals themselves. A number of anatomical and physiological - neural, hormonal and immunological - differentiations, however, are specific for mammals, providing them with new qualities and dimensions of stress reactions, of coping with these activations, and of possibilities for suffering and well-being. These new dimensions have not been created by the evolutionary process leading to them, but this process made use of existing possibilities for dimensionally new ways of activation and organisation in thermoregulated vertebrate organisms.

With the functional and structural differentiation of living systems the necessity increases to integrate the different tendencies generated by the various components into one smooth and effective action. With this necessity, metafunctional and metastructural properties of the systems gain importance, i.e. properties that contribute to compatible activations and to regulations of the various components. The combination of adaptive properties generated in several different domains - with possible differences in dimensionality and logic - in a new functional context results in a fitness advantage for a mental-type of dimension to be included in contributing to the adaptive integration of these different properties. This is a process that may eventually lead to an orientation of the organism that includes perceptive awareness and mental consciousness.

Structural developments, by continuing, completing and integrating existing patterns, may lead to structurally and/or functionally new performances and thereby gain access to a new dimension of organisation. The integrative use of new organisational possibilities does not create this new dimension of metastructural and metafunctional orientation and regulation, but makes use of existing possibilities in a new dimension so far not included to that extent in the organisation of this system. Rather, such a generation of a new type of orientation and regulation, tends to be "pulled out" by the possibilities of the newly included dimension, than "pushed out" by an impetus of the developing system generated in the old dimensions. In a descriptive, metaphorical way, it can be said that the evolutionary development of mentality in mammals became pulled forward by a specific cognitive-mental dimension of reality, and that their mentality, including in its most advanced forms a conscious and conscientious orientation, became composed in this dimension. Besides this new dimension of advanced orientation higher mammalian mentality continues to include the older physicochemical, anatomical-organological, physiological and psychosocial dimensions.

The conceptual view outlined in metaphorical terms above, characterising structural and procedural conditions of animal life at different levels of organisation, is being proposed as an invitation to theologians to examine from their perspective to what extent the concepts of this view could be understood as compatible with theological concepts of creation as expressed in the metaphorical terms of theological language, or with other concepts of cosmological "productivity" (F.W.J. Schelling 1799) or "creativity" (A.N. Whitehead 1929), and to explore and discuss compatibilities and incompatibilities of theological and biological concepts describing or referring to the same process: the origin and genesis of mind, mentality, intentionality and suffering, and its relevance for evolutionary organismic development. A co-operation between biologists and theologians in this field might be helpful for both. The evolution of orientation, individuality and intentionality in animals is still hardly understood and obviously requires new conceptualisations. On the other hand, modern theology cannot neglect recent empirical and theoretical investigations in this field. Such a co-operation would require continuing efforts sustained over many years: the contribution of the biologists including serious scientific orientations outside the field of their empirical investigations and outside their biological competences, the contribution of the theologians including systematic efforts outside their specific fields and outside theology.

REFERENCES

Bateson, Gregory 1972: *Steps to an Ecology of Mind*, San Francisco.

Haas, Adolf 1961: "Das Lebendige: Spiegel seiner selbst", *Scholastik* 36, 161-191.

Haas, Adolf 1964: "Die Stilähnlichkeit christlicher Glaubenstatsachen mit den beiden Lebensakten der Entwicklung", *Gott in Welt*, Bd. II, Freiburg-Basel-Wien, 756-778.

Hendrichs, Hubert 1992: "On Social Stress in Mammals", *Stress-adaptions from the Molecular to the Ecosystem Level*, Bielefeld, 105-110.

Hendrichs, Hubert 1994: Individual Psychosocial Structures in Higher Mammals: Possible Requirements for the Realisation of Human Mind and Morality", *Origins, Time and Complexity*, Vol. II, Genf, 39-46.

Hendrichs, Hubert 1996: The Complexity of Social and Mental Structures in Nonhuman Mammals", *Evolution, Order and Complexity*, London, 00-00.

König, Josef 1994: "Probleme des Begriffs der Entwicklung", *Kleine Schriften*, Freiburg-München, 223-244.

Lorenz, Konrad 1973: *Die Rückseite des Spiegels*, München.

Rahner, Karl 1961: "Die Hominisation als theologische Frage", *Das Problem der Hominisation*, Freiburg-Basel-Wien, 13-90.

Schelling, Friedrich W.J. 1799: *Erster Entwurf eines Systems der Naturphilosophie.* Jena-Leipzig.

Whitehead, Alfred N. 1929: *Process and Reality*. New York.

MYSTICISM OF NATURE
IN TEILHARD DE CHARDIN AND NIELS BOHR

JAMES F. SALMON
(*Washington, D.C., USA*)

In order to clarify the meaning of terms in this presentation, theology is taken as: "The study or science which treats of God, His nature and attributes, and his relation with man and the universe" (Oxford 1955, 2167). Nature is: "the sum total of all things in time and space; the entire physical universe" (Webster's 1976, 948). Mysticism may be defined as: "reliance on spiritual intuition as the means of acquiring knowledge of mysteries inaccessible to the understanding" (Oxford 1955, 1306). Mystic is: "One who seeks by contemplation and self-surrender to obtain union with or absorption into the Deity or who believes in the spiritual apprehension of truths inaccessible to the understanding" (Oxford 1955, 1306).

In recent years there has been an extended debate about the characteristics of mysticism. A dividing line can be imagined between a group of authors who favour a "common core" of all mystical experience wherever it is found, and a second group who emphasise radical differences among mystics. The former group includes Walter Stace, Ninian Smart and Aldous Huxley, but such scholars as Rudolf Otto, R.C. Zaehner and Gershom Scholem are among those who have proposed various categories by which mystics may be classified. Although "there is no general survey of modern theories of mysticism" (B. McGinn 1994, 265), differences proposed may be classified as due to theological, philosophical or psychological approaches. "No word in our language - not even socialism - has been employed more loosely than Mysticism" wrote Dean Inge in 1899 (W. Inge 1899, 335). And, more recently, Yale philosopher Louis Dupre writes: "No definition could be both meaningful and sufficiently comprehensive to include all experiences that, at some point or other, have been described as 'mystical'" (L. Dupre 1987, 10:245). Moreover, within the community of natural science, words like mystic and mysticism are used regularly as a derogatory reference.

This presentation examines the writings of two natural scientists who were said to be mystics and who spoke about mysticism, the physicist Niels Bohr and the geologist-paleontologist Pierre Teilhard de Chardin. Is it possible to determine a "common core" for them or was their experience directly related to their own personality, background, domain of study and therefore interpretation of experience? I will presume that the reader is familiar with the life, scientific accomplishments and honours of each of these scientists, so that we may concentrate on the examination of their writings. The sources used for Bohr are his published and unpublished correspondence and his limited public discussion of the topic.[1] The major sources for Teilhard used are his private journals,[2] letters and non-scientific publications, most of which were published posthumously.

In order to seek a "common core" I suggest the four classic characteristics of mystical experience proposed by William James, who as professor of both psychology and philosophy at Harvard was professionally neither natural scientist nor theologian (W. James 1960, 343-44). The first characteristic he proposed is "ineffability". "The subject of it immediately says that it defies expression, that no adequate report of its contents can be given words." A second important characteristic, "noetic quality", is described as "states of insight into depths of the truth unplumbed by the discursive intellect...full of significance and importance...and as a rule they carry with them a curious sense of authority for after-time". "These two characteristics will entitle any state to be called mystical in the sense in which I use the word. Two other qualities are less sharply marked, but are usually found". "Transiency" means that the mystical state is not sustained for long. "Except in rare instances, half an hour, or at most an hour or two" and, "when faded, their quality can but imperfectly be reproduced in memory." The fourth characteristic, "passivity", may be described as "when the characteristic sort of consciousness once has set in, the mystic feels as if his own will were in abeyance, and indeed sometimes as if he were grasped and held by a superior power." These characteristics might help to clarify Bohr's seemingly equivocal interpretation of mysticism. In his last interview with Thomas Kuhn, on the day before his death, Bohr recalled his interest in James's way of thinking: "William James is really wonderful in the way he makes it clear...that it is quite possible to analyse things ... - I mean simply if you have some things...they are so connected that if you try to separate them from each other it has nothing to do with the actual situation" (AHQP, p.5). Bohr's application of the notion of complementarity, "a principle which prescribes the necessity of applying mutually exclusive concepts in an exhaustive description of observations at or beyond the bounds of human experience," (Honner 1987, 18) has led some to classify him as a mystic.

Ken Wilbur criticises so-called New Age mysticisms in the preface to his anthology: "what does it mean that the founders of your modern science, the theorists and researchers who pioneered the very concepts you now worship implicitly, the very scientists presented in this volume, what does it mean that they were, every one of them, mystics" (K. Wilbur 1984, X)? It is noteworthy that, in the introduction to this anthology, Wilbur lists as mystics: "Einstein (2), Schroedinger (4), Heisenberg (5), Bohr (0), Eddington (3), Pauli (1), de Broglie (2), Jeans (2), and Planck (1)" (K. Wilbur 1984, 5). The number I added in the parenthesis lists the number of essays by the respective scientists in the anthology. But, interestingly, no essay by Bohr is included. In Bohr's effort to interpret "that we are both onlookers and actors in the great drama of existence" (N. Bohr 1934, 119), as revealed by the mutuality of spectator and actor in the quantum formalism of "that nature of which we ourselves are part" (N. Bohr 1958, 1), he manifested certain characteristics that led some friends and colleagues to suggest that he was a mystic. Bohr's patron, Carl Oseen, described his original quantum theory as a "fruitful mysticism" (BSC 27Jan. 1919, 4). Max Born found Bohr's "Copenhagen" approach "very mystical" (K. Przibram ed. 1968, 84) and for Albert Einstein it was a "tranquilizing philosophy - or religion" (K.Przibram ed. 1968, 31).

Bohr's ambivalence regarding mysticism is not difficult to find. In the draft of a letter written in 1919, while wrestling with fundamental questions in quantum theory, he admits an inclination "to take the most radical or rather mystical views imaginable" (M. Klein 1970, 20). In a letter to Werner Heisenberg in 1925 he writes "I am forcing myself these days with all my strength to familiarise myself with the mysticism of nature" (NBCW 5, 362). Such remarks are found throughout his private correspondence and notes. But merely to label Bohr a mystic without further clarification would not reveal the truth. Commenting on his suggestion to substitute 'reciprocity' for 'complementarity' Bohr writes to Wolfgang Pauli in 1929 that his "preference for artificial words is due, not so much to an urge for mysticism, as the endeavour to avoid this by the help of language itself" (BSC 31July 1925, 14). In another letter to his good friend Pauli, in 1955 he writes "I have always sought scientific inspiration in epistemology rather than in mysticism" (NBCW 6, 195).

In a lecture at Bologna in 1937, Bohr makes the interesting statement:

An immediate consequence of this situation is that observations regarding the behaviour of atomic objects obtained with different experimental arrangements cannot in general be combined in the usual way of classical physics.... Far from being inconsistent, the aspects of quantum phenomena revealed by experience obtained under such mutually exclusive conditions must thus be considered complementary in quite a novel way. The viewpoint of "complementarity" does, indeed, in no way mean an arbitrary renunciation as regards the analysis of atomic phenomena, but is on the contrary the expression of a rational synthesis of the wealth of experience in this field, which exceeds the limits to which the application of the concept of causality is naturally confined (N. Bohr 1958, 19).

In terms of the "principle of separability" (H. Folse 1989, 270) in classical physics, Bohr's "rational synthesis" contains both an ineffable and a noetic quality. No adequate report of content can be given, using a classical pictorial interpretation that is universally and unambiguously applied. But there is an "insight into the depths of truth unplumbed by the discursive intellect...full of significance and importance." On the other hand, I have not found any clear description of private mystical experience in Bohr; in fact all indications are that Bohr would deny any such personal experience. Hints of a scientist's experience of transiency, ineffability and passivity appear in an address in Copenhagen:

> It is not the recognition of our human limitations but our efforts to investigate the nature of these limitations that marks our time. It would only give us a poor picture of our possibilities if we were to compare our limitation with an insurmountable wall.... From a deeper and deeper exploration of our basic outlook greater and greater coherence is understood and thus we come to live under an ever richer impression of an eternal and infinite harmony, although we can only feel the vague presence of this harmony but never really grasp it. At every try, in accordance with its nature, it slips out of our hands. Nothing is firm, every thought—yes every word is only suitable to underline a coherence that in itself can never fully be described but always more deeply studied. These are then the conditions for human thought (MSS 11, 4).

To conclude, examples of James's four characteristics of mysticism can be observed in Niels Bohr. These characteristics are found however, only in Bohr's discussion of the paradoxes in nature that became evident in the quantum formalism. If Bohr was a mystic at all, his was at the edge of a mysticism of nature.

There seems to be little ambiguity in Teilhard de Chardin. His inner life was enriched by regular practice of the *Spiritual Exercises of Ignatius Loyola*, in which the concluding exercise is a "Contemplation for Obtaining Divine Love". The exercise envisions the world penetrated with the presence of God:

This is to reflect how God dwells in creatures: in the elements giving them existence, in the plants giving them life, in the animals conferring upon them sensation, in man bestowing understanding.

And later:

This is to consider how God works and labours for me in all creatures upon the face of the earth, that is, He conducts Himself as one who labours. Thus, in the heavens, the elements, the plants, the fruits, the cattle, etc., He gives being, conserves them, confers life and sensation, etc. Then I will reflect on myself (I. Loyola 1963, 102-3).

Teilhard writes about his Jesuit noviciate (first two years): "I seriously considered the possibility of completely giving up the 'Science of Rocks,' which I found so exciting in order to devote myself entirely to so-called 'supernatural' activities" (Teilhard 1978, 46). When he spoke of this separation to his novice director he was informed that the natural development of his talent and personal interests was the will of the Order and surely the Will of God. He later revealed that this was an important moment, and he never turned back. God's dwelling and working in matter was worthy of the highest reverence and study, and so eventually a loving marriage occurred in his interior life between science and theology. "I have the feeling that a synthesis has been effected naturally between the two currents that claim my allegiance" (Teilhard 1971, 97). Holy matter in all its forms created a divine milieu. His reflection about the reality of evolution during seminary studies made the whole cosmos "fundamentally and primarily living" (Teilhard 1969, 23). It also makes scientific research a powerful spiritual tool, as he notes in his journal:

It is necessary in order to have entirely overcome certain difficulties, not just to have faced them, but to have experienced them, - so as to have felt the impasse, or the limit. It is a great conquest to have got to the bottom of certain things, - not so as to be blasé, liberated by "scepticism," but so as to have understood that the value of the most beautiful and pleasant things is to be introductive or constructive....

- Item, it could be affirmed that the greatest reward of Research is to reach the point where stands (or indeed expands) the unfathomable Real; - the untouched Real; from this contact with the Mystery (or the Almighty), [which is] not only relative to our individual ignorance but relative to the totality of human Thought, an irreplaceable perception of the Being, of the Absolute emerges in us (Teilhard 1977, 20 Jan. 1920).

Possibly Teilhard's description of the experience of research could have been written by Bohr, or for that matter by anyone who has had it. It surely can be a high experience for one who does research into nature, and is probably the closest to Stace's "common core" (W. Stace 1960, 35-38) of mystical experience that might be acceptable to both Bohr and Teilhard. But the interpretation of the "unfathomable Real," "the Absolute", is personal.

Further insight is gained into Teilhard's theology of nature from journal notes some twenty-five years later:

> To be analysed, in what sense "Science leads to God": more and more true insofar as Research becomes sacred, constructive, revealer and actress of Evolution, - the latter uncovering an Omega. Science leads to the Divine, - is a modern access to the Divine, - and seeks to be continued into an Omega (Teilhard 1977, 19 Aug. 1944).

Since all research is impregnated with the Mystic (thanks to the love we have of Evolution), one understands that the last phases of anthropogenesis tend to a "pan-spiritual" *discovery* of God, — which will be the condition and the prelude of an "ECSTASY" (Teilhard 1977, 25 Oct. 1944).

Interpretation of these passages requires more space than is permitted here, but there seems little doubt that they reveal a well-developed spirituality of scientific research and a basis for nature mysticism. His "Three stories in the style of Benson" (Teilhard 1965, 41-55), written at the Front during the First World War, are perhaps the most powerful examples of cosmic mysticism in Teilhard - and profoundly Christian. A briefer example of his vision, which seems to incorporate the four characteristics of mysticism of William James is Teilhard's prayer:

> Lord, it is you who, through the imperceptible goadings of sense-beauty, penetrated my heart in order to make its life flow out into yourself. You came down into me by means of a tiny scrap of created reality; and then, suddenly, you unfurled your immensity before my eyes and displayed yourself to me as Universal Being.

So the basic mystical intuition issues in the discovery of a supra-real unity diffused throughout the immensity of the world.

In that *milieu*, at once divine and cosmic, in which he had at first observed only a simplification and as it were a spiritualisation of space, the seer, faithful to the light given him, now perceives the gradual delineation of the form and attributes of an ultimate *element* in which all things find their definitive consistency.

And then he begins to measure more exactly the joys, and the pressing demands, of that mysterious presence to which he has surrendered himself (Teilhard 1965, 91).

In conclusion, characteristics of a mysticism of nature can be found in both Niels Bohr and Teilhard de Chardin. Although Bohr uses words like "harmony" and Teilhard "unity", they do not manifest a "common core". Whereas Bohr's approach was at the edge of a philosophical mysticism of nature, Teilhard's was profoundly Christian and closely identified with a theological interpretation of his scientific research.

NOTES

1. I am indebted to John Honner, S.J. for valuable correspondence regarding this project. Citations from AHQP, BSC, and MSS come from his book *The Description of Nature*. Oxford: Clarendon Press, 1987, 235 pp.

2. I am indebted to Nicole and Karl Schmitz-Moormann for their suggesting Teilhard's personal journals as a rich source, and for their translations of pertinent texts into English.

REFERENCES

AHQP. *Archive for the History of Quantum Physics.*

Bohr, Niels. 1934: *Atomic Theory and the Theory of Nature*, New York.

Bohr, Niels. 1958: *Atomic Physics and Human Knowledge*, New York.

BSC. *Niels Bohr Scientific Correspondence.* Niels Bohr Archive, with microfilm number.

de Chardin, Teilhard. 1971: *Christianity and Evolution*, New York.

de Chardin, Teilhard. 1978: *The Heart of Matter*, New York.

de Chardin, Teilhard. 1969: *Human Energy*, New York.

de Chardin, Teilhard. 1965: *Hymn of the universe*, New York.

de Chardin, Teilhard. 1977: *Journal Tome I*. Paris.

Dupre, Louis. 1987: "Mysticism," in *The Encyclopedia of Religion*, ed. Mircea Eliade, New York, 10:245.

Folse, Henry. 1989: "Bohr on Bell," *Philosophical Consequences of Quantum Theory*, Notre Dame, 254-71.

Honner, John. 1987, *The Description of Nature*, Oxford.

Inge, William. 1899: *Christian Mysticism*, London.

James, William. 1960: *The Varieties of Religious Experience*, Garden City, New York.

Klein, K. 1970: "The First Phase of the Bohr-Einstein Dialogue," *Historical Studies in the Physical Sciences 2*: 20f.

Loyola, Ignatius. 1963: *The Spiritual Exercises of St. Ignatius*, Westminister, Maryland.

McGinn, Bernard. 1994: *The Foundations of Mysticism Vol.I*, New York.

MSS. *Niels Bohr Scientific Manuscripts*, Niels Bohr Archive, with microfilm number.

NBCW. 1972-: *Niels Bohr Collected Works*, Amsterdam, with volume number.

Oxford Universal Dictionary. 1955: Oxford.

Przibram K. ed. 1968: *Letters on Wave Mechanics*, London.

Stace, W. 1960: *Mysticism and Philosophy*, New York.

Webster's New World Dictionary. 1976: Cleveland, Ohio.

Wilbur, Ken ed. 1985: *Quantum Questions*, Boston.

A RECIPE FOR PHILIP HEFNER'S "THE HUMAN FACTOR"

HUBERT MEISINGER
(Bensheim-Auerbach, Germany)

Abstract: In his book "The Human Factor. Evolution, Culture and Religion" Philip Hefner develops an original approach to link scientific and theological concepts. Following Imre Lakatos, Hefner talks of *research programs* and *auxiliary hypotheses* in his theological program. The center, the hard core of it is his concept of the "created co-creator" which is inspiring for the dialog between science and theology. According to Hefner humankind with its two-natured character is a proposal for the future evolution of the planet. Altruistic love has an intrinsic character and is part of humankind as imago dei. Because of this Hefner says that sociobiological research on altruism is an archeological expedition for the purpose of illumining what biological building blocks make up the infrastructure of the biocultural *Homo sapiens*. But the quintessential human stance is forward-looking because of his cultural possibilities. Thus Jesus Christ is the paradigm, the model of what it means to be humans in the image of God, of what it means to be the human being that God intended.

Keywords: altruism, anthropology, created co-creator, imago dei, Lakatos, love command, research program, sociobiology.

1. GENERAL REMARKS

In his book "The Human Factor. Evolution, Culture and Religion" Philip Hefner has developed an original approach to link scientific and theological concepts. My intention (*cf.* Meisinger 1996, 281-291) is to give a short survey on the main thoughts of the book and some comments on it in order to enhance the ideas which are developed in the book - to take Hefner's words of the preface where he compares his way of reflection with the recipes of his maternal grandmother: a recipe for the "Human factor".

2. EVOLUTION AS *CREATIO CONTINUA*

2.1 SCIENTIFIC KNOWLEDGE AND THEOLOGICAL ANTHROPOLOGY -
HERNER'S PROGRAM OF MAN AS "CREATED CO-CREATOR"

The presupposition of Hefner's thoughts is that "large frameworks of meaning like those proposed by religion and metaphysics, are unavoidable and required if the human quest for meaning is to be fulfilled. At the same time, those frameworks are useless and empty if they are not brought into conjunction in a credible manner with the concrete data of our scientific and social experience" (Hefner 1993, 8). This is why science plays an important role for him in doing theology. His theological anthropology is based on scientific knowledge because in his opinion sciences try to determine how things really are. His intention is to create a wider frame of reference for interpreting life and for making possible an orientation in life. In this respect he could be called a constructive theologian. But unlike Gordon Kaufman (1993), the main exponent of constructive theology whose starting point is the construction of a concept of God, Hefner focuses on the meaning of myth and ritual. His overarching purpose is to "provide resources from the Christian tradition to revitalizing the myth-ritual-praxis constellation" (Hefner 1993, 224). Hefner does not intend to present a complete approach but a program that is interesting and stimulating for future discussions.

In principle Hefner follows the philosopher of science Imre Lakatos (1978), but not all of the details of his philosophical proposal fit with Hefner's theological method perfectly. Lakatos elaborated the notion of a *research program*: that is, that the goal of an intellectual proposal is to provide ideas that will prove to be fruitful if their suggestions are tested carefully. He distinguishes between a *hard core* of this program and *auxiliary hypotheses*. The hard core of a research program is the idea on which it is based. The auxiliary hypotheses are drawn from the hardcore. They are a kind of belt that protects the hard core, and it is these hypotheses that ought to be subjected to verification and falsification - not the hard core. Only when this belt is proven wrong, will the central idea also drop. If this is not the case, the research program is a fruitful enterprise to get constructive insights that enable us to gain new wisdom - thus it is forward looking into the future.

Hefner's theological program is based on this model. The central idea is the description of men as *created co-creator* which is surrounded by a belt of nine hypotheses. We will focus on the term *created co-creator* in order to understand the core of Hefner's program.

The adjective *created* indicates "that the human species did not design its own nature or its role in the world" (Hefner 1993, 36). It corresponds with the fact that human life is conditioned by its genetic and cultural presuppositions and by the ecosystem in which human life exists. In the end it depends on God's act of creation, that enables life to start with. Mankind is part of creation. The noun *co-creator* corresponds to the freedom of the human being who is able to make decisions on his own that participate in the intentional fulfilling of God's will. Thus an eschatological perspective appears that asks for the direction in which human beings and the process of evolution will evolve. Of course human beings are not totally free because they are created beings. There is a close relation between determinism and freedom - both are no opposites. The term does not say that human beings are identical with God the creator, but it points to a special quality of human beings as *imago dei*[1]. There the symbiosis between genes and culture reaches a (preliminary) perfection. Thus Hefner talks about homo sapiens as "a proposal for the future evolution of the planet" (Hefner 1993, 50). Human beings are the representatives of all creation.

Very important are Hefner's thoughts on the problem of altruism and Christian love. They will give us insights in the nature of human beings as *imago dei*.

2.2 HEFNER ON THE PROBLEM OF ALTRUISM AND CHRISTIAN LOVE

Hefner's main thesis is the following: "The concepts of altruism as articulated by the evolutionary biocultural sciences and the love command of the Hebrew-Christian tradition focus upon the same phenomenon: beneficent human behavior toward others, even those who are not genetic kin" (Hefner 1993, 197). Both have to be brought into conjunction. Otherwise Christian theology runs the risk of losing an adequate interpretation of its content. He concludes that "the theological elaboration of *agape* should not shy away from identifying it with altruism" (Hefner 1993, 208). According to Hefner, sociobiological models on altruism stress the gain for the altruist - which takes altruism out of altruism. It only is "a self-seeking strategy for attaining other goods. ... the Christian love command can be identified with the behavior associated with the biocultural evolutionary concept of altruism, but the meaning and status of altruism are not exhaused by those scientific concepts" (Hefner 1993, 208f). Thus Hefner does avoid a reductionistic view on the problem of altruism. In his opinion it is an important function of theology to integrate sociobiological theories on altruism within a greater frame of reference. Hefner says: "The significance of the theological concepts of altruistic love, elaborated from myth and rituals and also by the scientific understanding, is this: Theology suggests that theories of epigenetic rules or strategies of self-interest are not enough to complete our understanding of altruistic love; we require also ways of discussing the hypothesis that altruism is an intrinsic value, rooted in the fundamental character of reality" (Hefner 1993, 209). For Hefner, *agape* is rooted in God, "that is, in the way things really are" (Hefner 1993, 207). Thus, love is written in the fundamental nature of human reality. It does not have its origins within family-boundaries or comparable human relationships as sociobiological theories claim. Love is part of humankind as *imago dei*.

2.3 LOVE AND THE CREATED CO-CREATOR AS *IMAGO DEI*

Because of its intrinsic character, altruistic love belongs to the created co-creator as *imago dei*. It is part of God's act of creation. Thus according to Hefner sociobiological research on altruism is an "archeological expedition for the purpose of illumining what biological (including genetic) building blocks make up the infrastructure of this biocultural *Homo sapiens*" (Hefner 1994, 72). It investigates the past of human beings, his biological origin. Theologically speaking, evolutionary theory tries to describe a part of God's act of creation. Evolution belongs to the *creatio continua*, the sustaining and new-creating act of God. But this backward looking view has to be completed because "the quintessential human stance is forward-looking" (Hefner 1994, 71f). The human being is no prisoner of his biological constraints, but has the freedom to own decision-making that should correspond to what God intends with creation. According to Hefner human beings have the potential to actualize a radically new phase of evolution because of their cultural possibilities. Jesus Christ is recognized as the "paradigm, the model of what it means to be humans in the image of God, of what it means to be the human being that God intended" (Hefner 1993, 243). In light of this paradigm the will of God is the principle of universal love that breaks all boundaries. Only in love human beings make good use of freedom.

Thus sociobiological research on altruism is embedded twice. Firstly, it is incomplete as long as the intrinsic character of altruisic love is not seen. Love rootes in God, the way things really are. We can call this a *protological perspective*. Secondly, it is incomplete as long as it is focused on the origin of human beings. Human beings as part of creation aim for freedom and future. Important is the direction in which the two-natured character of the human being - who is a symbioses of genes and culture - will evolve. Only this *eschatological perspective* opens up the possibility to unrestricted love that fulfills the protologic-intrinsic character of human beings.

3. SOME COMMENTS ON HEFNER'S "HUMAN FACTOR"

That Hefner follows the philosophy of science of Lakatos is indeed unusual for a theologian - but very fruitful as e.g. Nancy Murphy (1990) also shows. To my mind this way of dealing with theology stresses its scientific character in the dialogue with the natural sciences. Both disciplines prove to be methodologically comparable, because also in theology one can talk about theories and hypotheses. The notion of *the hard core* fits theology where God is the center of all thinking. Both Hefner's theology of creation and a theology of revelation are "a proposal in the public marketplace of ideas that people of faith make for understanding human life and its meaning" (Hefner 1993, 18). Decisive is the persuasiveness that depends on the potentiality to interpret the processes and structures of the world fruitfully. This methodology of Hefner is provocative both for theology and the natural sciences, because two fields that are so widely separated are joined together. To be sure, some transformations have to take place. Further investigation is needed e.g. with respect to the question of novel facts that should be intended by a research program.

The difference between God and the world seems to be given up when Hefner talks about God as "the way things really are" (Hefner 1993, 207) and when natural sciences are an effort "to determine how things really are" (Hefner 1993, 101). Hefner should be cautious not to identify both, because it is widely accepted that the natural sciences do not investigate the world as it is (*"Welt an sich"*), but the world as we see it through our senses, our mind or scientific instruments. According to the theory of cognition there is a difference between reality and the way we realize or experience the world. This has to be taken into consideration in order to avoid that the natural sciences will become direct approaches towards God. This is beyond their potentialities. In addition, the relationship between the notion of experience in science and in theology has to be taken into account.

As far as his concept of the *created co-creator* is concerned Hefner himself discusses two problematic points which are almost opposed of each other. The first objection - theologically speaking - is that the *co* implies that "humans are somehow on the same level with God, at least in the significance of their actions. ... For the scientists, who are deeply impressed with the awesomeness of nature, it seems simply absurd to suggest that human beings are more than tiny actors on a stage whose dimensions in time and space are beyond our capacity to comprehend, let alone master" (Hefner 1993, 236). In a way the objection is anthropocentricm. The second objection is "that the image of created co-creator, when the directionality of its activity is placed as I have placed it, in service to natural order, is *too demeaning* of human beings to function as central symbol for the thematizing of our experience of ourselves in the world" (Hefner 1993, 237). Both objections - which are clearly at odds - hold that the term created co-creator would be the wrong interpretation of human being.

To my mind both objections stress one part of the term *created co-creator* in an inadmissible way - either the adjective *created* or the noun *co-creator*. This does not fit Hefner's approach. Both elements depend on each other reciprocally. The gain Hefner profits by these two objections is that both recognize "one of its [i.e. created co-creator imagery] most important dimensions - its tremendous dynamism and energy" (Hefner 1993, 237).

Freedom and determinism are two aspects of the *created co-creator* that also depend on each other reciprocally. "Not only are we apparently determined to be free creatures, but our freedom must be finally consonant with the objective course of our evolution. We can say that we are not only determined to be free, but we are free to be determined" (Hefner 1993, 121). According to Hefner, biological evolution is the medium by which God created the cultural free human being. And it is the task of human beings to search for what God intended us to be by this freedom. "The activity that we fashion to meet the requirements of our destiny should conform to the sacrifice of Christ for the whole world and in such self-giving we find our deepest harmony with our destiny" (Hefner 1987, 139).

The sacrifice of Christ is the paradigm for altruistic, universal love. As shown above that altruistic love has an intrinsic character because it is rooted in God. This could be criticized out of an humanistic perspective that foregoes a final cause. But in this case two opposite perspectives are confronted with each other and a fruitful discussion will not take place.

As far as Hefner's thoughts on altruism and *agape* are concerned the identification of both concepts could be problematic for some readers. To my mind it is also possible to differentiate between altruism and *agape* without separating both from each other. Indeed, both deal with the same phenomenon, "beneficent human behavior toward others, even those who are not genetic kin" (Hefner 1993, 197). But because *agape* is rooted in God, it makes up the greater frame of reference for altruism. Both concepts have similiarities and differences.

4. CONCLUDING COMMENT

Hefner's book contains a synthesis of modern thinking and theology that is fascinating and provocative. It does not provide a final picture of reality but presents a program that opens up further dialogue - within theology and between theology and science. It is a recipe itself for further investigation and interpretation of reality.

REFERENCES

Hefner, Philip. 1987: "Freedom in Evolutionary Perspective", *Free Will and Determinism*, ed. V. Mortensen and R. C. Sorensen, Aarhus, 121-141.

Hefner, Philip. 1993: *The Human Factor. Evolution, Culture and Religion*, Minneapolis: Fortress Press.

Hefner, Philip. 1994: "Entrusting the Life that has Evolved: A Response to Michael Ruse's Ruse", *Zygon. Journal of Religion and Science* 29, 67-73.

Kaufman, Gordon. 1993: *In Face of Mystery: A Constructive Theology*. Cambridge, MA: Harvard University Press.

Lakatos, Imre. 1978: *The Methodology of Scientific Research Programmes*. Cambridge: Cambridge University Press.

Meisinger, Hubert. 1996: *Liebesgebot und Altruismusforschung. Ein exegetischer Beitrag zum Dialog zwischen Theologie und Naturwissenschaft*. Novum Testamentum et Orbis Antiquus 33. Fribourg: Universitätsverlag and Göttingen: Vandenhoeck & Ruprecht.

Murphy, Nancy. 1990: *Theology in the Age of Scientific Reasoning*. Cornell Studies in the Philosophy of Religion. Ed. by William P. Alston. Ithaca and London: Cornell University Press.

NOTES

1. It is important to notice that this should not be understood in an anthropocentric way. On the contrary: "Because the human is made up of the basic stuff of the planet, the *imago* of God in that human being indicates that the world itself is capable of that special relationship to which the image of God points. The planetary ecosystem is a support system that stands in so intimate a relationship to humans that we are fully dependent upon it. Furthermore, the evolutionary processes that produced the ecosystem are the same processes that produced humans" (Hefner 1993, 239). In Hefner's (and my) opinion the anthropocentrism of the concept of the image of God requires revision today.

THE INTEREST OF NEUROBIOLOGY
FOR THEOLOGICAL ANTHROPOLOGY

BERNARD MICHOLLET
(*Lyon, France*)

The complexity of brain structure was completely unknown until very recently, and it is only in the beginning stages. Yet, some discoveries already show us that the growth of brain structure is not only the effect of a genetic program, but that brain building is also an interactive process. The concept of interaction has many consequences which would need a long analysis to show how it leads to some new anthropological implications. In the theological field, the idea of deterministic creation is dead, and with this, the conception of the human being as co-creator comes to light with new strength.

BRAIN STRUCTURE IS THE RESULT OF AN INTERACTIVE PROCESS

Before birth, the genetic program determines brain building. But the information it provides is less important than that of the whole brain.[1] Evidently genetic power structures the central nervous system and the main centers. For all human beings this mechanism is the same. But experiments upon animals show that clones do not have the same nervous system. This means that genetic identity does not produce the same nervous system.

Yet before birth, differences can appear. Environment has a large place in this development. But human brain organisation takes place for nearly the first twenty years of life. This is why environmental conditions are essential, for example, regarding nourishment. But cultural conditions also build brain, the first being language - in which the baby is immersed. Language gives particular structures to the cortex, which are not, however, strictly deterministic. Nevertheless, their importance is such that other possibilities are lost forever.

Brain building time is not a cumulative growth.[2] Several neuronal structures can appear. But only those which are more adapted remain. The approach, founded on observation, underlines the role of education and cultural environment. Affective life, linguistic and personal acquisitions have a neuronal basis - or more precisely, a brain structure basis. Even if it is not absolutely deterministic, brain structure largely defines the capabilities of a person. Though other abilities can be acquired in other ways, the basic brain structure remains. So mind-brain is not only the result of a genetic program, but also of an interactive process.

THE EPISTEMOLOGICAL LEVEL

The idea that the world has an influence on human psychology is not new. The influence of the *milieu*, social and cultural ideas, has been well known for a long time. What is new is that these influences are also biological. They are largely responsible for the structure of the brain. We know that there is a strong link between neurobiology and psychology even though we still are unable to choose the best theory to explain it. The human being is the center of a world of interactions. The brain as the biological basis of the mind is not independent of its human and material environment. The brain is the reflection of both a particular situation and a network of relationships. It is not a pure product of the genetic code. So mind is always a concrete mind. For this reason, its biological basis does not allow us to conclude the existence of a pure mind - unlimited and all-powerful.

The idea of interactive growth is the basis of this new research. Its value lies in systemic analysis[3], the paradigm[4] dominant in contemporary thought. Even though this paradigm would need more discussion, experimental results already exist. We only suggest that this approach should remain at the epistemological level and not become a new ontology.

As the result of interactions, brain structure is both a natural and artificial product. One of the most important consequences of this research is that old boundaries between nature and culture are no longer justified. The link between mind and the human person is so strong that the rapport between mind and "brain-interacting-with-its-world" must lead to anthropological consequences.

ANTHROPOLOGICAL CONSEQUENCES

The first question concerns freedom. In one sense, no one is independent of the world in its totality. Concretely, through his brain, a person is the product of biological, environmental and cultural factors. Immediately we see the crucial responsibility of each individual and of society for the growth of children. What is new in the nerosciences is the demonstration of the permanence of the biological inscription of interactions. Brain flexibility means that new acquisitions are possible in some cases, but not always.

Another question concerns the identity of the human subject. The genetic program permits the development of the basic brain structure. But then the human being learns more things after birth than do all other animals. The human brain has been evolving for years. So we cannot maintain a purely biological basis for one's identity. Genetic identity only means that one belongs to the human race. Brain complexity is such that several people can be quite different with the same genome.

But does this mean that a person is only the product of interactions?[5] It is clear today that we are all products of environmental conditions, relationships and culture, and that this is largely inscribed in our biological being. External conditions have a real impact on the structure of the brain. Common sense tells us that no one is shut up inside the boundaries of his education even if this is important. Even though limited, freedom is real.[6] One's identity is cultural - but not entirely since it is also written in one's brain. Mind is no longer considered as an empty blackboard ready to accept all sorts of information. It seems to be a framework which accepts some information more easily than other data.

Human mind with its particularities is individual. But it is also collective. It is not an isolated object. It carries certian common marks in its biological structure. Here we are not speaking of the ideas it receives later. These common marks are those of a culture or a specific group. In this sense, mind through brain has a collective dimension. The first collective dimension, specific to the human race, without precise characteristics, is the basic neuronal structure. This new collective dimension depends on the contribution of human education. The biological basis shows that the human mind must be thought of as an incarnate object. Mind is embodied in a singular "body-interacting-with-others".

The biological structre of the brain, the basis for mind, is beyond the distinction between natural and artificial, as well as between individual and collective. More precisely, today no one can define mind as a purely singular natural object which would later receive artificial, collective and bodily influences. This assertion could open doors to various types of metaphysics. However, we would not want to choose one that is too structured before asking the questions of creation theology. Only then, perhaps, could we admit a metaphysical support for theology.[7]

IMPACT ON THE IDEA OF CREATION

According to the classical vision, God creates humankind in his image. Everyone is unique and carries God's image. Sometimes theology forgets that creatures also come from earth.[8] Tradition has tried to define how God's image is in everyone. The answer given was that it is the essential part of man: one's reason[9], for example. This kind of question led to a separation between the pure image of God and concrete human people. Cartesian theory then increased the gap between these two human dimensions which were unkown in the biblical world.

Since brain is linked to mind, we can see that our knowledge about brain structure and its growth touches on an essential part of the human being. The idea that the human person is created independently of everything under God's blue sky, must be changed. Perhaps the idea of creation must have a more biblical approach as well as a richer significance thanks to recent scientific research. Our background is always this: God is the creator and he gives a personal and special spirit to each individual. The doctrine of creation needs a new interpretation in the light of the new scientific context.[10]

The relativisation of the distinction between the natural and artificial in the brain - essentially linked to mind - means that this distinction is no longer relevant for separating God's work from that of human beings. All human activities interact with God's work.[11] And God has chosen to associate man with his own. Does a purely human activity exist? And is there a place where God's creation is empty of humankind?[12]

God's creation is an interactive action in which man's part is very significant. Until modern times human activity as co-creation was not thought to be essential. Man had a vocation: working on earth to survive. His main work was to "paint the clay" shaped by God. Today he has become aware that he also works in shaping the clay. The human mind, through the biologically structured brain, is one of his major areas of creativity. In this, he has no choice. Only today have we come to recognize its importance.

In a theology of the Word of God individual being is not that of a pure creature passively bearing the world's imprint. An individual is also an active product of society. A human is not God's creature *despite* these conditions. He is God's creature *through* all these conditions including the biological ones. God's work is a collective work. God calls human beings to life. Concretely, humans belong to a natural environment, to a

cultrual world and to a human relationship. The creation of a person includes all these components. This raises the question of imperfectibilities
or illness. The mystery of God's tactfulness may not answer such questions quickly. The only answer which we have, seems to lie in a better
participation in God's creation. Creation is neither a grand manipulation
by God nor his solitary work.

TOWARDS A THEOLOGICAL ANTHROPOLOGY

God's creation is God's call to life mediated by human relations,
particular conditions of life, technical means (with ethical references), etc.
The basis of a theological anthropology is the vocation of man to be
co-creator.[13] Man is co-creator not only for a small part of the universe,
but also for his own identity.[14] Creation means radical separation between
God and his creature. In other words, freedom is the fundamental concept
of a creation theology. Without this, creation would be either without any
significance (no link whatever between God and the world) or an ema-
nated part of God (no autonomous existence). Thus man's freedom appears as the central concept of a creation theology. Evidently this takes
into account culture and evolution.

Without developing ethical consequences, we can note that a strong
distinction between the natural and artificial in this field cannot be maintained. Otherwise one eliminates the relevance of a creation theology. If
a creation theology belongs to a theology of the Word, free human response is at the center. that means that human responsibility is an ontological concept. Today neurobiology leads people to go beyond the
concept of a natural basis of studying human personal identity.

This dynamic conception has grown in the 20th century.[15] Man is
an objective co-creator of his mind through the power of his own brain.
He has more to do than simply follow nature passively. He has to grow
in awareness of the divine mission. Neurobiological discoveries, although
still limited, lead humans to respond to God's call through nature. Does
man wish to enter more deeply into this mission of co-creator?

CONCLUDING REMARK

When Augustine wanted to say something about God, he remembered
that the human person is in the image of God. So he thought it was
possible to find traces of him in man. Inspired by this idea, he built some
nice trinitarian models.

God's image is not indiependent of a natural and artificial *milieu*. The concept of image has to be rethought. Classically the divine image remains at the superior level of the human being: his reason, his capacity for love, his freedom, etc. According to this idea, concrete diversity is not taken into account. But we have seen that individual mind also has collective dimensions. this reminds us that humankind is created in God's image, and not simply as an individual. The same can be said for concrete diversity which means we have not to build images of God!

NOTES

1. For this see e.g. Jean-Pierre Changeux, *L'homme neuronal*, Paris 1983.
2. One of the theories used to explain this fact is neuronal darwinism: Gerald M. Edelman, *Bright Air, Brilliant Fire: On the Matter of Mind*, New York 1992.
3. This is a free use of the systemic thought of Ludwig and Bertalanffy.
4. For this concept *cf.* Thomas S. Kuhn, *The Structure of Scientific Revolutions*, Chicago 1962.
5. For such a conception see Daniel C. Dennet, *Consciousness Explained*, New York 1991.
6. We do not discuss here the case of the further limitation of freedom caused by illness. We will return to this question in the theological part of this paper.
7. Ian Barbour thinks metaphysics is necessary for theology to avoid simplifications. See e.g. Ian Barbour, *Religion in an Age of Science*, New York 1990.
8. The concrete story of Genesis 2 shows this dimension.
9. Thomas Aquinas develops the idea of *intellectus* as the human center.
10. For a good analysis of the concept of interpretation *cf.* Paur Ricoeur, *Le conflit des interprétations*, Paris 1969.
11. For the development of this idea see Arthur Peacocke, *Theology for a Scientific Age*, Minneapolis 1993.
12. The immensity of the universe is not an answer because we stay in the same world. Even with other universes, the universality of God's creative act would be marked by a particular engagement with man.
13. We retain this concept even if in a strict sense only God is creator. Human activity belongs to another metaphysical sphere.
14. Man is creator towrads the cosmos, towards himself and even towards God - if we consider the covenant: see Adolphe Gesche, *L'homme*, Paris 1993.
15. Pierre Teilhard de Chardin gave strength to these ideas. See also: Philip Hefner, *The Human Factor*, Minneapolis 1993.

Section 3

Mind and Nature

SUPERVENIENCE
AS A STRATEGY OF RELATING
PHYSICAL AND THEOLOGICAL PROPERTIES

DENNIS BIELFELDT

(*Brookings, USA*)

Abstract: In this paper I offer a non-dualistic strategy by which talk of God's immanent activity can be made compatible with a robust physicalism. Through the employment of the notion of "supervenience" - a very hot topic in the philosophy journals these past 15 years - I apply and extend Donald Davidson's notion of "anomalous monism" to theology. Just as mind-talk is not reducible to brain-talk (even though ultimately all that exists are neurophysiological events and processes), so too is talk of divine immanence not reducible to discourse about the physical (even though all that exists are physical events and processes). On my view the divine and physical comprise different "layers" of one ontic reality, layers whose respective property groups sustain a relationship of *metaphysical dependency* rather than *causal interaction*. Accordingly, the notion of *downward causation* is criticised as a way to relate higher-level and lower-level properties.

Keywords: Anomalous monism, divine immanence, downward causation, nonreductive materialism, physicalism, supervenience

I.

Theists of various religious traditions often ascribe intentional states to God. They say that God "knows" and "loves" His people, that He is sometimes "angry" with them, and that He ultimately "desires" their salvation. They claim further that God acts within history in accordance with these intentional states, for God creates, speaks, enjoins, chastises and redeems the world. Thus, believers frequently attribute to God both *propositional attitudes* and the divine *actions* that flow from them.[1]

Unfortunately, while religious people speak as if God actually possesses propositional states and really acts in history, philosophers and theologians have not been successful in clarifying precisely *how* such divine action is intelligible. This problem of the ontological status of God's "mighty acts in history" is not new, but was raised by both Hume and Kant who asked how a transcendent God could "cause" an event in the universe, when the category of causality properly applies only to re-lations among events already within the universe. The problem becomes even more acute when we try to conceive how such divine causality is possible without violating the causal closure of the physical order, a prin-ciple that many take to be a cardinal presupposition of all the natural sciences. While some continue to argue that a dualistic causal interaction-ism between the universe and God is philosophically defensible (Taliaferro 1994), many sense that such a dualism is rapidly losing general intelligi-bility today among people living in a first-world environment charac-terised by secularisation, democratisation, technology and the flow of information.[2]

I am pessimistic about the prospects of a nature-supernature dualism retaining plausibility in America and Europe over the next century, for I believe that in the next decades the naturalistic impulse driving the sci-ences will continue, that science will proceed to discover better explana-tory and predictive models, and that (regardless of the amount of indeterminacy the final quantum theory allows) God will be increasingly regarded as a causally inert, and therefore irrelevant, entity.[3] The result will be the further subjectivisation and privatisation of the notion of God, and an additional undermining of the belief that there can be truth-con-ditions for theological and religious language at all (Grigg 1995, 30-40).

I want therefore to explore another option for conceiving the con-nection between the divine and the physical, an option that rejects a du-alistic *causal* link between them in favour of a monistic *metaphysical* relation. I wish to explore the possibility of using the notion of *super-venience* - a hot topic in the philosophy journals these last fifteen years - to connect the propositional attitudes and actions of the divine to physi-cal actualisations. Assuming a nonreductive materialism not unlike that proposed by Willem Drees in *Religion, Science, and Naturalism* (Drees 1996), I shall argue that divine intent and action can be construed as "supervenient upon" or "realisable within" the processes of nature. I claim that just as the real properties referred to by the theories of chemistry, biology, physiology and psychology ultimately supervene upon micro-physics (without thereby adding new entities to the microphysical do-main), so too might theology refer to real theological properties which supervene upon physics (without increasing the ontological inventory of the physical order).

For purposes of this paper I shall presuppose the truth of *physicalism*, the view that everything is composed in some way out of subatomic en-tities of the kind that microphysics posits (Pettit 1993). Upon that basis I shall try to sketch how supervenience might be a philosophically legiti-mate avenue by which to conceive the immanence of God. My hope is that divine immanence can be superveniently connected to macrophysical actualisations in such a way that language about God's immanent intentionality and activity can be granted definite truth-conditions. If my argument is successful, I will have depicted how supervenience can provide the believer who sees God at work in the world with a philosophical option whereby she can make true or false statements about that divine activity, without at the same time compromising her scientific and philosophical scruples about the ultimate composition and causal structure of spatio-temporal reality.

II.

That believers ascribe intentionality and agency to God is compatible with an analogy many have noticed between the mind-body and God-universe relationships (Peacock 1993, 144ff).

1) Both mind and God are nonspatial, while the brain and universe are spatial.

2) Both mind and God are intentional, while the brain and universe are not.

3) Both mind and God have agent-action structures (a freedom issuing in action), while the brain and universe possess an event-event character.

4) Both mind and God, and brain and universe are intimately connected to time.[4]

5) Both mind-brain and God-universe causal connections are problematic, for they threaten the causal closure of the physical.

On the basis of the analogy's strength we should expect affinities between strategies in the philosophy of mind and theology.

1) Just as *Cartesian dualism* holds that the mind and brain are different ontic types possessing a problematic *interaction*, so does *theism* assert ontically distinct realms of nature and supernature that are somehow causally linked.

2) Just as Berkeley's *idealist dualism* claims that brain is but a bundle of ideas in the mind, so does the *idealistic monism* of the Upanishads assert that the material universe is but an idea within the divine Brahman.

3) Just as *logical behaviourism* advocates a *semantic reduction* of mental-conduct concepts to behavioural dispositions (Ryle

1949), so some attempt to semantically reduce God-talk to a less problematic discourse.[5]

4) Just as *type-type reductionist* theories claim via *empirical reduction* that mental properties are neurophysiological ones (Carnap 1932), so some might claim that the divine properties just are types of physical actualisations.[6]

5) Just as *eliminativism* holds that the very concept of the mental must be jettisoned, so does *atheism* call for an end to God-talk.

6) Just as *functionalism* reduces mind to a complex information-processing system disconnectable in principle from neurophysiology or other hardware (Putnam 1975), so might one claim that God is merely a complex organisation of infinite information (Tipler 1993).

7) Just as the ineliminable and irreducible *intentionality* of the psychological constitutes a different class of properties from the neurophysiological (though there may be a *token-token identity* of the two), and just as the first is capable of *downward causation* into the latter; so might one argue a *property dualism* between theological and physical properties with a corresponding downward causation from the former to the latter (Peacocke 1993, 157ff).

8) Just as psychological and neurophysiological properties are such that the former *supervene* on (or are "determined by") the latter (Teller 1983, 137), so might one argue that the theological supervenes on the physical.

I think (7) and (8) are the most interesting, for both take *physicalism* seriously, while allowing for an *anomalism* of the psychological or theological, e.g., they reject "bridge laws" between the two property groups (Davidson 1980, 222). Before examining them more closely, however, we must briefly look at (3), (4) and (5).

Despite the explanatory and predictive success of intentional explanations (Fodor 1987, 2-5 & Dennett 1978, 5ff.), *eliminative materialists* claim that they must be abandoned (Churchland 1984, 43ff.). Just as a mature chemistry expunged phlogiston from its theory, so too must a seasoned psychology jettison intentionality. However, most philosophers of mind have not gone so far. While they share with eliminativists common physicalist assumptions, they contend that the mental can neither be eliminated nor reduced to the physical through the semantic reduction of (3) or the empirical reduction of (4). They argue, in effect, that the explanations and predictions of "folk psychology" - explanations in terms of desire, belief and motivation - are sound.

Donald Davidson is well-known for his embrace of physicalism, his rejection of eliminativism and his denial of reduction. His anomalous monism asserts a token-token identity between the mental and neurophysical, while yet denying pyschophysical or psychological laws (Davidson 1980, 207-227). Davidson's position also allows for the claim that intentional explanations of human action are *causal*, for human action is better explained by the intentionality of the agent than by the description of her neurostates (Davidson 1980, 3-19).

Interestingly, while philosophers have allowed retention of intentional explanations in a world of "bodies in motion", they have rejected analogous theological explanations. Many assume their impossibility because God can neither be *within* nature (for only natural events, objects, properties and laws exist), nor can He causally affect it from the *outside* (for that would violate the causal closure of nature). But this rejection of the theological is unfortunate, because those called to faith are denied an avenue by which to think God. The entities their theological language quantifies over are baldly and roundly asserted not to exist, and their "theological theory" is denied explanatory and predictive power.

I suggest that just as many philosophers happily give some variant of a folk psychological account of human behaviour (without denying physicalism), so too ought believers be permitted an analogous theological account of the physical course of the universe (without being saddled with ontological dualism). If we allow mental states the status of a higher "conceptual level" irreducible to, yet realisable within neurophysiology, then could we not also regard immanent divine action as constituting a "conceptual level" irreducible to, yet realisable within nature and history? That one is allowed philosophical legitimacy while the other denied it, strikes me as simple prejudice. In order to explore how such a theological account might run, I turn to positions (7) and (8).

III.

Views similar to (7) are endorsed by a number of thinkers convinced of the fruitfulness of the mind-body/God-universe analogy. I am worried, however, about (7)'s advocacy of downward *causation* in relating the "higher-level" emergent properties of mind to "lower-level" neurophysiological properties (Peacocke 1993, 53-55 & Sperry, 201), for the notion is clearly problematic. Fortunately, just as downward causation is not required to legitimise the use of psychological categories like agency, freedom, belief and action, it is not needed either to validate employment of similar divine, intentional categories.

Emergentism claims a compatibilism between physicalism and the existence of a hierarchy of levels of organisational complexity (e.g., the physical, chemical, biological, psychological, sociological, etc.). It asserts that entities at each level possess properties specific to that level. While higher-level entities have arisen out of the physical, they have over time acquired properties appropriate to their higher organisational level. Accordingly, the objects over which psychology quantifies really exist and possess psychological properties. *Downward causation* claims that are causal power properties by which the course of actualisations at the lower-level are influenced are included in the set of properties of the higher-level group. Brian Mclaughlin explains:

> [Emergentism implies] that types of structures that compose certain special science kinds can affect the acceleration of a particle in ways unanticipated by laws concerning forces exerted by pairs of particles, general laws of motion, and the spatial or spatio-temporal arrangements of particles (Mclaughlin, 52).

In *Theology for a Scientific Age* Peacocke expresses the relationship this way:

> ... the changes at the micro-level ... are what they are because of their incorporation into the system as a whole, which is exerting specific constraints on its units, making them behave otherwise than they would do in isolation (Peacocke 1993, 53).

There is in the literature a temptation to think of this "system as a whole" as a higher level, which then causally affects actualisations of the parts existing at the lower level, thus "making them behave otherwise than they would" have. It is a simple step to apply this analogy to the God-world relation, and to conceive God as somehow acting in a non-interventionist way such that the units comprising all of history and nature "behave otherwise than they would" have without God. In a recent *Zygon* article James Nelson writes:

> The knowing of God's mind works like a program in a computer or as the patterns on a TV screen are shaped, without interfering with the physical laws of the system... God can be seen as such a higher reality, and the Creator Spirit as the enveloping supervenient power who acts in and through creation (Nelson 1995, 280).

Although Nelson is quick to point out that this is not "to be taken literally as an explanation of how God works" in the world, he definitely holds that the analogy can "make credible the meaning of the actions of God in creation" (Nelson 1995, 280).

Peacocke's application of downward causation is more nuanced, for he speaks of a relation between God and the "world-as-a-whole", with the particular world events then downwardly caused by the totality of the world-as-a-whole (Peacocke 1993, 161). Because the physical actualisations within the various subsystems are functionally related to the boundary constraints of the world-as-a-whole, and because God nonphysically establishes these boundary constraints, the physical actualisations of history and nature are functionally related to God's activity via top-down causation.

Unfortunately, there are considerable problems facing those wishing to employ downward causation for theological purposes. In the first place, one can question whether there is good scientific evidence for it. Brian McLaughlin points out that downward causation implies the existence of "configurational forces" which are in principle irreducible to "point-pair forces," and that there is not "a scintilla of evidence" for the former (McLaughlin 1992, 90-91). He believes, in fact, that the advent of quantum mechanics has seriously compromised the intelligibility of downward causal explanations, for it can actually explain the higher-level actualisations which previous theory had relegated to the effects of "the emergent" (McLaughlin 1992, 89).

A second problem recalls that downward causation is actually a mereological relation between the whole and its parts rather than a downward relation between levels. While it is true that particles will "behave otherwise" in a context than they would have in isolation, there is really no *causal* relation between the context and the particular particle actualisations, for the context itself is *comprised* of particular particle actualisations. The problem with discussions of downward causation is that there is a proclivity to reify the notion of a "context", as if it were some kind of thing that existed apart from its constituent parts. One is thus led to say that the context includes "boundary constraints", which downwardly influence microphysical actualisations, without thereby realising that these constraints themselves have a microphysical constitution.

In order to see this more clearly, allow C to be a context, and M1 and M2 to be particular configurations of particles. Assume the claim that C causes M1 rather than M2. (This is the standard downward-causal assertion.) Now consider C as having certain boundary constraints A. But physicalism asserts that C having A is realisable as some set of particular configurations Mc. If this is so, however, then the greater probability for M1 over M2 given C having A is just the greater probability of M1 over M2 given Mc rather than Md (C not possessing A). But it should not be surprising that Mc could cause M1 rather than M2, for such a fact is explainable by analysing the forces between the microparticles themselves. We certainly do not need to talk about a causal connection "between levels" in order to explain why particles in isolation "behave otherwise" than they do in complex configurations of other particles.

A third problem with downward causation is specific to Peacocke's theological extrapolation to God as the non-physical determiner of the boundary conditions of the world-as-a-whole. While it makes sense to talk about boundary conditions as the environment for Benard cells' actualisations, or of preceding history establishing the particular DNA for the organism's development, it makes less sense to speak of the boundary conditions for the world-as-a-whole. Willem Drees expresses this point very well in his criticism of Peacocke: When we start talking about 'the world-as-a-whole', the whole notion of a context, of an environment, becomes a metaphor. In science, we always deal with a context which is itself also captured in terms of the same laws of physics (Drees 1996, 104).

The problem is that the notion of 'boundary condition' has been extended beyond its proper limits of applicability. We do not know exactly what we mean when we say that the 'boundary condition' for the universe as such can be established nonphysically. We are misled by an analogy in a way similar to how the notion of causality was routinely "extended beyond the range of possible experience" in the period prior to Hume and Kant.

As a final point I question those who would argue that downward causation can somehow occur as a flow of information without an exchange of energy (Nelson 1995, 276). It seems clear, however, that this is problematic. A recent book in the philosophy of mind illustrates the problem.

> ... consider a certain quantity of the total energy in the universe, which is sufficient for and could be used for producing either to two distinct neurophysiological events, E1 or E2. Suppose that on the basis of event-causal laws and the previous succession of physical states, event E2 is predicted to occur if the mind is fully event-causally determined, but that E1 occurs instead as a result of the mind's contracausal agent causation of a freely chosen mental act. This result contradicts the event-causal determination of the mind's activity (Jaquette, 153).

Look carefully at the argument. While the total energy for E1 or E2 is the same, some energy is surely required in transferring the information to "switch on" E1 rather than E2 (Peacocke 1993, 370). But from where can such energy flow? If the energy is physical, then the emergent entity has no independent causal power, if not, then causal closure is violated. Because of all these problems, I believe (7) should be rejected.

IV.

(8) claims that physicalism is true, higher-level properties exist, and downward causation is false. Thus, it grants to theology a way of consistently and coherently modeling divine intentionality and agency without adopting dualism. What it attempts is a divine causal account of the universe's actualisations on the *agent-action* model, an account that simultaneously affirms the inviolateness of physical event-event causality. But how is agent-action divine causality realisable in a physical *event-event* system?

Following Donald Davidson, I assume that physical events are basic metaphysical entities *causally related* to each other yet describable in indefinitely many ways (Davidson 1980, 163-180). Furthermore, I assume as he does that *causal explanation* is a relation between descriptions of these events (Davidson 180, 161-162). My suggestion is that we allow one of these descriptions to be theological. Accordingly, causal explanation in theology would concern the relationship between events *theologically described*; it would link events which would simultaneously have physical (or possibly psychological or sociological) descriptions. My view thus asserts a *theological anomalous monism* in which the recognition of the holistic nature of theological discourse would prohibit type-type reductions to the physical, but which would nonetheless allow a token-token identity between physical events and the suitably described theological events of intentionality and agency. Just as we holistically ascribe belief, desire, expectation, preference and action to other people (for we do not assign beliefs to another person one by one on the basis of isolated verbal behaviours), so too do believers assign belief, preference and action to God holistically. It is apparent that when believers survey the vicissitudes of human history, they try somehow to make sense of divine action on the assumption of a type of "principle of charity," for (paraphrasing Davidson) they try "for a theory that finds Him consistent, a believer of truths, and a lover of the good" (Davidson 1980, 222). Let us turn now to an example.

Let us assume that God willed the hardening of Pharaoh's heart, and then the heart of Pharaoh was hardened. Obviously this can be captured by the proposition 'God willed the hardening of Pharaoh's heart, which caused it to be the case that the heart of Pharaoh was hardened.' Accordingly, the event e1 described by 'God's willing' caused the event e2 described by 'the heart of Pharaoh was hardened by God.' That these events e1 and e2 also have some physical descriptions does not, however, constitute a reductionism, for we could never in principle specify *which* physical descriptions refer to the same event as 'God's willing' or 'the heart of Pharaoh was hardened by God.' We thus cannot frame a bridge principle that would identify some type of physical event with a type-occurrence of God's willing. All we can say is that there is some event e2 that is describable by 'the heart of Pharaoh was hardened by God' and some physical description P1.

Notice that we can now quite properly say that since e1 caused e2, the theological description of e1, T1 *causally* explains e2 - whether it is described by physical description P2 or theological description T2. Accordingly, this strategy allows for construction of theological causal explanations for historical and natural events, a requirement for any theory of divine providence.

I further propose the use of *supervenience* in connecting the theological to the physical (Bielfeldt 1995). According to the basic intuition of supervenience, two possible worlds indistinguishable with respect to their subvenient physical properties are also indistinguishable with respect to their supervenient theological properties. Thus, there could not be a change in the process of divine action within the universe without a corresponding change in the physical organisation of the universe. Simply put, there would exist a function mapping some subset of physical actualisations within the universe onto the set of divine intention and action properties. The effect of this supervenience function would be to establish constraints on what divine immanence descriptions are permitted given a particular physical description of the world.

Three characteristics standardly thought to constitute the supervenience relation would hold between theological properties T, and macrophysical properties P.

1) [*Physical Monism*] All concrete particulars are P.

2) [*Antireductionism*] P and T constitute autonomous property groups, for one cannot be reduced to the other through nomological biconditionals.

3) [*Asymmetricality*] T is "consequent upon" or "realisable in" P, but not vice versa.

Paraphrasing Jaegwon Kim, we can formulate the supervenience relationship as follows (Kim 1993, 65):

T supervenes on P iff necessarily, for each x and each property F in T, if x has F, then there is a property G in P such that x has G, and necessarily if any y has G, it has F.

It is important here to distinguish between weak, strong and global supervenience. The formulation above is of strong supervenience, for it connects T and P rigidly; in all possible worlds if there is P there is T. This must be distinguished from weak supervenience which would state that in any particular possible world, if there is P there is T. The advantage of strong supervenience is that it sustains projection into counterfactual situations. After all, we might want to say that 'if God were to do X, then Y would have happened.' Since weak supervenience cannot relate T and P in worlds outside the actual it cannot account for counterfactuals - I shall consider it no further.

The strong supervenience relation applied to theology would state that the statement 'God willed the heart of Pharaoh to be hardened, and the heart of Pharaoh was hardened by God' is true because event T1 (God's willing the heart of Pharaoh to be hardened) is supervenient upon P1; P1 is causally sufficient to produce physical state P2; and T2 (the heart of Pharaoh was hardened by God) is supervenient upon P2. What is rejected in the supervenience strategy is any kind of causal interactionism between T and P states. Just as the nonreductive physicalist claims that the mental and neurophysiological are *distinct* noncausally related states having a metaphysical relation of dependency, so can the theological anomonalist monist maintain that the theological and the physical realms bear a noncausal, metaphysical relationship of dependency of the former upon the latter.

The objection naturally arises that God cannot be of the nature about which I speak. After all, what sense can it make to say that the "Lord of History" or "All-Determining Reality" is "consequent upon" physical actualisations? Does not this have it backward? Does not God determine the course of history? Is it not a contradiction of terms to assert that the actions of the "Lord of History" are themselves determined by history?

In responding to this it is critical that we avoid committing a category-mistake. We can, I believe, make legitimate sense of God as the "Lord of History" or as "All-Determining Reality" if we realise that such expressions are theological descriptions which can only refer to higher-level divine properties. To claim that "All-Determining Reality" logically entails that the higher-level properties about which the phrase speaks cannot themselves be determined by lower-level actualisations, is to misunderstand the domain of the phrase's applicability. God is "all-determining" because He is *causally-related* in the appropriate way to other entities and properties denoted by terms within the theological theory. In the same way that the "I," "agency," "freedom" and "responsibility" only make sense on a folk psychological description, so does "God," "divine determination" and "divine love" only make sense on a higher-level theological description. One can say "God is the Lord of History" in the same sense one can say "I am master of my own fate;" both are obviously false in the sense that the ultimate constituents of the world would include entities like God and the I, yet both are profoundly true in that each refer to events that do have some true physical description. Just as the I's freedom and responsibility is supervenient upon the

event-event actualisations of neurophysiology, so does God being the Lord
of History supervene upon the macrophysical events of the universe.

A final issue concerns the act of supervenience ascription. It is undeniably true that not all people see God at work in the world. But if not
all epistemic agents perceive the world through believer's eyes, it seems
unwarranted to claim that the theological domain constitutes an *ontological* supervenient group similar to the domains of the special sciences.
Perhaps theological supervenience is better characterised as a matter of
the consistent ascription of theological properties by the believing community, the only group which presumably can "see" God's providential
immanence in the course of historical and natural events. James Klagge's
exploration of the notion of ascriptive supervenience might be relevant
here, for it is a supervenience wherein two indiscernible subvenient descriptions could initially receive different supervenient ascriptions "if
judged by different people employing different [standards]" (Klagge 1988,
463). According to Klagge, ascriptive supervenience concerns the consistent *constraints* placed on judgements, not the fundamental *constitution*
of the world.

The supervenience proposal I have sketched is obviously fragmentary
and in need of considerable development and defence. Unfortunately, I
cannot provide that here. In this paper I have merely outlined a new and
potentially fruitful approach for relating physical and theological properties.

The supervenience strategy is a natural theology approach applying
only to the problem of God's immanence. Granting physicalism, it asserts
that while God's intentions do not causally influence the course of history,
historical events can be causally explained by His intentions. On this view
God is fully resident in the universe because His desires and beliefs issue
in divine actions - even though such desires, beliefs and actions are merely
alternate descriptions of the fundamental event-event physical realm.

NOTES

1. This is true despite the fact that in the classical theological tradition, the property of divine simplicity precluded God from possessing human-like propositional attitudes.

2. Richard Grigg argues persuasively that the notion of God as a supernatural agent is increasingly undermined today in the first-world due to the problem of theodicy (Grigg 1995, 28-46).

3. Eberhard Jüngel expresses the point well: "Science has no need of [God], neither as a ground of its own legitimation, nor as a reference to the ground of legitimation for that which science itself cannot legitimise" (Jüngel 1983, 3).

4. This statement must be qualified. In the dominant tradition going back to Augustine God is not thought to be within time, but is Himself <u>eternal</u> because all things are present simultaneously to Him.

5. One might argue that Kant is attempting such a reduction on "divine acceptation" when he writes: "Man may then hope to become acceptable to God (and so be saved) through a practical faith in this on of God... In other words, he, and he alone, is entitled to look upon himself as an object not unworthy of divine approval who is conscious of such a moral disposition as enables him to have a well-grounded confidence in himself, and to *believe* that, under like temptations and afflictions... he would be loyal unswervingly to the archetype of humanity..." (Kant 1934, 55).

6. A "type-type" reduction claims that for any property P in domain A (the reduced domain) there is some biconditional between P and some property S in domain B (the reducing domain). A "token-token" reduction asserts that for any x in A having property P, there is a y in B having S, and y=x. The second assumes an identity of "tokens" between domains without asserting their type entity. For example, Susan's particular headache may be identical with C-fibre stimulation C235aj without there being a law of nature saying that for all x, if x is the type of headache Susan had, then x has C-fibre stimulation C235aj. After all, one can imagine a Martian having a headache like Susan's but not having C-fibres at all.

7. The term "downward causation" seems to have been used first by D.T. Campbell in 1974 in describing biological systems (Campbell 1974).

8. Global supervenience states that once the distribution of P-properties across an entire world is fixed, the distribution of T-properties across that world is also determined. Unfortunately, global supervenience also permits local pockets in which strong or weak supervenience fail, and it allows for scenarios where a minuscule change in P-properties is consistent with an extensive change in T-properties. While these problems are not perhaps insurmountable, I will consider global supervenience further in this paper.

REFERENCES

Bielfeldt, Dennis. 1995: "God, Physicalism, and Supervenience", *Center for Theology and Natural Science Bulletin*, 15:3 (Summer 1995): 1-12.

Campbell, D. T. 1974: "'Downward Causation' in Hierarchically Organised Biological Systems." In F.J. Ayala & T. Dobzhansy, eds, *Studies in the Philosophy of Biology: Reduction and Related Problems*, Berkeley.

Carnap, Rudolf. 1959: "Psychology in Physical Language" (1932), *Logical Positivism*, A.J. Ayer, ed., New York, 165-198.

Churchland, Paul. 1984: *Matter and Consciousness*, Cambridge, MA.

Davidson, Donald. 1980: *Essays on Actions and Events*, Oxford.

Dennet, Daniel. 1978: *Brainstorms*, Montgomery, VT.

Drees, Willem. 1996: *Religion, Science, and Naturalism*, Cambridge.

Fodor, Jerry. 1987: *Psychosomatics*, Cambridge, MA.

Grigg, Richard. 1995: *When God Becomes Goddess*, New York.

Jacquette, Dale. 1994: *Philosophy of Mind*, Englewood Cliffs, NJ.

Kant, Immanuel. 1934: *Religion within the Limits of Reason Alone*, trans. by Theodore Greene and Hoyt Hudson, New York.

Kim, Jaegwon. 1993: *Supervenience and Mind*, Cambridge, MA.

Klagge, James. 1988: "Supervenience: Ontology and Ascriptive." *Australasian Journal of Philosophy*, 66, 461-469.

McLaughlin, Brian. 1992: "The Rise and Fall of British Empiricism," *Emergence or Reduction*, Beckermann, A., Flohr, H., and Kim, J., eds., Berlin.

Peacocke, Arthur. 1993. *Theology for a Scientific Age*, Minneapolis, MN.

Pettit, Phillip. 1993. "A Definition of Physicalism," *Analysis*, 53:4 (October 1993).

Putnam, Hilary. 1975: *Mind, Language, and Reality*. Cambridge, MA.

Ryle, Gilbert. 1949: *The Concept of Mind*, New York.

Sperry, Roger. 1984: "Roger Sperry" (1984), *The Omni Interviews*, Weintraub, P., ed., New York.

Taliaferro, Charles. 1994: *Consciousness and the Mind of God*, Cambridge.

Teller, Paul. 1983: "A Poor Man's Guide to Supervenience and Determination." *Southern Journal of Philosophy*, 22, 137-167.

Tipler, Frank. 1994: *The Physics of Immortality*, New York.

THE NEUROANTHROPOLOGICAL FABRIC
OF SPIRIT

JOHN A. TESKE
(*Elizabethtown, USA*)

It is the present contention that our spirituality is a product of the very processes of human evolution which make the social construction of human culture, human meaning and individual psychology possible, and even necessary. Evolutionarily adaptive characteristics of human neuropsychology require that we live in a social world, making the construction of personhood near-inevitable, and making a spiritual life possible. Our species is likely to have been evolutionarily advantaged by the extended childhoods and complex social interdependencies that the co-evolution of brain and language required (Deacon 1992). This included the capacity to function in an "as if" manner that intentional representations of the world make possible, and which allow us to operate within socially constituted understandings of the world, our fellows and ourselves. Such understandings are also grounded in prelinguistic and sub-doxastic capacities to co-ordinate our behaviour and our emotional lives with each other. The human nervous system is likely to have evolved in ways which require social interdependency, not only for the survival of groups but for the canalisation of individual nervous systems and the genesis of individual psychologies. We human persons, over and above but inclusive of our neural functioning, are constituted by our placement within larger social wholes, no less real for being symbolically generated, playing a potential emergent role as higher-order units in evolutionary processes. Indeed, "group selection" (Wilson & Sober 1994) may be the level at which archaic moral orders evolved to overcome the natural problems produced by genetic competition amongst members of a group (D. Campbell 1991). As such, neuro-psychological mechanisms are involved in both constructing and reaching beyond our individuality, processes of social construction which presuppose membership in a more extended hierarchy of social units, including relationships, families and wider communities.

When we understand that the self, our subjectivity, our internal life, is a socially constructed logical space, we have a handle on the constitution of individual spiritual lives. Jaynes (1976) and others (cf. Hermans, Kempen & van Loon 1992) argue that our very consciousness of self is constituted and organised metaphorically *as* a space. Metaphor is a central concept, given our ability to direct our lives toward conceptual objects, to live, as it were, metaphorically, "as if," in the virtual reality of symbolic systems. But this is also what allows us to build a meaningful communal life, and step beyond our own egos. Nevertheless, evolutionarily and historically contingent though they may be, the forms that constitute our selves are interiorized in a particular way, nested within the evolutionary biology of socially interdependent nervous systems, deeply interwoven with the neuroanthropological fabric. Spiritual life does not escape the sociohistorical and evolutionarily embodied contingencies by which it is constituted. The central focus of the present paper is to draw out some of the fibres of the neuroanthropological fabric from which our psychology, and our spiritual experience, is woven. The passions of faith, and "spiritual" questions about boundaries between self and other, alienation, will, surrender, communion and even the experience of grace may ultimately be understood more fully as embodied phenomena by attention to these fabrics.

The present work is part of a larger attempt to map out the constitution, and the embodiment of our spirituality, in terms of what we know about human minds and brains from contemporary cognitive and neurosciences. This is a project that is necessary for any kind of theological or religious system that is coherent with science, the only chance for its viability in a world dominated by a scientific episteme. Two years ago, in this forum (Teske 1996a), I argued that both our self-transcendence and the self-limitations that require it are made possible by our neuropsychology. I also argued that our individual integrity depended upon a boundary between internal and external life which was as much a product of historical social life as of evolutionary biology. Our very internality, at its deepest roots, may not be the individuated consciousness of an ego separate from others, but constituted by the sociohistorical nexus of our individual development. Nevertheless, the social nexus of our development is itself embedded within the biological unfolding our species. It is to the evolutionary and developmental background of our psychological and spiritual emergence, as understood through the glass of contemporary sciences of mind, that I turn here.

A further set of arguments has made it all the more important to understand the social interdependencies which, evolutionarily and developmentally, root the ontogenesis of human mental and spiritual life (Teske, 1996b). While neuropsychology is necessary for spirituality, the very characteristics which make spirituality possible also provide limits that *individuals* cannot alone transcend. Reflection, consciousness and self-knowledge require a neuro-psychology sufficient for symbolically representing a world and a self within it. But representations are always selective, abstract, constructed and partitioned, and therefore limited by bias and incompleteness, separation from the world, fabrication and self-deception, and the possibility of fragmentation and decay. The evidence from research on hemispheric specialisation, brain dysfunction and normal memory suggests that the unity and integrity of self and mind is a contingent achievement. Our sense of unity and integrity may be subdoxastic and subcortical, perhaps rooted in the limbic substrate of our emotional lives. Or it may depend upon the integrity of relation, the suggestion that the self may be incomplete, and insufficient for the work of integration, without a place in some larger system or community. The latter suggestion points to the interesting possibility that the healing of individual separation and fragmentation may be bound for failure without attention to the separation, fragmentation and destruction of the communities that constitute and maintain our individuality. Nevertheless, both emotional and relational life point to a likely reason why neuroscience cannot provide a complete account of human nature or human spirituality (Jones 1992). This is because many of the important characteristics of both mind and spirit are not only emergent properties of an individual's central nervous system (Sperry 1991), but may be *social* emergents, i.e. properties of a number of individuals (and a number of individual nervous systems) in interaction. It is the present contention that not only is this so, but that the evolutionary and developmental evidence will show us why and how our social interdependencies, our membership in larger human groups, are both necessary for and constitutive of much of what we believe to be characteristic of the mental and spiritual life of human beings. We will begin by addressing overarching issues of neuroplasticity and cognitive evolution, and then will sample more specific developmental changes, both evolutionary and ontogenetic, which may support the social constitution of mind and spirit.

One of the central principles necessary for understanding human development is that of our extensive neurobehavioural plasticity. The nature/nurture controversy has long given way to interactionist views. The last few decades have uncovered a great deal about how biological processes interact with the external world during growth and development, showing measurable effects on the anatomy, physiology and chemistry of the nervous system (Blonder 1991). While genetics do set some constraints, there is plasticity at every level of development (Nowakowski 1987). Cells and their interconnections proliferate, migrate, differentiate and are pruned directly by experience with the external world, affecting synaptic connections, dendritic growth, neurotransmitter synthesis and even vascularisation. We are left with a brain that is constantly being shaped, in structure and function, by its history of developmental interactions with the outside environment. David Hubel and Thorstein Wiesel, awarded the Nobel Prize in 1981, found that depriving cats or monkeys of certain visual stimuli (e.g. vertical lines) resulted in the loss of cells in the cortex for detecting them. Rats reared in enriched environments have larger neurons, greater dendritic spread, and greater enzyme production (Rosenzweig, Bennett and Diamond 1972). Greenough (1986, Greenough, Black and Wallace 1987) has provided evidence for remarkable plasticity even in the cerebellum for synaptic growth with skill development. He also provides evidence for both "experience-expectant" *over-productions* of synaptic connections for species-ubiquitous environmental information (experience itself selecting which connections remain), and for "experience-dependent" *novel* synaptic connections formed in response to idiosyncratic individual experience. There is also a growing body of evidence for neurobehavioural plasticity in human beings that extends across the lifespan: the dependence of left-hemisphere, language-area maturation on appropriate stimulation pre-puberty; the quantitative increases in left-hemisphere dominance for language produced by literacy; the *elimination* during adolescence and young adulthood of excess synapses in the principal sulcus, which appears to be necessary for fully mature delayed-response functioning; and the extensive dendritic growth in the learning and memory-crucial parahippocampal gyrus among normal elderly people (cf. Blonder 1991, Goldman-Rakic 1987).

Given the neurobehavioural plasticity of even the lowliest of mammalian species, it is clear that the cognitive abilities required for spirituality are not just genetically constrained, but epigenetically constructed and dependent on extensive environmental experience for their emergence. It is also clear that the developmental environment of human beings and their hominid ancestors is a socially mediated environment, an environment increasingly influenced by human activity, to the point of becoming a virtual reality of human artifacts. While this suggests a heavy influence of human culture and learned behaviour on the ontogenesis of human mental and spiritual life, we must be cautioned that, in the face of evidence for a number of human cultural and linguistic universals (cf. Brown 1991), cultural differences may themselves be relatively superficial. This suggests that, despite the importance of cultural and social supports in the ontogenesis of individual psychology, we had best acknowledge that it has deeper evolutionary roots. Nevertheless, Lewontin (1990) warns us about the limitations of the evidence for the biological evolution of human cognition, and Gould (1992) even suggests that many of our emergent cognitive skills (including, for example, literacy) may be maintained at levels of evolution higher than genes or organisms (e.g. populations, species), and therefore provide us no more than bookkeeping data at biological levels.

It should thus come as no surprise that there may be less than a one percent difference between the DNA of chimps and humans, suggesting that any determination of cognitive abilities not shared between us are likely to be epigenetic or even developmental (King and Wilson 1975). Evolutionary changes in cognitive abilities, despite their cultural amplification, may not involve radical changes at the neural level. "If psychological evolution, like morphological evolution, can be meaningfully thought of as innovations in ontogeny, then comparative psychologists should have no trouble accepting as a possibility that a major evolutionary change occurred quite recently in primate history" (Povinelli 1993, 506). Even human language capacities are likely to be polygenetic, shared with other developmental domains, tied to epigenetic and probabilistic maturational events and, given the multifunctional and individual variability of human brains, not strictly universal in functional organisation (Mueller 1996). Small differences in DNA must play a role in a number of differences between humans and other primates, including cortical investment in speech-related musculature, the double voice-box in the larynx, upright stance and bipedalism, female pelvic changes, the underdevelopment of human babies (requiring greater parental and social investment) and, perhaps most importantly for our purposes here, our brain size, particularly the disproportionate amounts of prefrontal cortex, hippocampus and cerebellum (responsible for complex motor sequencing, long-term memory and complex motor co-ordination respectively). Epigenetic plasticity alone could grant a huge role for culture as a storage device for processes replicative of human cognitive function.

The other general principle needed for understanding the ontogenesis of human cognition is the hypertrophy of prefrontal cortex (Deacon 1992). This is the major neurological change behind our being, relative even to other primates, linguistic or combinatorial savants, creatures that can live in symbolic virtual worlds, can construct meaningful narratives, can imagine their own origins and ends, and can conceive of God. Prefrontal hypertrophy, in combination with an overall neurobehavioural plasticity (and the concomitant roles of epigenesis and development in generating human cognition) also guarantees the colonisation of human neuropsychology by the prefrontal functions of attentional control, planning and complex motor sequencing, and so constitutes the particular character of higher cognitive functioning.

Terrence Deacon (1992) makes this case clearly. He accounts for the absence of even simple language-like symbolic systems in other primates by drawing our attention to the most robust and divergent neuroanatomical feature of human brains relative to other primate species. This is the enlargement of prefrontal cortex and the expansion of projection fields which contribute to the attentional-mnemonic supports critical to symbolic and associative learning. This prefrontal hypertrophy guarantees a predisposition to employ symbolic learning, and facilitates the computational learning behind the evolution of human cognition, consciousness and culture. This is the brain structure supporting the special demands of language which are the most modified by environment-related developmental changes, a system so overbuilt and failsafe that even retarded and brain-damaged human beings are still often capable of symbolisation. The primary evidence has to do with the fact that while other brain structures in human beings have grown in an unchanged ratio to body size and other brain structures, the ratio of neocortex to other structures is larger. This difference is produced by the action of homeobox genes producing disproportionate embryogenic growth in the dorsal half of the brain (Deacon 1992). The information for building these structures is not itself in the genes but in circuits and information from the environment, sculpted by the environment in a kind of neural Darwinism in which circuits are grown in a process of competition for space. The neocortical hypertrophy produces a kind of bias in the competition for space in which the structures of the brain most controlled by input from the outside world remain the same relative size but smaller than the rest of the neocortex. The prefrontal areas therefore inherit the largest share in competition for space, and increasingly come to dominate connections to other parts of the brain, especially those contiguous areas controlling vocalisation. These areas are distinct from the subcortically mediated systems controlling laughing, crying, and other vocalisation more resembling primate call systems. Novel functions are thereby produced by the disproportionate frontal impact. The evidence from electrical stimulation, cerebral blood flow and brain damage suggests that it is frontal cortex function that is behind our abilities to shift categorisation criteria, generate word lists, do syntactic analysis and generate the novel patterns that enable insight learning.

Deacon (1992) argues further that emergent frontal cortex functions are what give us entree to a symbolic "virtual reality". They allow us to make the step from indexical mappings of sign-event co-occurrences to symbolic re-presentations, in which similar things are connected not just by indexes but by other similarities. The result is that no representations are simple, and symbolic reference is always systemic. Once this systematicity is present, new symbolic associations can always be learned by restructuring, by retrospectively reorganising previous connections in respect to one another. This gives us a capacity for generating an abstract virtual world only indirectly connected to the concrete present, for representing possible and impossible futures, and for having access to an illimitable symbolic world. Moreover, once this capacity emerges, with its ontogenetic social and cultural supports, it becomes necessary for human reproductive success, as an individual human being lacking this capacity becomes locked out of the human social world. We become over-dependent on the symbolic transfer of learning, and enter a way of life driven by a compulsion to symbolise. We are also granted the capacity for symbolic empathy, via cortico-limbic ties allowing us to match arousal states to representations, to make believe, and to imagine the experience of fellow beings, from the sublime to previously unimaginable horrors. With the symbolic capacities made possible by prefrontal hypertrophy, human sociability is no longer based solely on genetic contributions, nor on animal communication and meaning, but on the symbolic transfer of sociohistorical learning, and the colonisation of human psychology by higher cognitive function. We can now examine more specific neurological structures and functions in terms of the evolution and ontogenesis of the human capacity (even the necessity) to live in a socially constructed, symbolic virtual reality.

Fairly primitive brain structures mediate arousal, which influences attentional selection, sometimes almost totally, but in ways mediated both by circumstances and past experience. Arousal is likely to be a prerequisite for attention, involving stimulation from the reticular formation, itself a distributed network which also includes cortical connections. Attention may also be controlled by rhythmic aspects of arousal, involving heart rate and muscular tension changes. However, not only is it clear that we need brain stem (and limbic) interactions to understand the cognition which is built upon them, but, given the extensive epigenetic and ontogenetic shaping of this relationship, we must also understand its embedding within a complex system of developmentally supportive social interchanges. The role of symbiotic caregiver-child interactions in the scaffolding of the child's ability to self-moderate arousal levels begins a process of social internalisation almost at birth, and roots an extensive system of object-relations (e.g. Mahler, Kohut). The social scaffolding of attention is also a prerequisite of linguistic communication (Sherwood and Bruner 1975).

The social scaffolding which structures the regulation of arousal and attentional mechanisms, and which contextualises our experiences of our bodies and their boundaries, emerges in and is mediated by the basic mammalian attachments that form the foundation of our emotional lives. Even in rats, the period of dependency required by the rearing of infants makes early social attachment adaptive and survival-relevant. The mother's role as regulator of physiological and behavioural systems in the infant is most evident in the synchrony and reciprocity of nursing, and responses of infants to separation may be a kind of withdrawal or release phenomenon (Hofer 1987). Given a much lengthier period of dependency in human child-rearing, attachment patterns and developmental experience within familial contexts are likely to be even more deeply determinative of the social and emotional patterning of adult lives. Tomkins (1979) and others provide accounts of how recognisably human affect complexes and fuller emotional scenarios are built out of biologically primary motivators over decades of biographical development. Our evolutionarily structured neuropsychology may require our attunement to, and functioning within, a hierarchically structured, socially interdependent world which requires, in turn, the development of fairly sophisticated cognitive and emotional elaborations of primary motivators. While such motivators may be constrained by the evolutionary contingencies embodied in our genetics, they are hardly determinative, but provide an envelope for understanding the role that cultural and biographical variations might play in the construction of different emotional tones, and different kinds of self/not-self and self/other emotional boundaries. James Ashbrook (1994) has characterised the early experience of separation from a loved object, and the emotional need to fill this separation with transitional objects and symbols (cf. Stern 1985, Winnicott 1965), as central to a spiritual "cry for the other," and as motivating the meaning-making which roots consciousness, creativity and faith.

Human emotional life, particularly as it is mediated by reciprocal connections between the limbic system and the neocortex, has been viewed as the locus of religious sentiment by a number of thinkers. MacLean (1988), as well as Ashbrook (1994), focus on early family dynamics, including maternal nursing, separation cries and sibling play. Robin Fox (1986) also implicates early learning, including the separation and stranger anxieties which appear between 6-15 months, concomitant with the myelinization of limbic circuit fibres. Nevertheless, Fox also offers a more detailed analysis of limbic-cortical connections, suggesting that it is a wired-in mechanism for the disruption of social categories that is behind both the alerting responses to minor cognitive mismatches, and the passionate upsets of horror, disgust and fear in response to more serious violations of social expectations. Areas of the brain that are involved in emotion are also involved in memory; it is the emotional charge of an event that most directly determines how well it is remembered. Fox reminds us that there are connections through the hippocampus which are vital to encoding new memories. The hippocampus itself, lying just beneath the frontal cortex, receives no direct sensory information, but only abstracted and cortically processed information passed via the cingulate gyrus to the hippocampus, and eventually back to the cortex. Selecting emotionally significant memories for long-term retention is necessary to avoid a kind of combinatorial explosion of memory in higher mammals. By a limbic-frontal linking of visual images and complex associations to emotionally significant information, especially that tied to initiation, trauma, drama, ritual and fear (precisely those experiences most strongly tied to learning and relearning of central social categories), these memories are the ones most likely to be consolidated over a period of years, as the plethora of more shallow memories are washed away in the accumulation of experience.

Este Armstrong (1991) provides allometric evidence of some limbic differences between human and primate brains, and supports the importance of attentional and memorial endowment of symbols with emotional significance and meaning. The amygdala, mediating negation and anxious aggression, septal areas, mediating positive feeling and sexual response, and the hippocampus, with its role in consolidating short-term, explicit memory (but not skill development) into long-term storage, are all larger than they are in primate brains, but are not scaled differently, suggesting that these structures do not serve radically new functions. Limbic structures that do scale differently include relatively smaller olfactory structures, and a relatively larger anterior thalamus. This is part of the Papez circuit, which brings emotional information into the cortex for further elaboration and conscious access.

Papez circuit structures like the hippocampus and cingulate gyrus (which can focus attention either on parietal information about extra-personal space, or on prefrontal information related to the "internal space" of subjectivity) are well placed for activation by association cortex, which plays the role of input to the limbic system, otherwise largely divorced from direct sensory input. As part of the Papez circuit, anterior thalamic structures may be critical for the brain's ability to remember cultural rules and events, and play a role in the emotional prioritising, and approach/avoidance valencing of symbolic representations of events.

Alternatively, cortical feedback, particularly inhibitory influences, are likely to be important for social co-operation, as human beings can approach and engage in joint social activities without direct expression of hostility or sexuality. Nevertheless, while there do appear to be some important, if subtle changes in limbic structures, and in the relationship between cortex and limbic system, much appears to be driven, in evolutionary if not motivational terms, by more radical changes in the cortex. Moreover, extensive cortical neuroplasticity makes possible, and may even require, cultural and institutional supports in order to produce cognitive development.

Some of the important prerequisites to human-level cognitive and cultural capacities, particularly to having subjective interior lives and to attributing the same to our fellows, are already present in our nearest primate relatives. Cheney and Seyfarth have provided evidence in chimpanzees for short-term planning, transitive and analogical reasoning, deliberate deception (with Smuts 1986), and even the attribution of mental states (1990). Gordon Gallup (1970) provided an early demonstration of the ability of chimps to recognise themselves in a mirror, an ability which emerges in human children between 18-24 months, and he has more recently reviewed evidence for the existence of this ability in 20 other species of apes, but in no monkeys. Premack and Woodruff (1978) have argued that self-recognition is an empirical marker for having a "theory of mind," and Gallup (1982) has presented a model in which self-recognition is taken to index both a capacity to introspect on mental experiences and the means to infer such experiences in other organisms. Povinelli (1993) extends Gallup's work, arguing that children lacking self-recognition fail to attribute mental states, and are incapable of introspection-based social strategies. He also points out that the self-conscious emotions emerge at about the same time as self-recognition. It is clear that self-recognition is a necessary, if not sufficient index for a number of higher cognitive abilities, and Povinelli provides experimental demonstrations of the attribution of mental states and of false beliefs in both chimps and older children which are lacking in monkeys and younger children. It is clear that socially-relevant cognitive abilities like reflective consciousness, attributions of intent, perspective-taking, role reversal, attention to knowledge over behaviour and the attributions of false belief necessary both for deception and its detection require a number of years for their development in human children, but may be available to many adult apes. Nevertheless, it is to the emergence of specifically human cognitive capacities, and their needs for extensive linguistic and cultural support, that we now turn.

Merlin Donald (1991, 1993) argues that any comprehensive theory of human cognitive evolution must bridge the huge gap between the animal kingdom and the uniquely human invention of symbols. He bridges this gap by suggesting the evolutionary emergence of an ability he calls "autocuing," the self-initiated recall of specific items of memory independent of the immediate environment. This ability would provide our hominid ancestors with their first representational ability to "think about" things unrelated to the immediately present environment, and with new voluntary retrieval paths to their already present knowledge base. Donald's suggestion is not only consistent with a prefrontal hypertrophy allowing different access routes to limbically mediated memory, but also is a separate and preliminary step to the evolution of language. There are both anatomic and cultural signs of a major evolutionary landmark with the emergence of homo erectus (1.5-0.3 million years ago), the cultural achievements in particular (e.g. sophisticated stone tools, long-distance hunting, seasonal adaptations) requiring memory improvements. Nevertheless, these changes are not likely to have been accompanied by language, the anatomic and cultural signs for which do not appear for another million years.

Donald (1993) suggests that prelinguistic autocuing allows non-verbal representational skills, the existence of which is also consistent with the autonomy of non-verbal forms of human intelligence and which, accompanied by cortically mediated improvements in motor control, would allow the development of mimetic skills advanced enough to support tool-making, skill refinement and a flexible social organisation superior to that of apes. Mimetic skills, based on a memory system that, in an extended kinematic imagination, enables the voluntary and systematic rehearsal and refinement of movements (seen frequently even in human children, but rarely in apes), allow for an implementable self-image, have supramodal characteristics like rhythm (also absent in apes), and make purposive, alterable sequencing possible. Like the sophisticated mimetic and expressive abilities of illiterate deaf-mutes, the culture of homo erectus may have been the complex mimetic one in which we can still see our symbolic and linguistic culture to be embedded. This includes crafts, games, social rituals, expressive scenarios and even many athletic skills, non-verbal skills unaffected by even profound aphasias.

According to Donald (1991, 1993), it is with emergence of the modern vocal tract and its motor control that we see, with the emergence of archaic homo sapiens between 500-100 thousand years ago, evidence for real language. Donald suggests that this second evolutionary landmark corresponds to the evolution of "lexical invention," the capacity to invent and retrieve thousands of words and the rules for their combination (perhaps in a second phase of "grammatical invention"), allowing the construction of narrative commentaries. Portable, efficient, true symbols can not only disambiguate mimetic messages (or contrast with them to produce more complex, layered meanings) but provide a second form of retrievable knowledge, and a second-order modeling. The shift from re-enacting to storytelling also takes the teller outside the story, and allows freer examination, reassembling and sharing of components. This makes possible the incredible speed of language differentiation, the production of collective, standardised narratives in mythology and religion, and provides a narrative frame for the governance of pre-existing mimetic institutions. Indeed, while we may form and maintain our social constitution largely by routinisation, by daily habits, and by group rituals, its meaning may depend upon non-automatised, second-order, symbolic monitoring and commentary.

Goodenough (1993) contends that the elaboration of grammatical arguments not only facilitates the planning and co-ordinating of social interaction within domestic groups (especially familial groups with the increasingly long periods of child-dependency needed for learning the burgeoning culture) and allows for the cumulation of shared experience, but makes it possible to inform others about nonpresent events of which they were not a part. Grammatical markers for subject and object, indications of time, place, reality/unreality, beneficiary and relationship provide the materials for the elaboration of symbolic systems of belief, and pave the way for the post-narrative, post-communicative emergence of private speech, tied to reflective language, divorced from activity and indispensable for individual belief.

It is Donald's (1991, 1993) third stage of cognitive development, that of the externalisation of memory, which makes all the more clear the necessity of social interdependency for human cognitive evolution. Mimesis and language, although themselves co-evolved with culture, still depend on the internal memory capacity of individuals, however expanded it may be by virtue of its colonisation by prefrontal hypertrophy. Biological memory is impermanent, its medium is fixed, and its format is constrained. Indeed, the evolution of internal memory capacities may itself have depended on ways of editing and pruning them. However, the emergence of literacy, and other skills involving symbioses with symbolic external storage, allows memory to be externalised in ways that are enduring, refinable, and even capable of reformatting. External storage also, via the use of a spatialised external information space, allows us to harness vision for reflective thought, to change the part of the brain used for thinking, to interrelate information and images in novel ways, and to develop new cognitive strategies which are socially organised, and can be institutionalised to survive the replacement of member individuals.

External storage thus makes possible an even more thorough invasion and use of the brain by cultural programming, especially institutionalised education, the development and elaboration of new devices (from wax tablets to manipulable computer imaging systems), and new visual symbolic codes. This culminates in the deliberate construction of artifacts which produce particular internal mind-states in recipients, states which, like the world of a novel, may be artefact-dependent for their maintenance. This may change the role of biological memory to be more symbiotic with cultural artifacts, increase demands on certain areas of the brain which, given its neuroplasticity, can expand their territory at the expense of other functions, producing, for example, the loss of rote verbal skills and visual imagination that may come with literacy. Finally, we also face a danger to individual integrity. "Free access to external memory tends to pull apart the unity of mind, fragmenting experience, undermining the simpler mythic thought structures humans have grown rather attached to" (Donald 1993, 164). Nevertheless, this is not the place to rehearse an analysis of the effects of post-modernism on self-identity (but see Cushman 1990, Gergen 1991 and Giddens 1991).

The central point here is that human brains are not evolved to develop in isolation. They are complexly, flexibly and only loosely constrained by genetics to internalise a whole range of sociocultural practices. Our brains internalise social practice in ways that, by virtue of our neuroplasticity and prefrontal hypertrophy, profoundly influence our psychological functioning, down to our neurophysiology. Walter Freeman (1995) makes the point that our brains have evolved primarily as organs of social co-operation and understanding, involving the construction of symbolic representation and the development of mechanisms to reach social agreement. Barresi and Moore (1995) have mapped the complexities of how increasingly sophisticated social organisms represent multiple levels of intent, depending on the use of imagination and the extent to which different participants intentions are integrated. Freeman suggests the possibility that our ancestors learned to adapt neurohormonal mechanisms for the reproduction and care of young to reshaping otherwise relatively slow accretions of synaptic change with experience. He suggests that social bonding, the emergence of shared meaning, and the co-ordination of activity facilitates the unlearning of individual value systems via socially co-operative action, and encourages us to focus not on individual but societal aspects of neurodynamics and neurochemistry. Evolutionary psychologists like Robert Wright (1994) have begun some of this work; a case in point is Wright's (1995) sophisticated analysis of how the relationship between social oppression, low self-esteem, and the low levels of impulse control associated with decreased serotonin might provide a deeper understanding of urban violence.

The origination of putatively individual cognitive activity in social context is amply documented in the psychological literature (Rogoff and Chavajay 1995), and such activities may not only have social origins, but actually be socially distributed, including even memory and problem solving. Early social embedding is a sine qua non. of the development of higher functions like language and meaning (Vygotsky 1978, Wertsch 1979). Human intellect cannot be separated from the technologies that extend it; specific linguistic practices result in specific cognitive skills; learning is situated in communities of practice; cognition is socialised by learning "cognitive values" about what and what not to think about; habitual relations can be institutionalised in ways that result in their being viewed as externally imposed; and later generations can lose awareness of intentional structures buried in history. As Benzon and Hays (1990) have made clear, cultural evolution itself can be seen to have produced whole new patterns of thought, as rationalisation first appeared in Ancient Greece, theorising in Renaissance Italy, and model-building in 20th century Europe.

Space limitations forbid a more detailed explication of how our subjective internality, our emotional experience, and our very existence as well-bounded, autonomous and responsible selves are socially constructed. Further work will also be needed to extend such an account to the sociohistorical constitution of individual souls and spirituality, which have a reality as obdurate and of the same kind as do selves. It has been our present purpose to lay the foundation for such an explication in the neuroanthropological fabrics of our evolutionary and ontogenetic development. We have seen that our extensive neuroplasticity, and our prefrontal hypertrophy, make extensive experiential shaping of our nervous systems necessary and that, given our extended social dependency well into maturity, that shaping is likely to be socially mediated. We have seen that during the course of mind/culture co-evolution, this shaping has also come to include, by virtue of the cortical colonisation of many neurological functions, the entrainment of attention and arousal to social contingencies; the elaboration of emotional scenarios from social interdependency, particularly the regulation provided by early familial attachment; and the whole sequence of mimetic, linguistic and ultimately institutional and artefact-dependent cultural symbioses enabling the emergence of our sophisticated and emotionally engaging cognitive abilities. Finally it is the culture, the community, the family and other human relationships which differentiate and constitute our individual psychology, out of which it is differentiated, and provide the emergent capacities for transcending its limitations.

REFERENCES

Armstrong, Este. 1991: "The Limbic System and Culture: An Allometric Analysis of the Neocortex and Limbic Nuclei." *Human Nature* 2(2): 117-36.

Ashbrook, James B. 1994: "The Cry for the Other: The Biocultural Womb of Human Development." *Zygon: Journal of Religion and Science 29* (September): 297-314.

Barresi, John, and Chris Moore. 1996: "Intentional Relations and Social Understanding." *Behavioural and Brain Sciences* (Forthcoming).

Benzon, William L., and David G. Hays. 1990: "The Evolution of Cognition." *Journal of Social and Biological Structures* 13: 297-320.

Blonder, Lee X. 1991: "Human Neuropsychology and the Concept of Culture." *Human Nature* 2(2): 83-116.

Brown, Donald. 1991: *Human Universals*. New York: McGraw-Hill.

Campbell, Donald T. 1991: "A Naturalistic theory of Archaic Moral Orders." *Zygon: Journal of Religion and Science* 26 (March): 91-114.

Cheney, Dorothy, and Robert Seyfarth. 1990: "Attending to Behaviour versus Attending to Knowledge: Examining Monkeys' Attributions of Mental States." *Animal Behaviour* 40: 742-53.

Cheney, Dorothy, Robert Seyfarth and Barbara Smuts. 1986: "Social Relationships and Social Cognition in Nonhuman Primates." *Science* 234: 1361-66.

Cushman, Philip. 1990: "Why the Self Is Empty: Toward a Historically Situated Psychology." *American Psychologist* 45: 599-611.

Deacon, Terrence W. 1992: "Brain-Language Co-evolution." In *The Evolution of Human Language*, eds. J. A. Hawkins and M. Gell-Mann, 49-83. Reading, MA: Addison-Wesley.

Donald, Merlin. 1991: *Origins of the Modern Mind*. Cambridge, MA: Harvard University Press.

Donald, Merlin. 1993: "Human Cognitive Evolution: What We Were, What We Are Becoming." *Social Research 60 (Spring)*: 143-70.

Fox, Robin. 1986: "The Passionate Mind: Brains, Dreams, Memory, and Social Categories." *Zygon: Journal of Religion and Science* 21 (March): 31-47.

Freeman, Walter J. 1995: *Societies of Brains: A Neuroscience of Love and Hate*. Hillsdale, NJ: Erlbaum.

Gallup, Gordon G., Jr. 1970: "Chimpanzees: Self-recognition." *Science* 167: 86-87:

Gallup, Gordon G., Jr: 1982: "Self-awareness and the Emergence of Mind in Primates:" *American Journal of Primatology* 2: 237-48:

Gallup, Gordon G., Jr: 1991: "Toward a Comparative Psychology of Self-awareness: Species Limitations and Cognitive Consequences." In *The Self: An Interdisciplinary Approach*, eds. G. R. Goethals and J. Strauss, 121-35. New York: Springer-Verlag.

Gergen, Kenneth J. 1991: *The Saturated Self: Dilemmas of Identity in Contemporary Life*. New York: Basic Books.

Giddens, Anthony. 1991: *Modernity and Self-Identity: Self and Society in the Late Modern Age*. Stanford, CA: Stanford University Press.

Goldman-Rakic, Patricia S. 1987: "Development of Cortical circuitry and Cognitive Function." *Child Development* 58: 601-22.

Goodenough, Ward H. 1993: "Evolution of the Human Capacity or Beliefs." *Zygon: Journal of Religion and Science* 28 (March): 5-27.

Gould, Stephen J. 1992: "The Confusion Over Evolution." *New York Review of Books* (19 November): 47-54.

Greenough, William T. 1986: "What's Special About Development? Thoughts on the Basis of Experience-Sensitive Synaptic Plasticity." In *Developmental Neuropsychology*, eds. W. Greenough and J. M. Jurastin, 387-408. New York: Academic Press.

Greenough, William T., James E. Black and Christopher S. Wallace. 1987: "Experience and Brain Development." *Child Development* 58: 539-59.

Hermans, Hubert J. M., Harry J. G. Kempen and Rens J. P. van Loon. 1992: "The Dialogical Self: Beyond Individualism and Rationalism." *American Psychologist* 47: 23-33.

Hofer, Myron A. 1987: "Early Social Relationships: A Psychobiologist's View." *Child Development* 58: 633-47.

Jaynes, Julian. 1976: *The Origins of Consciousness in the Breakdown of the Bicameral Mind*. Boston: Houghton Mifflin.

Jones, James W. 1992: "Can Neuroscience Provide a Complete Account of Human Nature? A Reply to Roger Sperry." *Zygon: Journal of Religion and Science* 27 (June): 187-202.

King, M.C., and A. C. Wilson. 1975: "Evolution at Two Levels in Humans and Chimpanzees." *Science* 188: 107-16.

Lewontin, R. C. 1990: "The Evolution of Cognition." In *Thinking: An Invitation to Cognitive Science* (Vol. 3), Daniel N. Osherson and Edward E. Smith, eds., 229-246. Cambridge, MA: Massachusetts Institute of Technology Press.

Mueller, Ralph-Axel. 1996: "Innateness, Autonomy, Universality? Neurobiological Approaches to Language." *Behavioural and Brain Sciences* (forthcoming).

Nowakowski, R. S. 1987: "Basic Concepts of CNS Development." *Child Development* 58: 568-95.

Povinelli, Daniel J. 1993: "Reconstructing the Evolution of Mind." *American Psychologist* 48: 493-509.

Premack, D., and G. Woodruff. 1978: "Does the Chimpanzee Have a Theory of Mind?" *Behavioural and Brain Sciences* 1: 515-26.

Rogoff, Barbara, and Pablo Chavajay. 1995: "What's Become of Research on the Cultural Basis of Cognitive Development?" *American Psychologist* 50: 859-77.

Sherwood, Virginia, and Jerome S. Bruner. 1975: "Early Rule Structure: The Case of 'Peekaboo'." In *Life Sentences: Aspects of the Social Role of Language*, Rom Harre, ed., 55-62: New York: Wiley.

Sperry, Roger W. 1991: "Search for Beliefs to Live By Consistent with Science" *Zygon: Journal of Religion and Science* 26 (June): 237-258.

Squire, Larry R. 1986: "Mechanisms of Memory." *Science* 232: 1612-1619.

Stern, Daniel N. 1985: *The Interpersonal World of the Infant.* New York: Basic Books.

Teske, John A. 1996a: "The Modularity of Mind and the Construction of Spirit." *Studies in Science and Theology*, vol. 3, N.H. Gregersen and M.W.S. Parsons, eds., 200-207. Geneva: Labor et Fides.

Teske, John A. 1996b: "The Spiritual Limits of Neuropsychological Life." *Zygon: Journal of Religion and Science* 31 (June): 209-234.

Tomkins, Silvan S. 1979: "Script Theory." in *Nebraska Symposium on Motivation*, vol. 26, H.E. Howe and R.A. Dienstbier, eds., 208-236. Lincoln, NE: University of Nebraska Press.

Wilson, David S. and Elliott Sober. 1994: "Re-Introducing Group Selection to the Human Behavioural Sciences." *Behavioural and Brain Sciences* 17: 585-607.

Winnicott, D. W. 1965: *The Maturational Processes and the Facilitating Environment. New York:* International Universities Press.

Wright, Robert. 1994: *The Moral Animal: The New Science of Evolutionary Psychology.* New York: Pantheon.

Wright, Robert. 1995: "The Biology of Violence." *The New Yorker* (13 March): 68-77.

THE PHYSICAL WORLD AS A FUNCTION OF
THE OBSERVER'S CONSCIOUSNESS

S. SIPAROV
(St.-Petersburg, Russia)

Abstract: There are two basic ideas, which form the foundation of any theory: determinism and randomness, the latter being also described in terms of mathematical structures, providing the possibility to predict. It is shown that we can discover any deterministic motion while observing a random process - thus, making the consciousness of the observer the creator of a physical law observed. The world that can be created through such practice can possess various properties, which do not belong to the world described by traditional science. Nevertheless, the developed approach eliminates some difficulties in modern theories, while the possible system of axioms for a flickering universe has a similar level of complexity. So, the well known controversy between the laws of nature and our concepts of these laws is solved by stating that the laws of nature are just proclaimed by the consciousness of the observer and the following experimental observation is only to the effect of confirming them and making them obvious to another consciousness.

1. PLATO'S WORLD AND RORSCHACH'S WORLD

The 20th century is marked with the revival of interest in Plato's philosophy, which has obtained the new sense and new popularity (Slawianowski, 1996) due to the revolution in physics - origination and success of quantum theory. The direct and inexcludable participation of the observer in any experiment, participation which completes in the interpretation of results, now as seventy years ago, strikes the imagination of the researcher with the intrusion of mathematical theory into physical practice. The creature of consciousness radically determines the world around it.

During the process of cognition we, first of all, fix the image of the phenomenon in consciousness, and then regard its interrelations with other images, which were fixed before. Thus, we get the "shadow of the shadow", which has an invented and sometimes fanciful character, and presents a model of the phenomenon observed. Since rational thinking is based on logic, and its language is mathematics, we use both to describe the model's behaviour and to predict it. Turning again to the world, we make experiments, i.e. observe "shadows themselves", and find, whether the laws of consciousness, which are true for this very phenomenon's model, coincide with the cognized (in the same sense) laws of the surrounding world. Sometimes the role of consciousness, creating laws for the model and transferring them to the world, is seen clearly, as, for example, in quantum mechanics, where the observer can by no means be considered to be passive: he, his consciousness, his way of observation, which is the "choice of the question" (J. Wheeler, 1988) on the base of the model adopted, takes equal part in the reality creation. But it can be shown (S. Siparov, 1994, 2) that not only quantum mechanics or relativity theory have the conventional character, but classical mechanics as well.

The possibility to describe the world mathematically is a postulate, in frames of which we can distinguish two systems of axioms, leading either to the construction of deterministic equations for fields and motions, or to the interpretation of phenomena with regard to their random character and use of equations, stemming from the probability theory.

The recognition of the conventional character of every physical theory leads to the following.

In psychology there is the well-known Rorschach test: ink is splashed over a sheet of paper, then the sheet is folded in two to get a symmetrical, but formless image, and an examinee is asked to say, what this blot resembles to him. His psychological features are judged based on the examinee's associations. If we let him put onto the paper several points or lines in accordance with what he sees, and then show the result to another person, this last one will see the same image as the first one, though if we show him the initial blot, his answer may be well different. The same will take place if we ask the examinee just to show and name what he sees, without making any additional drawings. In this case the second person, having immediately observed what the first has named, will probably try to see something of his own.

When a researcher forms his notion of the phenomenon, and then makes an attempt to test it in experiment (interpreting the results in a corresponding way), and achieves "success", something like the introduction of additional lines into the Rorschach blot takes place. Adding a structure (especially mathematical), which is maximally formalised in accordance with human logics, the observer promotes the transformation of the "opinion" into "idea" (in Plato's terms), accessible for another observer's perception - "recollection". When more and more new lines are "drawn" (new experiments, *interpreted* in a corresponding way, are performed), more and more people see the picture that the first observer has discovered, the "idea" materialises. There is one important thing: to inform another person, another consciousness of one's notion of the world the noncontradictive language is needed (or else how to show the very notion of one's own?).

In Plato's world there are primary "ideas" correlated by laws. All that man can do is to formulate "opinions" with concern for the "shadows" he observes. In the language constructed to do this the primary "idea" is present in the direct form, and the most natural way to deal with it is to use the deterministic description. But the obvious successes in the use of the probabilistic approach, especially in quantum theory, demand, first, to correlate probabilistic and deterministic approaches, and, secondly, to *discover* the active role of the observer's consciousness in world formation.

Imagine a world of the Rorschach type. We can think of the universe, which possesses *inherent* random properties, in the same sense that we use, while speaking of homogeneity of space-time. Its space and time characteristics are its appearance and disappearance in random points and moments of time. What can be *observed* in such a universe? Whatever one likes. The universe is flickering or twinkling, and even the habitual notions of space and time have an emphasised artificial character. In the Rorschach world the active role of the observer is put forward. Out of the chaos of sensory signals the arbitrary picture is taken, and then it is made observable for the other observer by the choice of experiments and the use of the noncontradictive language. The lack of paradoxes in the structure of such a world is, thus, a result of consciousnesses interacting by means of logically noncontradictive (from their point of view) language. Here, Plato's primary becomes secondary, the "idea" is *constructed* on the base of individual "opinions", which are the manifestation of the subject's free will.

Is it possible to present a formal procedure, uniting these opinions into the noncontradictive whole? To introduce a function of observer's consciousness, which, on the one hand, *has to be arbitrary*, and on the other - can be used to get verifiable results? The first steps in this direction will be given in the next section.

So, the world is chaos, and the consciousness "produces" structures and forms, imparts space and time characteristics to them, dispenses properties, objectifies them in the process of interaction with other consciousnesses, and then investigates them, finding out *what* has been created, i.e. it investigates *itself*, analysing the results of its own activity. The denser is the Noosphere, the more definite and solid is the *evident* world around, and it is only in micro phenomena that we can still find out and realise our role and possibilities.

Whose consciousness was the first one? Who has "drawn" the first line in the chaotic picture in such a way that it separated light from darkness? Who suggested the idea of giving definite names to observable things, thus forming the noncontradictive language? Who tried to explain the very existence and the way of the world's existence through the idea of an indivisible Trinity and through miracles, which were the manifestation of pure free will?

The plurality of consciousnesses materialises the world, and it is only natural to advance in the most economic way, introducing as few new essences as possible (Occam). Nevertheless, it is possible to bring into being the world, which possesses properties different from known ones. One should only claim them and create the noncontradictive procedure of demonstration. The trouble with the latter is the huge and swiftly increasing quantity of cognized, which demands insertion into the correlated description.

2. INTERPRETING OBSERVATIONS

Imagine a line, an axis, on which there is a randomly moving particle. In the simplest case, which is usually discussed, this particle makes a dx meters jump every dt seconds, either in positive or in negative direction randomly. This model (random walk) is well known and has a lot of applications for statistical processes description. It follows from reasoning, that the average displacement of the particle $\langle x \rangle = 0$, while the average square displacement is proportional to the square root of the number of jumps (or steps).

Let this walk take place in the darkness, and use a stroboscope with frequency of flashes much less than the frequency of jumps to observe the particle's motion. Through the series of time and displacement measurements we will find that the observed displacement is a square root function of time, and guess that the particle moves randomly with constant jump lengths and periods. Since we know a priori (where from? It is only Newton's first law of inertial motion, which is the *axiom*, though the main one) that a *free* particle moves in a straight uniform way, and we haven't switched on any fields, we can start thinking of the origin of these jumps.

Imagine now that the jump lengths and periods *depend on time* in such a way that during every flash of the stroboscope we see that the particle's displacement increases uniformly. In this case we are satisfied to conclude that the particle moves freely. By the way, is it possible to find this jump dependence on time? Yes, it is, see section 4. What does it mean? It means that we can in the same way find another jump dependence on time that will give, for example, the uniformly accelerated motion of the particle, while observing it with the help of stroboscope.

And we will look for an attraction source (gravity? electrostatics?) or consider the reference frame being accelerated.

Is it nonsense? We see what we see. But we know beforehand and continue to believe that the axiom of inertia is true, which up to now has been the most convenient, most economic way to think. Even the realisation of the observer's consciousness role in quantum mechanics couldn't shake it. The invention appeared to be highly suitable. The correction to Rorschach picture is very convincing.

And at last, why stroboscope? Because what we can observe in the microworld is *always* a kind of stroboscopic experiment, no continuity is possible.

The conventional character of every physical theory was clearly realised in the beginning of the century (H. Poincare 1898). Nowadays the theme of discussion (F. Kapra 1994, H. Stapp 1994) is the necessity to introduce into a theory some function of the observer's consciousness in the direct way. And although the problem of the interaction between the consciousness and the world around is treated in different ways in physics and theology (S. Siparov 1994,1), the answers to it have a tendency to converge.

3. FROM THE POINT OF VIEW OF PHYSICS

As it has been mentioned in section 1, the main axiom (A) in natural science is the possibility to describe the physical processes in the world around in the language of logics and mathematics, belonging to the human consciousness, and the two approaches are possible. In the first one the concept of the system's Lagrange function is introduced and the minimal action principle is postulated. Let's call the possibility of such an approach the Ad-axiom (determinism). The results of the Ad-axiom usage are the differential equations of motion - mathematical structures, providing the possibility to get the dependence of the co-ordinates on time, if the initial conditions and the types of physical fields are known. To check these results we have to fulfil the measurements, i.e. the direct definition of co-ordinates at different moments of time. After that the calculated and the experimental results are compared. If there are discrepancies, they speak of the dissipative forces and of the energy dissipation. The latter means that we have to pass from regarding several bodies in frames of the Ad-axiom to regarding the additional system, containing a large number of bodies, for which the As-axiom (statistics) is considered to be true: to describe the behaviour of the many body system the formal apparatus of the Probability Theory and Random Processes Theory can be used. The mentioned discrepancies between the theoretic predictions and the experimental results in mechanics can be used to calculate the physical constants for the thermodynamic (statistical) process. In this approach we also get the mathematical structures (and some of them also have the meaning of the differential equations of motion), with the help of which we can predict the system's behaviour.

It is important to note that if we try to calculate the motion of microscopic molecules (forming the many body system), we face the impossibility of the direct co-ordinates and times measurements and factually *compare the results* of A and A axioms usage, thus, demanding our description to be noncontradictive.

There is one more important circumstance. While the size of the system's bodies becomes disappearingly small we start exerting the irreversible influence upon the results of the direct measurement, and, as it was discussed in (J. Wheeler, 1988), not only by instruments but by the very way of asking questions. This situation is treated in the Quantum Theory. The latter again uses statistical ideas essentially, and the deterministic motion in the direct sense is now neither described nor observed. The micro level, at which the deterministic effects of the Ad-axiom of classical mechanics fail to be true, is defined by the Heisenberg uncertainty relation. Planck's constant h is the quantitative characteristic of the classical mechanics applicability.

So, there is a transition region, where the Ad-axiom effects do not work with the decrease of the objects' scale, and where the As-axiom effects become senseless with the increase of the objects' scale. As to the direct measurements - they are impossible for the above mentioned reason.

Whence the conventional character of the micro phenomena description is clear to the majority of scientists, the conventional character of the Ad-axiom and its effects is recognised more rarely (S. Siparov 1994, 2). This is due to the tradition of interpretation of the experimental data in the direct measurements. Constructing a theory we speak of the space-time homogeneity or of its curvature. And in the same way we can speak of the random properties of the physical world, i.e. stochastic properties can appear not only in the microscopic level (G. Catania 1990), but in the macroscopic level as well and be observed in the direct measurements data interpreted in the corresponding way. The influence of the observer's consciousness, which must obviously be considered in the microworld (F. Kapra 1994), have to be considered in the physics of the macro phenomena too.

4. FUNCTION OF OBSERVER'S CONSCIOUSNESS CONSTRUCTION

Let's turn to the construction of this function of observer's consciousness and use the above mentioned random walk model, developing the ideas presented in (S. Siparov, 1994 (2)). The average square displacement in the simplest case of constant step length dx and time interval between steps δt is

$$\langle x^2 \rangle^{\frac{1}{2}} = \sqrt{b \frac{(\delta x)^2 t}{\delta t}} \qquad (1)$$

where b is a dimensionless constant. If we demand that the ratio δx/δt is neither zero nor infinity, then we can get (W. Feller 1966) the so called Focker-Planck equation, which, provided the boundary and initial conditions are given, makes it possible to calculate the probability to find the randomly walking particle in the certain area of the point x at the moment t. This model is very convenient to describe diffusion (in frames of the As-approach), the equation for which exactly coincides in form with the Focker-Planck equation, but the result of its solution is regarded as the dependence of the diffusing matter concentration on time and co-ordinate. The instantaneous distribution of the matter over all the samples is usually ignored for the sake of "physical reasons" - the same reasons we used while choosing the finite ratio δx/δt. This is a simple example of what is taking place, while we use a formal mathematical model, taking into consideration only that part which suits us, and calling it the physical law if we manage to observe the coincidence of predicted results with the experimental ones.

Let's preserve the form of the eq. (1) for time dependant δx and δt regard it as a solution of the dynamics equation, where $\langle x^2 \rangle^{\frac{1}{2}}$ plays a role of displacement (the particular features of this assumption will be discussed later). Passing from δx and δt to $X(t)$ and $T(t)$ and preserving the form of eq. (1), we get

$$\langle x^2 \rangle^{\frac{1}{2}} = \sqrt{b \frac{X^2(t)t}{T(t)}} \qquad (2)$$

Writing eq. (2) in such a form, we used the ergodic hypothesis, according to which the average over the number of realisations (left hand part) is equal to the average in a single realisation when $t \rightarrow \infty$ (right hand part). Let us find such $X(t)$ and $T(t)$ that the displacement $\langle x^2 \rangle^{\frac{1}{2}}$ is a linear function of t. (Then observing the particle motion with the help of a stroboscope we shall discover that it moves uniformly.) To do this let's demand the time derivative of the displacement be constant. This means that we consider only those (random) points, visited by the particle, which lie in the vicinity of the given linear function $x_1(t) = vt$, v = const. Calculating the derivative we get

$$C_s = \sqrt{\frac{bt}{T}}\frac{dX}{dt} - \frac{X}{2T}\sqrt{\frac{bt}{T}}\frac{dT}{dt} + \frac{X}{2}\sqrt{\frac{b}{tT}} - v = 0 \qquad (3)$$

Let the function $T(t)$ be arbitrary. If the set of points, visited by the particle, is dense enough, then during a single flash of a stroboscope, lasting for τ seconds (and $\tau \gg T(t)$), the points will be observed, for which the jump lengths $X(t)$ will suffice the condition (3). This makes it possible to *observe* the straight uniform movement of the particle, while the scattering of points on the plot (due to the random character of the process) can be interpreted as an experimental error.

In the same way we can find the conditions corresponding to the other motion types - uniformly accelerated, etc. The choice of the linear function $x_1(t)$ and the condition $C_s = 0$ in the form of eq. (3) is due to their correspondence to the postulate of inertial reference systems existence. Nevertheless, it is clear that in the same set of visited points we can *observe* other different motions, if we use other functions . So, the C_s function (where C stands for consciousness and s for stochastic), is a function of the observer's consciousness. The necessity of such function introduction was discussed in (F. Kapra 1994, H. Stapp 1994, G. Catania 1990). In the same way the necessity of the unified approach to the description of micro and macro phenomena is realised long ago (R.P. Feynman, A.R. Hibbs 1965) but up to now this problem is not solved.

To deal with the arbitrariness in $T(t)$ choice during the experimental investigation of the macroscopic objects of classical mechanics, it is enough to demand that for large t the value of $T(t)$ is essentially less than t, which is usual for any observation.

5. CONSEQUENCES

Returning to the concept of the world, based on the assumption that it has some inherent random properties - in the same sense that we use while speaking about the homogeneity of the space-time as a postulate - we see that the main law of the twinkling universe is that very changeability which J. Wheeler proclaimed in (J. Wheeler, 1979).

The approach under discussion appears to be noncontradictive, though far from giving an immediate exhaustive picture for every branch of physics. Nevertheless, the place of this approach among existing theories can be shown.

1. Constructing mechanics, we can preserve the structure of the Lagrange formalism with the only difference that in the minimal action principle we should pass from the variational problem with the fixed ends to the variational problem with the free ends, while the role of the transversality condition will be played by the condition:

$$
\begin{cases}
(L-v\dfrac{\partial L}{\partial v})\Big|_{t=t} T(t)-(L-v\dfrac{\partial L}{\partial v})\Big|_{t=T_1} T_1+\dfrac{\partial L}{\partial v}\Big|_{t=t} X(t)-\dfrac{\partial L}{\partial v}\Big|_{t=T_1} X(T_1)=0 \\
C_s=0
\end{cases}
\tag{4}
$$

If there are no fields due to the particular sources, and the particle moves freely (in the twinkling space-time), and we would like it to move in a straight uniform way, then we should use C_s defined by eq. (3) and solve the system (4) to find the free Lagrangian L_0. In the approach under discussion we can speak about homogeneity and isotropy of space-time only with concern for a certain procedure of averaging over some area and time interval near the (t,x) point.

2. We can also regard the reference system in which the free particle moves according to eq. (1), i.e. it has the acceleration, decreasing with time as $t^{-3/2}$. Such a system will become an inertial one at large t (in the corresponding units). This is a good analogy of the situation in general relativity, when the space-time region far from material masses has a disappearingly small curvature.

3. While constructing the electrodynamics in the randomly twinkling space-time under discussion we can use the corresponding results for the discrete space (K.E. Plohotnikov, 1988).

4. In the quantum mechanics the transfer of traditional random properties of the microscopic object to the space-time (G. Catania, 1990) will make it possible to describe the quantum-instrument interaction from the unified point of view. Besides, the finiteness of the first interval fits the ideas and results of (D. Kobe, V. Aquilera-Navarro 1994), where the energy-time uncertainty relation derivation is discussed.

5. In the special relativity theory the appearance of the second postulate about the limit velocity value is related to the Maxwell's theory of electromagnetism. But if a particle moves according to eq. (2), then we have the limit velocity value inherent to such approach. Really, for example, for the simplest case of eq. (1) the $x(t)$ plot is the distribution of points near the parabola branch. Calculating the dispersions $D(t)$ and $D(t+dt)$, assuming that $dt \gg \delta t$, we shall find the limit velocity value $v = (1/2)dD(t)/dt$. This means that though the "superlight" speed is possible, its observation can take place only if the single measurement time τ is less than dt (or $\tau < T(t)$ in a more complicated case). Such a motion in the vicinity of the parabola branch is due to the choice of $\langle x^2 \rangle^{1/2}$ as a displacement.

6. The parabola has two branches, and the randomly moving particle can be found in turn near both of them. As it is shown in (W. Feller 1966), such transitions are more rare than it seems at first sight, moreover, their frequency vanishes as $t^{-1/2}$. Such transitions are analogous to the transitions from the expansion stage to the contraction stage in the universe evolution as it is discussed in Fridman's approach to general relativity.

7. As it was shown by E. Recami in (E. Recami 1979), when observing the superlight cosmological objects, described in frames of the generalised relativity theory, the first thing we shall see will be a single flash in a certain point, then it will double and at the first stage of the observations the velocity of these two flashes divergence will follow the law of $t^{-1/2}$. This corresponds to the assumption that at small times (in corresponding units), when $T(t)$ is not small enough to suffice the condition $t > T(t)$, the motion is described by the formula (2), which also suggests that the velocity is proportional to $t^{-1/2}$.

We can see that the two independent basic postulates (inertial systems existence and limit velocity value existence) are replaced by a single one - world's random properties existence - from which both mentioned are corollary. In traditional theory the observation results into the state of the quantum object. In this approach the observer takes part in the creation of the whole world. The equations of physical laws stand only for certain structures, imposed on the world and generated by the observer's consciousness. Among the random points-events those are observed which fit the chosen structure in the best way. This means that the consciousness that has formed an arbitrary picture of the world, imparted it with some properties, and constructed the noncontradictive structure to describe this picture, will observe it, thus observing itself. The results of such observation, presented to the other consciousness would help to form in this consciousness the same picture with the same properties, and at last materialise the world.

REFERENCES

G. Catania. "The need for a probabilistic interpretation of Quantum Mechanics: causes and results". Proc. Conf. on Found. of Math. and Phys., Perugia, 1990.

W. Feller. An Introduction to Probability Theory and its Applications. John Wiley and Sons, Inc., New York, 1966 (rus trans.)

R.P. Feynman, A.R. Hibbs. Quantum Mechanics and Path Integrals. McGraw-Hill Book Company, New York, 1965 (rus. trans.)

F. Kapra. Dao of Physics. (rus trans. 1994).

D.H. Kobe, V.C. Aquilera-Navarro. "Derivation of the energy- time uncertainty relation". Phys. Rev. A, v.50, No.2, p.933-938, 1994.

K.E. Plohotnikov. Rus. Doklady Academii Nauk, v.301, 1362, 1988.

H. Poincare. "Rev. Metaphys. Morales", v.6,1,1898.

E. Recami. "Relativity Theory and its Generalization", Astrofisica e Cosmologia Gravitazione Quanti e Relativita, (Guinti Barbera, Firenze, 1979).

S. Siparov. "Inversion in the cognition process and reorganization of personality". Contributed to the 5th Conf. of the ESSSAT, Munich, 1994 (1).

S. Siparov. "Conventional Character of Physical Theories". Proc. Conf. "Physical Interpretations of Relativity Theory", London, 1994 (2).

Slawianowski J.J. "Platonism as a Spontaneous Way of Thinking in Modern Physics." Report to the 6th Conference of the ESSSAT, Cracow, 1996.

H.P. Stapp. "Theoretical model of a purported empirical violation of the predictions of quantum theory". Phys. Rev. A, vol. 50, No.1, p.18, 1994.

J.A. Wheeler. "Quantum and universe", Astrofisica e Cosmologia Gravitazione Quanti e Relativita, Guinti Barbera, Firenze, 1979 (rus. trans).

J.A. Wheeler. World as system self-synthesised by quantum networking. IBM J. Res. Develop. vol. 32, No.1, 1988.

OXYTOCIN IS A MANY SPLENDID THING: BIOCHEMICALS USURP THE DIVINE

KEVIN SHARPE

(Concord, USA)

Abstract: Certain biochemicals occur with particular animal, including human behaviours. Parental and filial love, for instance, correlate with the presence of oxytocin and vasopressin in the brain, and they in turn induce the symptoms of loving. Love is in part an adaptive trait that functions with hormones.

In the Christian view, God is love, the same sort of love. But we hardly expect the Divine to possess veins with oxytocin flowing through them. Or if with Saint John we believe that love comes from God, then we need to understand how love can derive from both biology and the Divine when we would not say the same about many "sinful" behaviours. Is it reasonable to include loving as a prerequisite for a person's salvation if the individual is missing the part of the brain responsible for moral conduct?

A tension therefore exists between neuroscience and spiritual thought, a tension that calls for a rethinking of the spiritual doctrine of divine love.

Keywords: Brain, determinism, the divine, hormones, love, neuroscience, oxytocin, parental behaviour, science and spiritual thought, vasopressin.

In the summer of 1848, an explosion shot a steel rod through the brain of Phineas Gage, the supervisor of a work gang laying railroad tracks in Vermont. Before the incident he was even-tempered with a strong, ambitious, social and positive character. Afterwards, he was fitful and irreverent, obstinate, unable to stick at anything for long, and indifferent to other people. Despite emphatic admonitions, he swore so foully that women were advised to stay in his presence for only a few minutes. From the accident he lost not only the sight of his left eye, but also his sociability (Damasio 1994).

A child in school steals, cheats, fights and lies. No matter what adults try, they cannot change him into a responsible and loving boy. Teachers blame his family background; parents call for a special educational program; counsellors work on building self-esteem. The current system considers outside intervention the cure. But does the problem lie outside or inside the boy?

"A natural chemical called oxytocin is found to underlie love," writes Robert Wright (Wright 1994, 351).

Inside your brain lies a hypothalamus, the organ that controls "primitive" behaviours such as sex, aggression and feeding (Insel, Carter 1995). It produces the two hormones, oxytocin and vasopressin, which then pass through a stalk down to the posterior pituitary gland at the base of the brain for storage and secretion (Greenblatt, Mahesh 1996). Both of these biochemicals evolved from the primordial hormone vasatocin which still endures in lower vertebrates. They also share a similar molecular structure, differing in only two out of their nine amino acids, the building blocks of proteins (Carter, Getz 1993). When released into the body, they bind to specific targets called receptors located in the brain and elsewhere, like keys fitting into locks. The receptors then effect other body parts and, finally, behaviour (Insel, Carter 1995).

Medicine has long known the effects of oxytocin on the female reproductive system. It naturally stimulates contractions in the uterus right through the birth process by locking onto specific receptors in the muscles of the uterus, causing them to contract. Not surprisingly, the name "oxytocin" derives from the Greek for "swift birth" (Hardy, Carter 1995). Obstetricians inject a synthetic form of it to arouse contractions when labour flags. (The Nobel-prize work of Vincent du Vigneaud in 1953 pioneered its and vasopressin's synthesis.) It also helps control excessive bleeding after delivery. Within seconds after her baby begins to suckle, oxytocin prompts the mother's mammary glands to release milk. As every mother and observant father knows, even the cry of a hungry baby can prematurely stimulate milk let-down, so susceptible is oxytocin release to emotional influences. It also plays a role in coitus, nipple eroticism the milk ejection reflex, and female sexual responsiveness (Ludwig 1995; Sarlin 1981).

Research into the source and functions of oxytocin continues. Neuroendocrinologist Hans Zingg of McGill University led a study on the role of the hypothalamus-regulated oxytocin levels that prompt labour in animals. His team's 1992 report states that the uterus, not the hypothalamus, produces this oxytocin. Similar evidence occurs in humans (Ezzell 1992a; Lefebvre, et al. 1992).

Maurice Manning and his colleagues in the Department of Biochemistry at the Medical College of Ohio in Toledo, developed several synthetic oxytocin "antagonists". These copycat proteins chemically resemble oxytocin and bind to the appropriate receptors, elbowing out the real things, and thus block the effects the receptors induce (Insel, Carter 1995).

For those mothers who experience premature labour, injecting an oxytocin antagonist can suppress contractions (Radetsky 1994).

Oxytocin's companion hormone, vasopressin, plays a key role in maintaining the volume of water in the body at a constant level, and maintaining the concentration of dissolved substances within narrow limits in the body fluids outside the body cells. Specifically male functions of certain animals, such as marking territorial boundaries with scent, also involve vasopressin (Insel, Carter 1995).

Recent research with vasopressin and oxytocin enters fields other than medicine. Oxytocin receptors could play roles in social behaviour aside from those already known (Oxytocin Receptors 1992). Peter Klopfer of Duke University recognised the association of social bonds between mothers and their offspring with the release of oxytocin, and suggested it might be the hormone of "motherly love". Physiological changes might prepare an expectant mother for her new role. Niles Newton of Northwestern University speculates that the secretion of oxytocin influences maternal and sexual bonds (Carter, Getz 1993).

In depth research on the role of these hormones in mammals gained momentum. When first presented with pups, a virgin female laboratory rat usually ignores them, is frightened of them, or eats them. She will tolerate them only when they are introduced to her many times over several days. Then she may even care for the youngsters by licking them, retrieving them when they stray from her side, and crouching over them protectively. But a pregnant rat responds to pups caringly within minutes, even before delivery of her own. In a classic experiment from 1968, Joseph Terkel and Jay Rosenblatt of Rutgers University injected virgin female rats with blood from rats that had just given birth. It took the virgins less time to nurture pups than normally (Hardy, Carter 1995).

Parent rats can mistreat their children if antagonists block their oxytocin receptors, according to the research of Cort Pedersen and Jack Caldwell at the University of North Carolina, and Gustav Jirikowski at Scripps Research Laboratory (Schrof 1991). Parent rats injected with antagonists to block their oxytocin receptors mistreat their offspring. Oxytocin release also induces grooming behaviour in rats (van Erp, et al. 1995), and when administered to sociable mice, it boosts the instinct for cuddling to a frenzied pitch (Schrof 1991).

Voles are small, brown, nondescript mammals of the genus Microtus which live under seeds and grasses (Carter, Getz 1993). Members of one species, the prairie vole, share elaborate systems of burrows and feeding tunnels. Males and females form long-lasting bonds, unlike most rodents, raising their young together. But montane (or mountain) voles occupy separate burrows and avoid each other except to mate - which they do often and indiscriminately. Mother montane voles usually abandon their pups sixteen days after birth, and fathers never see their offspring. When a predator plucks a youngster from its nest, it neither calls for help nor surges with stress-related hormones. In comparison with their prairie cousins, the high-meadow montane voles lack family values and are exceptionally asocial (Ezzell 1992b; Insel, Carter 1995). Why?

Mapping the oxytocin receptors of vole brains to see where the hormone acts reveals many more in key areas of prairie brains than in montane's (Insel, Carter 1995). Thomas Insel, now at Emory University, and Larry Shapiro of the National Institute of Mental Health's (NIMH) facility in Poolesville, Maryland, found that prairie voles have three times the number of oxytocin receptors in their prelimbic cortex - and seven times more in their nucleus accumbens - than do montane voles. And during the brief period in which female montane voles nurse their young, the number of their oxytocin receptors surges (Ezzell 1992b). Thus the distribution pattern of oxytocin receptors matches with monogamy and care for offspring, suggesting that oxytocin plays an essential role in social organisation (Carter, Getz 1993; Winslow, et al. 1993). We should not conclude, however, that this represents a cause-and-effect relationship between the hormone and behaviour (Insel, Carter 1995). Further research does lead to this conclusion, however.

As soon as the female prairie vole becomes sexually active, she and a male will copulate repeatedly, more than fifty times over 36-48 hours. After such a bout, she becomes more socially exclusive, preferring her mate to unfamiliar males. This discovery by Diane Witt of the University of Maryland suggests that mating instils long-term pair bonding. Copulation causes the release of oxytocin; is this the critical factor in developing her social preferences (Insel, Carter 1995)? Jessie Williams, also of the University of Maryland, found that a female prairie vole rapidly forms a preference for a male if exposed to oxytocin for six hours. But when administered with an antagonist to block the oxytocin receptors, oxytocin ceases its social effect. Oxytocin causes rodents to form monogamous pairs, shaping their sexual and parental behaviour, and their social organisation (Carter, Getz 1993; Ezzell 1992b).

Studies of domestic sheep by Barry Keverne, Keith Kendrick and their colleagues at the University of Cambridge, add to this picture of the behavioural effects of oxytocin. As a lamb moves down its mother's birth canal, it stimulates nerves that trigger the release of oxytocin. Only with it present at birth, or injected so it reaches the brain the same time mother ewe meets her new-born, does she bond with her offspring. She rejects her lamb if something blocks its release. High levels of oxytocin also occur in her milk, suggesting the hormone helps forge a mutual attachment between the mother and her infant (Hardy, Carter 1995).

What about males' sexual and parental behaviour? After the initial sexual bout, a male prairie vole prefers his mate and ferociously guards against rivals, even in her absence (Insel, Carter 1995). James Winslow, while at the NIMH in Poolesville, found that a male isolated from females and injected with vasopressin becomes aggressive and attacks other males. If exposed to a female and injected with vasopressin, a male develops a preference for her even if they do not mate. Administering a vasopressin antagonist to a male ready to mate does not prevent repeated and intense copulation. But afterwards he does not fend off intruders or prefer his partner. (Females respond very little to vasopressin (Carter, Getz 1993; Insel, Carter 1995).) On the other hand, an oxytocin antagonist alters neither the male's mate preference nor his guarding behaviour. Zuo-Xin Wang, Craig Ferris and Geert De Vries, of the University of Massachusetts in Amherst, found that vasopressin also increases (and a vasopressin antagonist decreases) the amount of time he spends with his pups, which he would typically and naturally do by retrieving them and huddling over them; many biologists believe such paternal care for the young anchors male monogamy (Carter, Getz 1993; Hardy, Carter 1995; Insel, Carter 1995). Only vasopressin, then, accounts for male sexual and parental behaviour.

Vasopressin and oxytocin are crucial for pair bonding, eliciting parental care and nurturing, and defending the family (Carter, Getz 1993; Hardy, Carter 1995). While oxytocin encourages social contact, however, vasopressin compels the males' antisocial, guarding behaviour after copulation. The hormones counter each other; their behavioural and cellular functions oppose each other in some circumstances. Perhaps oxytocin blocks the unfriendliness induced by vasopressin. No matter what the mechanism involved, vasopressin and oxytocin together determine for many species if a pair bond, nurture and care for their young, and defend the family. Monogamy and polygyny express the net outcome of what happens when oxytocin and vasopressin activate different circuits in the brain (Carter, Getz 1993; Insel, Carter 1995).

What about humans? The human brain manufactures vasopressin and oxytocin, which bind to receptors there; our forebrain contains many oxytocin receptors, Swedish researchers report (Ezzell 1992b). Though they are large molecules and do not readily penetrate the blood-brain barrier, they exist in larger-than-normal quantities in the brain when hard at work elsewhere in the body. Thus they could in principle influence our social behaviour (Ezzell 1992a; Insel, Carter 1995). Much maternal behaviour in an expectant mother arises from hormonal changes that her system induces, and after birth it usually stems from hormones her offspring stimulates (Rosenblatt 1994). A sensitive period for this bonding occurs an hour after birth - when her oxytocin level rises markedly (Nissen, et al. 1995). Breast feeding causes some of the stimulation. In addition, the hormones released by it benefit the mother's mental health and her ability to deal with stress; they calm her (Hardy, Carter 1995).

A British study of male medical students shows that vasopressin enters the bloodstream during sexual arousal, and oxytocin at orgasm (Carmichael, et al. 1994; Insel, Carter 1995). In both female and male humans, oxytocin levels rise dramatically during sex, and may promote the associated feelings of love and infatuation (Schrof 1991). Kerstin Uvnös-Moberg of the Karolinska Institute in Stockholm has shown that a simple touch can release oxytocin (Carter, Getz 1993). We share many of the oxytocin and vasopressin responses of other animals.

According to *Webster's New World Dictionary*, love is "a deep and tender feeling of affection for or attachment or devotion to a person or persons;...a feeling of [unity and co-operation] and good will toward other people;...a strong, usually passionate, affection of one person for another, based in part on sexual attraction." "Agape" it defines as "spontaneous, altruistic love." Oxytocin fosters friendship, love and nurturance. With vasopressin, it provides the chemistry of human attachment: sticking with your sexual partner and attention to your offspring. Says Cort Pedersen, "Human relations are influenced by the model of the parent-child relationship in that they include the notions of nurturing, care, help" (Schrof 1991). These behaviours we call love; earlier times would call it charity. Love derives from the positive effects of oxytocin and vasopressin.

"Children need love," writes Harold Hulbert in a 1949 issue of the *Reader's Digest*, "especially when they do not deserve it." Sometimes we love despite ourselves, and the involuntary release of oxytocin serves well the survival of our offspring, and with them, our genes. Can we decide to love, and do so, even if this means the decision prompts the release of hormones? This is a crucial question. Though oxytocin and vasopressin from the hypothalamus seem to mandate social attachments among voles, they and other hormones do not fully determine what happens. No hormone acts alone (Schrof 1991). A mother's behaviour and experience, for instance, both affect and are affected; exposure to pups reorganises the neural pathways in a mother rat's brain, making her respond faster to pups in the future no matter what her hormone level (Hardy, Carter 1995). A human mother can make her milk let-down by thinking about it; the thought spurs the release of oxytocin which in turn primes her mammary glands. Many factors - especially the complex activities in our cerebral cortex - intrude on the effects of the hormone in humans (Insel, Carter 1995). That does not mean we can take the opposite position to the naturalist and say that in humans love is only a product of the will. Love is an adaptive trait, both a willed and an involuntary phenomenon (often a combination of both), but it always involves the release of biochemicals.

I write the above though it is at this point speculative. For instance, why is it that quite different mammals exhibit monogamy? Sue Carter of the University of Maryland, and Lowell Getz of the University of Illinois, suggest it may result from the interactions between the adrenal and gonadal hormones in early life, but at this time it is only a hypothesis open to further exploration. Further, excessive amounts of oxytocin in the brain feature in a type of obsessive-compulsive disorder, the sort that sparks fears of germ contamination that lead to hours of hand washing each day—to the point of rubbing off skin and disrupting all other activities. It is the type that consists of repeated, upsetting thoughts or images linked to acts that a person feels compelled to carry out (Bower 1994; Leckman 1994). So oxytocin induces negative effects and only sometimes can we associate it with love. (You could look at the disorder, though, as a way of over-caring, carrying the usual results of oxytocin to an extreme.) It is appealing to ascribe the love role to oxytocin, but it is difficult to prove a causal association objectively, especially with such a large number of variables. Further, the roles of vasopressin and oxytocin are difficult to document, even in animals, and many questions remain unexplored or only partly explored (Carter, Getz 1993). We need to be cautious when we extrapolate data derived from animal or limited human studies. The important point, though, is that love has a biological rootedness, despite what else it involves.

Social bonds have a biology (Carter, Getz 1993). Love is in part a physical trait derived from evolution. Parental and filial love are associated with the hormones oxytocin and vasopressin which promote the behaviours and symptoms of loving. When people love this way, these chemicals occur in their bodies in larger-than-normal amounts. Love functions with them. The dictionary also defines love as "God's tender regard and concern for [hu]mankind." "Love is from God; everyone who loves is born of God and knows God," writes Saint John (1 John 4:7-8, *The New Testament and Psalms: An Inclusive Version*). Jesus talks of his wanting to gather together the people of Jerusalem "as a hen gathers her brood under her wings" (Matthew 23:37). The Gospel of John compares the love of the Divine to a good shepherd who would die for the sheep (John 10:17). Parental, filial, altruistic love - the oxytocin-vasopressin behaviour - originates in the Divine. But this leads to a confusion: the hormonal behaviour of love arises from both the biology of our bodies and from the Divine. It has two different sources. We may not say the same about many "sinful" behaviours.

Saint John continues his epistle with these words: "Whoever does not love does not know God, for God is love." The Divine is love; does that mean the Divine is pure oxytocin and, because God is a male, also vasopressin? Since we have them, should the Divine possess two hands, each with five fingers? Does the Divine crave food and sex, and does the chemical oxytocin flow through divine veins when the Divine loves? Of course not. The Divine is not a biological being that evolved under environmental pressures, and so does not have hands and fingers, the need for food and sex, or veins throbbing with oxytocin. Love evolved biologically; it pertains to organic creatures - voles, rats, sheep, humans - that developed under the imperative to survive genetically. An adaptive trait like love features specifically in animals like humans. So, why should the Divine have love? Love and biochemicals and genes belong together.

Not only does the Divine love us, but the New Testament urges us to love one another. If love derives largely from involuntary releases of biochemicals, is it reasonable to urge people to love each other? Could Gage, the man with a hole through his head, have changed his ways?

These difficult questions challenge the traditional view of the nature of the Divine and the Divine's relationship to us humans. They ask about the association of love with the Divine. So what is a spiritual understanding of love in the light of this new research? What role does the Divine play in love? An answer could take several paths. It could justify the elevation of love from the animal to the level of the Divine. Or it could make sense of how a divine property could become one that, with its biochemical associates, biological beings experience. Or it could start its understanding of the Divine from scratch, asking anew what is the nature of the Divine. To say that the Divine's relationship with the universe and humans is or is like love requires serious reconstruction and justification.

Whatever, an answer should emphasise the relevance of scientific and spiritual ideas for each other. This means actively exploring such points of contact as the nature and origin of love, its connection with the Divine, and the relationship between the Divine and human beings. In the larger enterprise of the partnership between scientific and spiritual ideas, it means working out a flexible system of spiritual ideas that moves with scientific advances, that builds on the findings of science and adopts a method like science's. It means exploring the spiritual scientifically, offering hypotheses and insights for scientific scrutiny. And it means promoting a science that seeks advances in spiritual thought. Spiritual thinkers and scientists could see themselves working in tandem with each other.

BIBLIOGRAPHY

Bower, B. 1994: "Hormone Shows Link to Some Obsessions," *Science News* 146 (29 October), 277.

Carmichael, M. S., V. L. Warburton, Dixen J. and J. M. Davidson. 1994: "Relationships Among Cardiovascular, Muscular, and Oxytocin Responses During Human Sexual Activity," *Archives of Sexual Behaviour* 23 (February), 59-79.

Carter, C. Sue, and Lowell L. Getz. 1993: "Monogamy and the Prairie Vole," *Scientific American* 268 (June), 100-106.

Damasio, Antonio R. 1994: *Descartes' Error: Emotion, Reason, and the Human Brain*, New York: Avon.

Ezzell, Carol. 1992a: "Explanation for Premature and Delayed Labour," *Science News* 141 (13 June), 389.

———. 1992b: "Brain Receptors Shape Volves Family Values," *Science News* 142 (4 July), 6-7.

Greenblatt, Robert B., and Virendra B. Mahesh. 1996: "Important Human Hormones," *Collier's Encyclopedia*, Cognito article # 17147687.

Hardy, Sarah Blaffer, and C. Sue Carter. 1995: "Hormonal Cocktails for Two," *Natural History* 104 (December), 34.

Insel, Thomas R., and C. Sue Carter. 1995: "The Monogamous Brain," *Natural History* 104 (August), 13-14.

Leckman, James F. 1994: "Elevated Cerebrospinal Fluid Levels of Oxytocin in Obsessive-compulsive Disorder: Comparison with Tourette's Syndrome and Healthy Controls," *Archives of General Psychiatry* 51, 782-792.

Lefebvre, Diana L., Adel Giaid, Hugh Bennett, Richard Larivire and Hans H. Zingg. 1992: "Oxytocin Gene Expression in Rat Uterus," *Science* 256 (12 June), 1553-1555.

Ludwig, M. 1995: "Functional Role of Intrahypothalamic Release of Oxytocin and Vasopressin: Consequences and Controversies," *American Journal of Physiology* 268 (April), E537-E545.

Nissen, E., G. Lilja, A. M. Widstrom and K. Uvnas-Moberg. 1995: "Elevation of Oxytocin Levels Early Post Partum in Women," *Acta Obstetricia et Gynecologica Scandinavica* 74 (August), 530-533.

"Oxytocin Receptors Linked to Social Behaviour," 1992: *BioScience* 42 (April), 327.

Radetsky, Peter. 1994: "Stopping Premature Births Before It's Too Late," *Science* 266 (2 December), 1486-1488.

Rosenblatt, J. S. 1994: "Psychobiology of Maternal Behaviour: Contribution to the Clinical Understanding of Maternal Behaviour Among Humans," *Acta Paediatrica*, Supplement 397 (June), 3-8.

Sarlin, C. N. 1981: "The Role of Breast-feeding in Psycho-Sexual Development and the Achievement of the Genital Phase," *Journal of the American Psychoanalytic Association* 29(3), 631-641.

Schrof, Joannie M. 1991: "Hormone of Love: The Chemistry of Romance and Nurturance," *U.S. News & World Report* 110 (24 June), 62.

Van Erp, A. M., M. R. Kruk, J. G. Veening, T. A. Roeling and W. Meelis. 1995: "Neuronal Substrate of Electrically Induced Grooming in the PVH of the Rat: Involvement of Oxytocinergic Systems?" *Physiology and Behaviour* 57 (May), 882-885.

Winslow, J. T., L. Shapiro, C. S. Carter and T. R. Insel. 1993: "Oxytocin and Complex Social Behaviour: Species Comparison," *Psychopharmacology Bulletin* 29(3), 409-414.

Wright, Robert. 1994: *The Moral Animal: The New Science of Evolutionary Psychology*, New York: Pantheon Books.

Section 4

Methodological Issues

THE ROLE OF PHILOSOPHY
IN THE SCIENCE-THEOLOGY DIALOGUE

Tempelton Lecture delivered by
JEAN LADRIÈRE
(*Louvain-la-Neuve, Belgium*)

Abstract: The conditions for a fruitful dialogue between science and theology are reciprocal understanding and reciprocal fructification. This implies hetero-understanding and co-referentiality. Those conditions can be met only through the intervention of a mediating agency. Philosophy appears as able to provide that mediation. More precisely, it is in the transcendental field, uncovered by modern philosophy, that science and theology can meet each other.
More concretely, the questions that are at the point of encounter between them are in part of an epistemological kind (forms of language, forms of intelligibility, criteria of validity, specific realities), and in part they concern the very content of science and theology (interpretability of science for theology and reciprocally, relation of science and theology to the general horizon of sense, existence as field of encounter). Beyond its task of clarification, with respect to those questions, philosophy has also the more fundamental task of explaining what science and theology have in common, despite their differences. In order to give account of the specificity of theology a distinction is introduced between the order of constitution and the order of event.
Keywords: Constitution, dialogue, event, existence, intelligibility, interpretation, mediation, reference, transcendental, field, validity.

At first sight, it seems that there is no reason to introduce a third term in the context of the science-theology dialogue. Science and theology are two spiritual powers, intrinsically autonomous. Each of them is able to pursue its own work, according to its own methods, without having to take account of the other's work. If a dialogue arises between them it is by virtue of a free decision on both parts. This does not mean at all, of course, that they have no good reasons, each one from its own point of view, to take such a decision. Theology could be induced, by the demands of its own task, to search for information about significant scientific achievements, on the supposition that they could be of some help in its endeavour to understand better the word in which it has to explain the meaning of Revelation. Or it could suppose that some scientific views could really suggest new metaphors, useful for the formulation of its own theses, or even new ways of understanding the tradition of faith, as it is apparently the case for process theology, whose conception of God owes something to the evolutionary conception of the visible world. And, in the same way, science could be interested in the achievements of theology, considered as an intellectual enterprise highly worthy of consideration, in the conviction that it is always fruitful for a particular field of research to have at least some knowledge of the way in which the work is progressing in other fields. Or it could even address some definite questions to theology about problems that it is able to detect and to formulate clearly but for which its own methods do not appear as relevant, in the belief that, after all, scientific research comes perhaps to touch, in its own way, some aspects of reality, which belong properly to that border territory where the visible world comes in contact with the realm of the invisible, and that only theology has perhaps something to say about it.

Assuming that such a will to enter into a dialogue actually exists, we have to wonder what are the conditions of a really fruitful exchange. It is easy to recognise that there is a minimal requirement: the possibility, on both parts, to understand the language of the other. But that condition, elementary as it is, has in fact far-reaching implications. To understand the language of the other is not only to understand the meaning of the words he is using, it is to enter into the specific problematic to which he is trying to give expression by his words, and thereby into the project of understanding from which his discourse receives its deep meaning. But in order to capture what is at stake in a problematic, it is necessary to have some access to the specific kind of reality that gives rise to that problematic, and thus a minimum of understanding of that reality, that kind of familiarity which reduces the distance, makes accessible or reveals a presence. It thus appears that this minimal condition is already very demanding: to understand the language of the other is already to enter into his own experience, his point of view, the very perspective from which he is speaking. And the adoption of another perspective asks the abandonment of one's own point of view.

But there is a stronger condition, under which the dialogue could reveal its most fruitful effects: the possibility of arriving, through and by the dialogue, not only to an understanding of the other's perspective but to an enlightenment of one's own research from the point of view of the other. Under such a condition, the dialogue becomes really an exchange where the one receives from the other the capacity of having a better understanding of what he is trying to do. His research, by itself, has certainly an intrinsic meaning, which is perhaps sufficient to justify his endeavour. But, seen from another perspective, it can perhaps receive a deeper or more inclusive meaning, with respect to which the intrinsic meaning is only very partial. It is besides not only the meaning of the research as such which could be so enlarged and transformed, but also the very content of the discipline, and this is true as well for the particular theses as for the world view which is implied in the explicit assertions.

Now a direct confrontation, based simply on the juxtaposition of two discourses, will have as a result, to make strongly apparent the differences which separate them from each other, differences in the languages used, in the problems treated, in the methods applied, in the assessment of criteria. It would be perhaps a comparison, certainly not a dialogue. The will to enter into a dialogue aims evidently at something else: a reciprocal understanding and a reciprocal fructification, this second aim presupposing the first one.

Understanding is the name of a process, whose objective is the seizing of a meaning. But a meaning is not a well defined entity, be it of an ideal order, which could be grasped in a simple act of apprehension. It is rather a set of indications which orientate the mind in a certain direction, which induces it to see the world in a certain way, in a particular perspective. This is already true of a simple predicate. A predicative term has the function, in the context of language, to open a given perspective upon the world. This perspective is suggested by the paradigmatic cases where this term has already been used. But those cases are presented as only particular examples and let open the possibility of extensions in which the predicate will be used about other objects. Each new application of the predicate reveals a supplementary aspect of the property designated by the predicate, even if the new shade added to the already available specifications is extremely tenuous. This shows that meaning is not fixed once and for all but can evolve, becoming more restricted or on the contrary broader according to the history of the usage which is made of the predicate. The meaning has thus a character of potentiality: it is what makes the predicate applicable to certain objects, relevant for the description of those objects, the class of objects for which it is relevant not being closed. The actual applications transform partially the potentiality of the meaning in effectivity, but this transformation is, in principle, a never ending process. What can be said for the case of a predicate is valid a fortiori for the larger linguistic units, such as sentences and sequences of sentences forming a discourse. The task of understanding consists in entering in that potentiality of the meaning and so to participate, so to say, in the process by which it is progressively actualised. This process is directional: it aims at a semantic situation which would be the saturation of the meaning, it is to say a situation where all the potentiality of the meaning would have been exhausted. But that situation has only the character of a limit. This implies that the task of understanding is, in principle at least, infinite.

Now science as well as theology express themselves in articulated discourses made of sentences of different kinds that are organised according to some definite principles of construction, such as hermeneutic argumentation or report of an empirical confirmation. But behind those explicit embodiments of the scientific or theological creative activity, there is an aiming at understanding which works silently, does not appear as such in the manifest discourse, but which is the real moving force that animates the work of expression. What is searched for is a knowing capable of sustaining the pretension of being in accordance with the exigencies of truth. The task of understanding a particular discipline is thus divided in two steps: there is the understanding of the explicit discourse, and there is the understanding of that aiming, which underlies the discourse. But this one is the key for the first one. Now that aiming, which relates itself to an adequate understanding of a particular reality, is itself a self-understanding of the discipline concerned. This one is led in its concrete work by a constitutive project, which is active but not quite clear to itself. It becomes more and more precise and more perceptible as the work advances, revealing itself to itself by the product which it generates. And correlatively the self-understanding succeeds in catching more of the meaning of its own enterprise. The understanding of a discipline is thus fundamentally, before being the understanding of its explicit discourse, understanding of its internal aiming, it is to say of its own self-understanding. And to understand such a self-understanding is to enter into the movement of that self-understanding, that is, into the progressive self-discovery of the discipline concerned. To understand in such a way is to understand with the other, to perform again his own performance, to assume for oneself the internal act by which the other assumes for himself his constituting project.

But this implies that a true understanding of the other cannot be obtained from inside. To interpret another field of research from one's own point of view is necessarily to reduce it to that point of view and so to miss what was precisely to be discovered in the other. On the other hand the interpreter cannot take purely and simply the place of the other: the dialogue demands that every participant remains himself. Thus mutual understanding requires that each one come out of himself while remaining nevertheless himself. This is possible only if there is so to say a common place between the two participants in the dialogue, in other words a mediating agency. Let us call that process of mutual understanding hetero-understanding".

Now, as demanded by our stronger condition, that reciprocal understanding must lead toward a reciprocal fructification and from that move which enables each protagonist of the dialogue to enter in the self-understanding of the other. He must be able also to come back to himself and to wonder what would be implied for his own self-understanding in what he has learned from the self-understanding of the other, as well for what concerns his fundamental project as for what concerns his particular theses. The aim of that second process is of course not to transform oneself in the other but to deepen one's own self-understanding, to become more faithful to one's constituting intention. But the possibility of such an interiorisation of the other must be founded upon a real basis. And that basis cannot be but the reference to a common domain of reality. Theology, for example, will be able to take advantage of such or such scientific theory only on the condition that the domain of reality for which that theory is relevant could reveal itself as belonging to its own field of study. Of course, such a condition does not ask that this overlapping between the two domains be immediately visible. At first sight the fragment of the real to which the theory under consideration is pertaining could appear as completely alien to the domain of theology. But a reflection on the constitution of that reality could show that it sends back to a more fundamental domain and that this one belongs precisely to theology, even if it is only by implication and not as a primary evidence. Let us call this process of recognising a common domain of reference co-referentiality".

Now we must raise the question: how are hetero-understanding and co-referentiality possible? As already mentioned, each one of the protagonists must be able to go out of himself without however transforming himself in the other. They need a mediation, that is, an intermediary field which would be a common field where an encounter is made possible, according to the conditions demanded by an authentic dialogue. That common mediating field exists: it is philosophy. We can already say, on the basis of what precedes, that the role of philosophy, in the dialogue between science and theology, is to be, between them, a mediating agency. But that assertion must be justified.

In order to ensure a dialogue, a mediation is needed. The status of mediation, in general, is to bring together two terms, apparently heterogeneous, by creating between them a communication, through the intervention of a third term. In order to play its role, that third term must replace what was only a contiguity by a relation of continuity. Therefore, it must be partially homogeneous to each one of the terms which it unites, it is to say it must have something of the nature of both of them. Could we say that philosophy has precisely that quality which would make of it the mediating term we are searching for? Could we say that it has some similarity with science on the one hand and with theology on the other hand?

It is appropriate to recall here the Aristotelian conception of philosophy, which has deeply influenced the western philosophical tradition. For Aristotle, as it is well known, science, episteme, is authentic knowledge,

governed by the idea of apodicticity. And such a knowledge is knowledge
of the principles and from the principles. Philosophy, the discourse of
wisdom, is science in the highest sense: it is the knowledge of the first
principles and the first causes", as it is explained in the first book of the
Metaphysics. It is therefore the most universal one ; and by having the
science of the supremely universal, the philosopher knows everything,
because all the particular cases fall under the universal." Two precisions
are given about that universality of the philosophical knowing. In the beginning of Book gamma, we find the famous sentence: There is a science
which is studying the being as being and the attributes which belong essentially to it." This expresses indeed the most general point of view which
is conceivable by the human mind about reality: the absolutely first principles, object of the highest science, "are necessarily also the elements of
the being as being." But in the Books epsilon and kappa, Aristotle explains
that "the first science has as object beings at the same time separated and
motionless." And he is led to distinguish three kinds of "theoretical philosophy": mathematics, physics and theology. This one, which is also
called "first philosophy", deserves that title because "it is certain that if
the divine is present somewhere, it is present in that motionless and separated nature." That double precision about the object of philosophy has
raised a very difficult problem of interpretation. The solution of that difficulty must be found very probably in the idea that, for Aristotle, being
is primarily substance and that those beings which are outside the realm
of motion are substances in the most perfect way. But, however that question of interpretation may be, we find in those texts of the Metaphysics
that very interesting indication that in the idea of philosophy there are at
the same time some fundamental characters which make of it a science
and some fundamental characters which make of it a theology.

The most profound inspiration which is at the root of the idea of
science remains certainly relevant for what we call usually "science" today as well for what we call nowadays "philosophy"; but we have to take
account of the splitting which has occurred in the modern times between
those two realms of theoretical reason. Husserl, still in the beginning of
this century, has defended the idea of philosophy "as rigorous science".
But, even in his conception, philosophy has been led to revise completely
its self-understanding and to conceive its proper task as clearly distinct
from the task of science. Nevertheless, something remains, in the present
state of philosophy, of what Aristotle explained so decidedly. It could be
said that philosophy aims at the understanding of reality as such, in its
very unfolding as reality, and therefore, by the same movement, of the
totality. Such an understanding must be articulated in concepts and the
concepts in which that radical universality can be thought must have the
status of principles. A principle is, according to the metaphor used by
Aristotle, "the source from which being, or generation or knowledge de-

rives." We find here again the idea of science. And it must be underlined that what we call science today retains fundamentally also that function of the principles. The ideal of the theoretical explanation is well to be able to deduce all the properties of the object from some highly general hypothesised statements. It is thus clear that, through that idea of a knowing according to principles, philosophy and science still belong to a common ground.

On the other hand, while studying the structure of the real in totality, philosophy is led to meet the problem of finitude: how is the status of the finite being possible? The search for the principles has been specified as the search for the foundations. Reflection shows that the finite being is not able to be its own foundation. What is then the nature of the foundation? Is it a prime mover, as for Aristotle, or the One, as for Plotinus, or the universal and unique substance, as for Spinoza, or a personal reality as in the metaphysics of creation? Without entering in the discussions that punctuate the history of metaphysics, it can be said at least that, while trying to find an answer to the question of the foundation, philosophy aims formally at that reality to which religious thinking and experience are referring when they speak of God. The formal point of view of philosophy orientates thus the thinking, if not, properly speaking, toward the God of faith, at least toward that region of being which is the ontological place of the divine being. We could think here to the term "heavens", used metaphorically by the Christian prayer to designate the proper realm of God. In this sense at any rate, philosophy can be considered as having also a proximity of essence with theology. By uncovering the universal perspective, which contains in itself the requirement of the foundation, it thus discovers a domain of encounter between the sciences, understood as endeavour of understanding according to principles, and the realm of the divine, to which, for its part, religious faith is referring.

But we meet here a difficulty of great magnitude. Christian theology does not speak of God as metaphysical principle, be it in the context of a conception of God as creator, but, to take again the words of Pascal, of the God of Abraham, of Isaac, of Jacob, of the God of Jesus-Christ, "not of the philosophers and of the learned ones". And it can speak of God in this sense only because God himself has revealed himself to mankind in an historical process, which has its decisive and in a sense definitive moment in the life, the death and the resurrection of Christ. It is in those events that the Christian faith recognises the reality of God and the salvation which is offered to us in Jesus Christ. That means that theology relates itself to an existential reality and that its discourse is soteriological, not cosmological nor ontological.

Now, we must take account, in relation to the question which is thus raised, of the internal evolution of philosophy to which it has been referred already. There is a decisive turning point in the history of western philosophy, which is very explicitly present in the philosophy of Kant, but which is of course of a much wider scope than what is proper to that particular philosophy. When it became apparent, especially after the publication of the Principia Mathematica of Newton, that the methods of physics were able to provide by themselves fundamental principles capable of giving account in an extraordinarily adequate way of the natural phenomena, philosophy had to redefine its own methods and, first of all, to conceive more precisely its specific object. The answer to the challenge presented by the new science was the discovery of the transcendental point of view, which, after all, can be considered as being but a specification of the old idea of the ascent toward the realm of the principles. In kantian terms, the domain of the transcendental is the domain of the conditions of possibility. This domain is of course not another realm of reality. The real reveals itself to us under the form of the phenomena, in the Greek sense of the word: what appears, what shows itself, what gives itself to be seen, what comes in presence. But the intelligibility of the phenomenon, what gives to it to come in the field of presence and to give itself to be understood, is not given as phenomenon. Nevertheless it belongs to the very structure of the real, as coming to us in what it shows of itself, in the phenomena. The transcendental is that stratum in the structure of the worldly reality, which is responsible for its phenomenalisation. Kant built a theory of the transcendental in the perspective, inherited from Descartes, which gives a methodological primacy to the knowing subject, with this justification that after all reality as such is accessible and meaningful for us only in the measure where it shows itself to us and that this donation is necessarily for us as receivers, that is, as subjects.

The idea of the transcendental has been revived in the beginning of this century by Husserl, in his project of philosophy as phenomenology, science of the phenomenalisation of the phenomena. In his works there is still to a certain extent a priority given to the subjectivist conception of philosophy, but in the course of the century phenomenology has tried to free itself from the opposition between subject and object and to construct itself with the aid of concepts neutral so to say with respect to that distinction, for example the concept of experience, as denoting that process in which an uprising of sense occurs. And phenomenology can be defined in that context as self-understanding of experience.

Its ambition is to discover in the last instance not so much how experience is structured but how it happens, how the general field of sense is constituted and how the particular fields of emergence of sense are constituted, how the general field that embraces all occurrences determines itself as nature, as life, as self-consciousness, as knowing, as will, as affectivity. Now experience is encounter, revelation of the world, but it is at the same time assumption of the self in its relation to the world, in the undertakings of knowing and of acting. As relation to itself, experience is the existence as such, that way of being real which consists in being oneself while always transcending oneself, in the movement of unceasing overcoming in which existence aims at something like the truth of itself. Existence, considered in that perspective of coming to itself, in the form of a radical question with respect to its own being, and correlatively in the feeling of a radical responsibility toward itself, is destiny.

Phenomenology places itself in a point of view from which it is able, at the same time, to show how science is possible and how it enters into the reality of history, and to show how existence unfolds itself and what is properly at stake in its becoming. The domain to which belong the conditions of possibility concerning science and those concerning existence can be called the domain of the original. In that term, which evokes an origin, we find something like an echo of the old notion of principle. There we have to do with an irreducible "datum", something which is simply given, as a matter of fact, and which can only be received such as it is. This "datum", which is uncovered by a kind of reductive analysis, coming back to the original, is not different from what appears visibly in perception, from what is immediately understood in the objects such as they show themselves, from what is naturally experienced in action, but that multiform reality which affects us in those different modalities of donation is seen, from the point of view of the original, in its uprising, in its genesis, in its unfolding, in the process of becoming phenomenon, of entering into experience.

Phenomenology analyses the relationship between man and the cosmic world, trying to describe how the world gives itself to existence, in perception and in action, and making explicit thereby the initial presupposition of science, that fundamental correlation which makes the world accessible and understandable. Science as such gives itself the task of articulating that intelligibility in conceptual representations, which, at best, take the form of theories. The role of phenomenology, with respect to that work, is to establish the possibility of theorisation, by showing the inrootedness of theoretical thought in perception. The analysis made by Husserl of "the origin of geometry" is a good example of that kind of achievement[1].

On the other hand, phenomenology shows also the possibility of the religious experience, not of course on the side of the initiative of God, but on the side of the human being, by analysing the receptivity which is the subjective condition of the experience of faith, as belonging to the very structure of existence in as much as it is destiny. That constitutive capacity of existence to be affected, in its very being, in its most essential possibilities, is the place in which it can be touched by the Word of God and by the grace of salvation. That capacity is reverberated in the structure of language, which lends itself to become the vehicle by which the Word of God says itself to the human being. As the language of theology is itself based on the primary language in which faith expresses itself, by showing the possibility, inscribed in the very texture of human language, of becoming the perceptible bearer of Revelation, the philosophical analysis of religious experience shows also the possibility of the theological language.

The two perspectives belong to the same field of genesis, which can be called, in a kantian terminology, the transcendental field. In that field science and theology can rejoin each other as emerging from the same fundamental realm of possibilities, inscribed in the very structure of existence. This transcendental field is the mediating agency that was searched for. And philosophy, as discourse of the transcendental, is the mediating discourse between the one of science and the one of theology.

* * *

But we must now try to show more concretely how philosophy plays this role, by evoking rapidly different questions which are precisely at the point of encounter between science and theology. For a part, those questions are of an epistemological nature, for another part they concern the very content of science and of theology. Among the epistemological questions, we could draw our attention more especially on the following ones, which are particularly significant: forms of language, forms of intelligibility, criteria of validity, specific realities.

The role of language is to convey meanings and to make possible communication about the different aspects of experience. The central philosophical problem raised by language concerns precisely the nature of meaning and the way in which meaning becomes a phenomenon and can manifest itself concretely and take an objective form, enabling exchange and recognition. Language, taken in its objective reality, is precisely the medium through which meaning is phenomenalised. The problem of the nature of meaning is inseparable from the problem of its phenomenalisation which consists in understanding how a system of conventional signs, which is purely combinatorial, can be the carrier of that fluid and impalpable entity which is called meaning. That problem is quite general and, as such, is the same for all types of language, but it takes particular specifications according to the kind of reality to which a particular language refers. A first task of philosophy, in the context of the dialogue science-theology, is to provide a detailed analysis of the ways in which the general problem of meaning is particularised in the case of science on the one hand and of theology on the other hand. The understanding of the mode of functioning of the other's language is a first step in the dialogue. In the two cases we have to do with the same fundamental difficulty: the language used must be able to speak of a reality that is not directly accessible to perception and therefore cannot have recourse to the simple means of reference which suffice for the description of the perceived world.

Science has to do with remote aspects of the constitution of empirical reality, for which it appears that ordinary language is no more appropriate. In the measure of the possible it has recourse to mathematical representations in order to describe the functioning of those hidden aspects of the World. But in order to explain the physical meaning of those representations it must use commentaries, formulated with the aid of ordinary language but which are not completely adequate, in such a way that they have to be corrected by some restrictive clauses. In some cases it happens that apparently contradictory commentaries must be invoked in order to convey a sufficiently adequate description of the object studied. The way in which the meanings are suggested is thus a very complex one and, in order to understand correctly what is exactly said, it is necessary to be fully conscious of the complicated interplay between abstract representation and use of images, through which a very subtle meaning can find its way.

Theology has to do with a spiritual reality which is accessible only, in its concrete effectivity, in the life of faith. Its language is so to say of the second order. It receives the content of what it tries to express in a systematic and elucidative way from the language of faith itself, in which the *kerygma* of revelation makes itself manifest. Its specificity comes from the mission to which it is devoted: to make explicit, as far as it is possible, the intrinsic intelligibility of the objective meaning of what is announced by the language of faith. But in order to assume that task, it has of course to enter itself in the dynamics of that meaning and in this sense its project is of an hermeneutic character. What it tries to do is to give to the very meaning conveyed by the source-language, the language of faith, something like a space of resonance where it will be able to give to hear its intelligible harmonics. The language of faith has recourse to analogies and metaphors in order to refer to the reality which it is making present. The use of parables in the Gospel is particularly representative of the way in which the language of faith can evoke what it calls itself "the kingdom of God". The language of theology, in the measure where it aims at making explicit what makes the language of faith understandable for human reason, has recourse to some terms borrowed from philosophy, whose help is appropriate in the measure where, for its part, philosophy tries to speak of the invisible which is at the principle of visible reality. But in order to use those terms in a relevant way, with respect to its proper task, it has to transmute their original meaning in order to make of them adequate carriers of the religious meanings which come from the source-language. That transmutation occurs according to the logic of a particular analogy, which reflects, on the level of that speculative language, the original analogy which is used by the language of faith, the analogy of faith, based in its turn on the kind of correlation which faith establishes itself between its own meaningfulness and the constitutive receptivity of the human soul.

That question of the types of language leads us immediately to the question of the forms of intelligibility. Here again we meet a philosophical problem of great import. In general terms, the intelligibility of a fragment of reality is what makes it understandable, apprehensible by that power of clarity which philosophical tradition has called "reason" and which is able to capture in the appearing reality that internal principle of enlightenment that is in it its value of universality. That the real as such is intrinsically intelligible is a basic philosophical thesis, in which is asserted the constitutive correspondence between the structure of reality and the structure of human reason. If the concept of reason is taken in a broad sense, as it is the case in that thesis, it can be said that the intelligibility of a fragment of reality is also its rationality, what makes it accessible to reason. Now what is proper to science and theology in that respect is the way in which each of them succeeds in making explicit the intrinsic intelligibility of their respective domains.

Very briefly, it can be said that science uses as a tool, in its proper mode of understanding, the method of model-building, which has been used already with great success by Greek science and which plays a central role in modern science. In relation with a real domain for which a formal theory has been elaborated, a model is an abstract structure on which that theory is realised and which, in the measure where the theory is verified, appears as an analogical representation of the real domain considered. The intelligibility of this one is, so to say, shown indirectly upon the model. It is the proper internal intelligibility of the model, what could be called its structural intelligibility, which projects itself onto the real domain and thus makes it intelligible in its turn by proxy. We understand the real object by understanding its model, or, as the case may be, its different possible models. The tool used by theology in order to make explicit the internal rationality of the content of faith is that remarkable property of the speculative concept, borrowed from philosophy, to lend itself to the dynamics of analogy. This one makes use of the meaning, which is already conveyed by the concept in its original context and takes advantage of the potentiality which is inherent to that meaning, in order to appropriate it to the new context constituted by the theological project, itself regulated by its relation with the sources through which it is in contact with its proper domain of reality. The original concept gives something of the suggesting power of its meaning, but that contribution is transmuted by its insertion in the field of attraction constituted by the content of faith, as assumed by the theological reflection. We have to do thus with two very different modes of reflecting intelligibility, but they have a common ground which is precisely the very idea of intelligibility and, correlatively, of rationality, in the broad sense of the term. And it is why the intervention of philosophy is clarifying and beneficial to the dialogue.

A third question which is relevant in our context is the question of validity. This question is raised already in the case of the most elementary statements, asserted with the claim of being valid. It is of course closely connected with the concept of truth and goes back to one of the most classical philosophical problems, concerning the status and the role of that fundamental value. When we have to do with a set of statements constituting a "theory" in the broad sense of the word, it is implicitly admitted that we have to be able to judge it with respect to its validity and, correlatively, to its acceptability. The problem is then not only to make more precise that idea of validity but also to build a criterion of judgement about that validity. The concept of truth, which has been built precisely in order to give a definite status to the vague idea of validity, has received different meanings, but it can be said that, finally, those different versions of the concept send back to a canonical sense, based upon the idea of correspondence. If that is accepted, the practical problem is to determine how the supposed correspondence can be ascertained.

In the case of science, that problem takes primarily the form of the problem of assessment of a theory. As a direct comparison with the empirical data is not possible, the method used is a comparison between some of the statements, which can be deduced from the theory and some of the empirical statements already accepted as valid. But that method meets two difficulties. On the one hand that process of indirect verification can never be considered as definitively conclusive, since it is not possible to test empirically all the statements deducible, in principle, from the theory, and since, therefore, it is always possible to encounter some day a case that would disprove the theory. And on the other hand the acceptation of an empirical statement depends finally on a decision which can be pragmatically justified but which is not based itself on a process of verification according to the canonical method. The status of the "basic statements" is necessarily different from the status of the statements which are based on them. This entails that the truth of a scientific theory must be considered as always relative to a process of verification which can never come to a definitive end. This does not contradict the fact that there are theories which have passed successfully so many tests that they can be confidently considered as firmly established and highly reliable in practice. It must be added that very often a theory which appears to be invalid with respect to certain tests can be perfectly accepted as practically valid on the condition that its domain of relevance be strictly delimited.

In the case of theological statements, the criterion that imposes itself for the assessment of their value is their faithfulness to the source-language from which it depends. The process being of an hermeneutic nature, the validity must be measured by its capacity to follow the suggestions enclosed in the original meanings and to unfold them without distortion. But the judgement in this case presupposes, on the part of the judging agency, a familiarity with the meaning sufficient to make it possible to recognise in a theological commentary the authentic presence of the original meaning. And this raises finally the theological problem of the competence of the judge. To a certain extent theology has to be judged by theology: the judgement is itself an hermeneutic process, primarily with respect to the sources but secondarily, and nevertheless importantly also, with respect to the theological text itself submitted to the judgement. But there is no guarantee that a discussion between theologies will always be able to settle a difficulty. From a purely speculative point of view, the question could remain open. But from the practical point of view of the life of faith, in certain circumstances appeal must be made to an authority, recognised as an authentic representative of the tradition and as direct witness of the real content of faith. This introduces the theological criterion of the recourse to the magisterium. In all this context, by helping to clarify what is at stake in this question of validity, philosophy helps also the protagonists to recognise more adequately how their respective projects meet the problem of truth.

In relation to that question, we have to take account also of the question concerning the respective realities wherewith science and theology are concerned. If there is a question of validity, it is evidently in function of the relation that is supposed to be established between a particular discourse and the reality upon which it is bearing. The philosophical problem here is to determine more precisely what "reality" in general means, and from there what "reality" in the case of particular methods of inquiry means.

As far as science is concerned, it is normally accepted that it refers to the reality of the visible world, such as it discloses itself primordially in perception. But the success of the scientific method depends from some methodological measures through which the point of view taken with respect to that reality has been strictly defined. The distinction introduced between primary and secondary qualities, in the seventeenth century, is a good example of such measures. More generally, it can be said that the "natural world" which science investigates is not the world of perception as such but a reduced world, extracted so to say from the world of perception and accessible. at least in principle, to a method of representation by mathematical structures. The implicit presupposition which is present in the constitution of that reduced nature is that the world, as science is viewing it, is a coherent totality, completely accessible to empirical investigation and to mathematical representation, and which contains in itself all the properties by which all its appearances can be explained. The understanding of such a reality consists in reconstructing the connections between the particular phenomena, ideally by deduction from very general principles, supposed immanent in that reality itself and mirrored in our representations. It could be said that the proper domain of science is cosmological.

Theology, on the other hand, being relative to what is made manifest in the language of faith, refers itself, in its discourse, to a reality which is of an event-like status, the salvation in Jesus Christ. That reality is present in human history and gives signs of its presence which are visible in the world, but it is not at all worldly, since it implies an encounter between God and mankind, which culminates in the event of the Incarnation of the eternal divine Logos. Made, in its visibility, by successive events which constitute a specific history, it introduces in the human world a new temporality, which is essentially determined by its eschatological structure. And it appeals, in the concrete life of man, to that dimension of existence where it is a question for itself, about its quality, its meaning, its destiny, where it becomes fully conscious of that adversity which affects human condition and to which theology refers as the presence of evil in the world, and where it raises also the request of hope, in the expectation of what could be for it a salvation. It could thus be said that the proper domain of theology is existential. This does not mean at all that it is of a purely subjective character. It is wholly objective, being based primarily on the intervention of God in human history. If it can be called "existential" it is because it concerns human existence as such in its destinal character.

We have to encounter now questions concerning the very content of science and of theology. Three of them will be taken here in consideration: interpretability of science for theology and reciprocally, relation of science and theology to the general horizon of sense, existence as field of encounter between science and theology.

As already recalled, science has recourse to abstract representations, which, in the most successful cases, take the form of mathematical representations. Those representations are accompanied by commentaries expressed in ordinary language, which simplify the understanding of the representations themselves. But we must perhaps distinguish between the commentaries which have a purely pedagogical role and which make use of more or less suggestive images, and those commentaries which are really intrinsic, in this sense that they are necessary in order to indicate what kind of information is really provided by the representation. That question is connected with the preceding one: to explain what is properly described by a representation is to ask to what kind of reality it refers. This type of question is perfectly illustrated by the problem of the interpretation of quantum mechanics. We have to do there with a formal theory which gives very accurate predictions but which can be used even without precision about the exact referential correlate of the "wave function". Nevertheless it seems that the explanatory power of the theory remains uncertain as long as we have no explanation about that reference. The different interpretations that are in discussion are not extrinsic aids giving an approximate idea of the scope of the theory but an indispensable component of a satisfactory understanding of the theory itself. There are also questions which are not intrinsic to the understanding of a theory but which can be raised about a theory, supposed correctly understood. Those questions belong to what can be called "philosophy of nature". For example, the structure of quantum mechanics suggests questions about the role of chance in the constitution of the physical world. The same type of question is suggested also, in another context, by evolutionary biology, the question concerning then the domain of life. Analogously there are questions which are suggested by the so-called "human sciences" and which belong by themselves to the philosophy of mind, for example concerning the possibility of a free will. The answer which can be given to questions of that type depends, of course, on the way in which the theory under consideration is understood and thus they send back to questions of the preceding type. In any case it seems that the scientific conceptions do have an interest for theology not so much in the formal representations as such but mainly in the interpretations which elucidate their meaning and in the contribution which those interpretations can bring to some philosophical problems. Now it seems that the problems of interpretation cannot be treated without making explicit some fundamental presuppositions which are implied in the way in which the theory is constructed and in particular in the way in which the hypotheses are formulated. And those presuppositions are of a philosophical nature. The role of philosophy, on the other hand, is evident in the case of the problems which appear at the juncture between physical sciences and philosophy of nature or between human sciences and philosophy of mind.

In the case of theology, it seems, a philosophical interpretation of the preceding type is not necessary, since the discourse of theology is formulated in terms of ordinary language, enriched by specific concepts whose meaning is explained explicitly by the contexts of their use. Nevertheless, from the point of view of a purely scientific thinking, accepting only the kind of facts which are accessible by the methods of science, the reality to which the theological discourse is referring could be considered as completely meaningless, And theology itself could be considered therefore as devoid of any interest. Now there is a philosophical approach to religious experience and religious discourse, both on the basis of the metaphysical question of foundation and on the basis of the phenomenological analysis of religious experience as reported for example by mystics. Without substituting itself for theology philosophy can thus show that theology is perfectly meaningful, as corresponding at least to fundamental possibilities which belong to the structure of human existence, and this could be acceptable even for somebody for whom the existence of God remains completely doubtful. Such a philosophical interpretation of the theological discourse would be able to make it understandable by scientific thinking and thus contribute to the dialogue also in the direction from theology toward science.

The question concerning the type of reality which is implied respectively in the work of science and in the work of theology is essentially a question of reference. But there is another aspect of that question about the reality concerned: it is the question of meaning, understood in its strictest sense, as distinct from the question of reference. In other words, it is the question of the point of view under which the reality concerned is considered, or of the particular perspective which is opened about that reality. That perspective is determined by the project of understanding which is at the basis of a discipline. And in the dialogue it is important to recognise as clearly as possible what is that project: it specifies exactly what can be expected from the discourse which it sets in motion. Here again the philosophical analysis can clarify what is at stake and how the general problem of sense is refracted in the particular disciplines that are in discussion. The concept of sense is one of the most elusive ones. As it designates that by virtue of which there are meanings in our life and in our discourses, it would be rather circular to ask its meaning. But nevertheless the content of the idea of sense can be suggested by the different contexts where we are led to say that some situation, action or word is sensed or senseless. What is clear is that this concept is of a strategic importance in the analysis of human existence, since it designates that horizon from which language, action, encounter, thinking, volition, affectivity, receive what makes of them components of a form of life penetrated by a fundamental and universal clarity, for which the world is understandable and which can be present to itself as responsible of its own being. Human life is so to say immersed in a stream of particular meanings which constitutes, in its totality, the life of sense. The question which can be raised for what concerns the dialogue science-theology is to specify what are their respective contributions to the life of sense. That contribution consists, for each of them, in the way in which they suscitate their own meanings, the particular kind of clarity which they project on reality. Science starts from the world of perception but constitutes itself, as already recalled, by a process of separation which transforms that world in the constructed world of scientific representations. The link with the first world however is not lost: what science is doing is to reconstruct the world disclosed in perception in such a way as to give account of the appearance by going beyond the appearance and to make thus apparent its intrinsic intelligibility. Its contribution to the life of sense is thus precisely to reveal that intelligibility. Theology explains how the form of life induced by Christian faith confers to human existence a new meaning, by introducing it in the process of salvation whose finality is to make man a participant of the very life of God. It concerns thus existence as destiny, and its contribution to the life of sense is to illuminate existence by making clearer for it what Christian predication really means for it. We find again here, naturally, the difference between a cosmological and an existential domain. But we find also positive indications about the possibility of encounter between science and theology.

What philosophy, as mediation between science and theology, can suggest, finally, is that the appropriate place for the effective encounter between them is existence, understood as the mode of being which is characteristic of human reality and viewed as the concrete carrier of the life of sense. Both science and theology contribute to the self-understanding by which existence becomes aware of its significance. Science gives it to understand how it is inserted in the cosmic and in the socio-historical world, and theology gives it to understand how it is called to inscribe itself freely in the life of faith. It is in the relationship between those two components of the self-understanding of existence that science and theology can meet each other concretely in an authentic exchange. And that relationship constitutes the general framework in which the particular questions raised on the borders of science and theology can be adequately treated. It is the case for example for the questions of the origin of the universe, of the origin of man, of the relation between contingency and necessity, of what is called "the anthropological difference", of the meaning of ethics, of the different forms of historicity, of the signification of the plurality of religions, of the psychological bases of religious experience, and so on.

In this general framework, for each of the problems which are arising, the way in which science and theology will be put in contact with each other will consist in putting in contact the meanings that the two sides of the problem have for existence. On the one hand we have to do with a presentation of models which function as instruments of intelligibility. On the other hand we have to do with the presentation of a *kerygma*. The scientific model will have a relevance for theology only in the measure where it gets in touch with existence there where the theological word, in its turn, gets in touch with it, that is to say in its ultimate self-understanding. This means that the scientific discourse must be understood not only as an objective knowing, which would remain external with respect to the life of existence, but as affecting existence in its apprehension of itself. For example, it can suggest that mankind is lost in the universe and that this one is completely unconcerned about his fate, or that the universe is for him a favourable dwelling place which he can habitate. It can suggest that human destiny is completely determined by the laws which govern the course of the cosmos, or that man has the power to orientate the natural determinisms, at least partly, according to his own finalities. It can suggest that human life is carried away in a cyclic time or that it is immersed in an evolutionary time. Each one of those alternatives, having a direct meaning for existence as such, raises a definite question for theology.

And, on the other hand, the theological word will have a relevance for science only in the measure where it is able to give rise in the scientific thinking to a resonance which will make it receptive for what the theological word is suggesting. And such a state of resonance can arise only if that word gets in touch with scientific thought there where it is sensitive to the presentiment of a meaning which is beyond its reach, be it through the experience of limits, or through the discovery of the profundity of the cosmic reality, or in the feeling of the enigmatic character of the world. But that sensitivity for what is beyond its own possibilities can be aroused only if it is in contact with a reality which is already by itself openness to a possible encounter with something which is beyond its own limits. That reality is existence, there where it can be reached by the theological word. This means that theology will have a relevance with respect to scientific thinking only if it can get in touch with it through the mediation of existence.

But beyond the task of clarification which is called for by those different questions, there is, for philosophy, a task which has a methodological priority because it refers to the very possibility of the dialogue: to explain what science and theology have in common, despite their differences. Theology itself gives a decisive indication here when it thinks

itself as science. We could cite here a well known text of Saint Thomas:
" Definitely, theology is a science. [...] It proceeds indeed from principles
belonging to a superior science, which is nothing else here than the very
science of God and of the blessed" (*Summa Theologiae*, I, qu. 1, art. 2).
Saint Thomas refers here explicitly to the Aristotelian idea of science: it
is a knowing according to principles. What specifies theology is that it
receives its principles from God himself, in the Revelation. Some years
ago Mgr. Tshibangu took again that question of the scientificity of theology in a book entitled *Theology as science in the twentieth century*[2].
He examines, in this book, in what measure the modern idea of science,
as emerging from the historical development of the so-called "positive
sciences", remains relevant for theology. One of his main concerns is
precisely to show in what sense theology must be recognised as a "positive science". His argument is that "theology is characterised first and
foremost as science of a "'given' which imposes itself to us" (p. 160).
This characterisation, however, important as it is, does not eliminate the
reference to the classical conception which, as we have seen, conveys the
leading idea of authentic knowing. It would be appropriate to add that
the contribution of modern science is perhaps rather to underline the capacity of science to ensure systematically by its own means its progress,
at the same time in extension and in growth of intelligibility. This is made
possible by the self-reflection of science, which controls critically its own
procedures. It is also appropriate to recall that theology also includes in
its work that self-critical moment. In any case it refers itself to the objective factuality disclosed by the word of Revelation in as much as it
lends itself to a reflexive reappropriation aiming at the intrinsic intelligibility of that factuality. The disclosure of that intelligibility is understanding. Here lies the justification of the recourse to the idea of science:
the best way of obtaining understanding is to read what is given in the
light of its principles. It is important to notice that philosophy has not at
all invented a priori the idea of science. This idea was suggested by the
different practices of argumentation aiming at a true knowledge. The role
of philosophy has been to bring out what was implicitly operating in
those practices. It has still today the task of reflecting on what is implicitly
active in the different disciplines which, in many different ways, participate of the idea of science. And theology is among those disciplines.

But a part of this general task is to show where lies the distinctive
difference between theology and the other sciences, or in what sense exactly theology can be said to be a "positive science". And here it could
be useful to introduce a distinction between the order of constitution and
the order of event. The constitution is what gives a reality to be what it
is, its kind of being, its properties, its potentialities, the principles of its
becoming. In metaphysical or in theological terms we could say that the
constitution of the world is what it is by creation. It is a central aspect

of creation that the created reality is endowed with all the capacities which must enable it to attain by itself its natural finality. The event is what occurs as something new, as unexpected, as a discontinuity in the course of a becoming, bringing new possibilities, opening new perspectives. This concept applies to what happens in history as purely contingent facts. But it applies in a particularly strong sense to the historical process of salvation such as it is understood by faith. The theological concept of "economy" expresses exactly the event-like character of what is, essentially, the object of theology. It refers to that divine plan, evoked by Saint Paul in the Epistle to the Ephesians (3.9), which was hidden in God from all eternity and which is now revealed through Jesus Christ and through the Holy Spirit. The factuality which makes of theology a "positive science" is the reality of that *oikonomia* in which is revealed the meaning of those signs through which the grace of salvation is bestowed on us. But redemption is at the same time the opening of a new life and restoration of an integrity which has been lost. The order of redemption presupposes and brings to its fulfilment the order of creation. It is that relation between those two orders which is the key of the relation between science and theology. It is the task of theology to explain it. Philosophy, for its part, could help theology in proposing the concepts by means of which that task could be accomplished. The last word belongs to theology.

NOTES

1. E. HUSSERL, "Die Frage nach der Ursprung der Geometrie als intentional-historisches Problem" (1936), *Revue Internationale de Philosophie* (Bruxelles), 1939, 203-225. Trad. franç. par J. DERRIDA: *L'origine de la geometric*, Paris, Presses Universitaires de France, 1962.

2. T. TSHIBANGU, *La theologie comme science au XXème siecle*, Kinshasa, Presses Universitaires du Zaire, 1980, 248 p.

THE LANGUAGE OF SCIENCE
AND THE LANGUAGE OF THEOLOGY

ALFRED KRACHER

(*Iowa, USA*)

Abstract: The notion of incommensurability has been advanced to claim that adherents of rival scientific theories cannot fully understand each other. If this is true even within science, is there any hope for understanding between the scientist and the theologian? Serious consideration must be given to the philosophical criticism of incommensurability, i.e., arguments that show how communication across theories, and by extension across disciplines, is possible. The parallel consideration of (a) rival scientific theories of light, and (b) scientific and theological understandings of creation show that problems arise from potentially resolvable misunderstandings rather than an unremediable lack of understanding. Some theologians have tried to minimise communication problems by adopting a "scientific" way of speaking, for example by transferring the scientific concept of complementarity into the science-theology dialogue. However, since the subject matters are irreducibly different, this approach creates its own problems. Analysing potential language problems between science and theology can lead to some practical suggestions on how to improve mutual understanding.

How does dialogue between different areas of thought take place? In our post-positivist age the idea of a neutral language in which disagreements and misunderstandings can be adjudicated has become discredited. Instead a notion has gained ground that theoretical systems may be *incommensurable* (Kuhn 1970; Feyerabend 1981, 147-161). This is a disturbing thought when we consider the prospects for a dialogue between very different areas, such as science and theology.

While the notion of incommensurability has been applied to different views of the same subject, for example, archaic vs. classical Greek art, or Newtonian vs. relativistic physics (Feyerabend, 1988), its proponents have paid less attention to how it may affect dialogue between different fields. However, arguments about incommensurability give us every reason to suspect that communication between fields is no less difficult than between rival systems within the same field. Do scientists and theologians actually talk to each other in any meaningful way, or is it all an illusion; does the dialogue, to paraphrase Feyerabend (1988, 226), merely consist in "argumentation by equivocation"?

In this paper I want to ask first how communication across fields such as scientific disciplines and theologies is possible, and then examine some strategies that purport to facilitate this dialogue. It will be seen that some practical conclusions for the science-religion dialogue can be drawn from this consideration.

The issue of understanding arises only if there is a perceived necessity for dialogue. There are at least two necessary requirements for this. First, there has to be some overlap in subject matter between science and theology. If we conceive of theology as limited to unobservable reality, juxtaposed to a strictly empirical science, dialogue is neither possible nor necessary. Second, there has to be a kind of epistemological common ground to get the dialogue started. Something has to be shared that can be used as a medium of exchange. Nancey Murphy (1990, 120), for example, claims that within Catholic theology modernism can be reconstructed as a "research program" in the sense of Lakatos, but (neo)scholasticism cannot. Murphy does not elaborate on the latter,[1] but one possible reason that emerges from her discussion is that neo-scholastics may want to deny that anything they deal with has the same ontological status as data in science.

Murphy's reconstruction does not necessarily make modernism commensurable with whatever scientific system it may come in contact (for example, anthropology or psychology). However, with regard to neo-scholasticism and natural science the question does not even arise. The practical manifestation of this is the frequently encountered attitude that there is literally "nothing to talk about" between (this type of) theology and science. But the demand that two phenomena that are thus completely disjointed can lay coequal claim to being about "reality" would likely lead to an intolerable case of cognitive dissonance, and most people seem to intuitively reject it.

There are epistemological as well as psychological reasons for rejecting this balkanisation of reality. The traditional kind of theology in question here depends on a form of realism. To the extent that science and theology are both about reality, they will necessarily encounter one another in at least some quadrants of this reality-space. At the time of Galileo, when the object of science was largely the inanimate world, it was perhaps plausible to believe in some kind of demarcation that would keep science and theology in separate areas. But in the age of psychology, ethnology and evolutionary biology this kind of separation is untenable.

The only way to maintain the separation is to give up traditional notions of "reality". This causes little difficulty for science, which can get along fine with an instrumentalist epistemology. There are theologies, such as fideist or existentialist ones, that likewise can survive giving up realism, but to traditional, dogmatic theology this move is fatal. This kind of theology is either about some of the same aspects of reality that are also within the domain of science, and hence has to engage in some kind of communication with it, or it is about nothing.

Rather than retreating into isolationism, it makes much more sense to assume that there is a range of issues on which scientists and theologians do actually want to conduct a dialogue, because there is a sense that in some areas their disciplines overlap. The titles of previous conferences in this series provide an exemplary list of such issues. But what are the prospects that mutual understanding is actually possible?

To illustrate similarities and differences between the situations of intra-disciplinary rivalry and cross-disciplinary dialogue let us look, in a somewhat simplistic way, at the semantic problems in the understanding of two concepts, *light and creation*.[2] When Newton was expounding his scientific theory of light, the existence of light corpuscles was a constitutive element of his concept. He could not argue about the properties of light without implying something about the behaviour of particles. Huygens, on the other hand, interpreted the same properties as the behaviour of waves. Thus, proponents of the incommensurability thesis would say, they were really talking about different things. They could not make a rational choice as to who was right, because they could not understand each other.

Not so, says Bishop (1991). What Newton meant by the term *light* depended, like all our terms, to some extent on the situation in which he used it. When he told his servant, "bring me a light", the servant, who probably didn't even know about waves and corpuscles, understood him quite well. Huygens may not have shared all of Newton's implications of the term *light*, but he certainly did not understand *any less* than the servant. Newton and Huygens could build on this limited understanding, which one may call the "vernacular residue" of meaning, and reach at least agreement that they had rival theories about the same phenomenon. That neither scientist changed his mind was not due to the epistemological impossibility of rational choice, but to the contingent fact that the evidence on either side was insufficient.

The semantic basis of understanding between the rivals can be seen in two different ways. Either the definition of *light* that served as their starting point was essentially ostensive, then this fact provided them with a referential foothold they had in common. Or, if their definition was indeed in terms of their abstract theories, they were capable of deliberately bracketing out those aspects of the definition that they did not share. Thus both of them worked with a definition of *light* that was less restrictive[3] than they perhaps would have preferred, but rich enough to allow them some form of mutual understanding.

Reaching even this minimal level of understanding is not always easy in the science-theology dialogue. Many scientists who talk about *creation* project their own interest in physical origins onto the concept without being aware that this is precisely the aspect they have to bracket out if they want to have a meaningful talk with theologians (Kracher 1994). By now it should be clear that, unlike the situation between the particle and wave theories of light, creation as used in theological discourse is *not* a rival physical theory for the origin of the world. Strictly speaking, it never has been, because the modern notion of a physical origin cannot be imputed to pre-scientific narratives. History has not falsified creation stories, but merely clarified the distinction between factual and symbolic narratives. That creation stories are still often treated as if they were originally meant to describe physical origins merely underlines the difficulties in clarifying concepts.

In the case of creation stories it turns out to be impossible to invoke a referential foothold, because the nature of the referent is partly what is at issue. When Newton and Huygens disagreed about the nature of light, they did have a range of phenomena they could agree on. Conversely, it is a matter of considerable consequence whether we regard the scientists' *universe* and the theologians' *creation* as identical, and there is no agreement about the answer. The scientific emphasis on facticity, as contrasted with the ethical dimension constitutive of the term *creation*, makes it difficult to maintain the identity of the two concepts (Kracher 1994).

Of course, scientists and theologians might simply agree that their uses of *creation* are equivocal, but that does not quite resolve the misunderstanding either. It would make little sense to say that to a scientist the statement "God created the world" is false, while for a theologian it is true, because the verb *to create* has entirely different meanings to them.[4] A more sophisticated conceptual investigation is required before we can connect the statement to both the scientific and the theological context in a meaningful way.

Even if there are such examples of genuine semantic obstacles, which cannot be immediately resolved, Bishop's analysis suggests that they do not necessarily become worse with increasing distance between fields. Usually it is precisely the situation of rival theories about particular physical phenomena where concepts become so "rarefied", so detached from their everyday use, that the recourse to less restrictive definitions (or vernacular "fuzziness", as it is sometimes called) might be in jeopardy. It may simply mean that scientists and theologians will have to stay with a simpler language, which may be imprecise, but carry enough contextual richness to allow for common ground. In a sense, such recourse to non-technical language matches the non-technical content of the dialogue. It is not the intradisciplinary details that scientists and theologians usually want to talk about, but questions like how we live our lives in the age of science. Epistemology aside, questions that are of such general importance need to be discussed in a sufficiently general language to engage the public affected by the issue at hand. Both theology and science have at times deserved the reproach of being unnecessarily arcane when they have tried to make points of public importance.

Is it always possible to work with a vernacular residue? Perhaps, but sometimes this layer of meaning is so thin that it cannot carry the dialogue. When a concept of this kind is used in one area it may look vacuous to the dialogue partner. This applies in particular to some of the Aristotelian categories popular in theology, but next to meaningless in science. It takes a great deal of work, for example, to make the concept of *final causes* scientifically intelligible; *substance* does have a vernacular meaning, but it is too vague to be of much use to a scientist. This is not to deny the possibility that Aristotelian concepts can be given a meaningful new definition by contemporary philosophers - Whitehead is an example of that. The point is rather that these concepts are still only useful within the system in which they are thus redefined. They do not have sufficient generally accepted content to help scientists and theologians understand each other.

Even short of the problem of stark vacuity, concepts reduced to the mutually understandable residue of meaning are necessarily fuzzy. This may have the advantage of making them rich enough for dialogue, but the required vagueness has its drawbacks. There is a danger that each side will refuse to take the other side seriously, since its concepts look primitive and crude from across the disciplinary boundary. Theologians have to convince scientists that this is not a deficiency inherent in theology, but dictated by the nature of the dialogue.

In this situation it is tempting to propose more contemporary terms for conducting the debate. In particular, scientific terms can import new and fruitful metaphors into other fields. This, however, has its own dangers. Scientific concepts can only become fruitful to other fields if they are sufficiently specific to give some force to their metaphorical use. There is no call to invoke the names of Einstein or Heisenberg, rather like patron saints, when one uses words such as *relativity* or *uncertainty* in their everyday meaning.

In the science-religion dialogue, *complementarity* is a case in point. If it is indeed understood in the sense in which Bohr first introduced it into physics, it has a valid place in philosophy and theology. The fact that there is serious discussion about the range of appropriate uses testifies to the fruitfulness of the concept. But this discussion also shows that concepts borrowed from science are only of use within a limited area of theology. It may be possible to employ complementarity as a way to conceptualise divine action in a world of physical laws, which is certainly important, but extending it to larger fields diminishes its usefulness by diluting its content. Unfortunately the same specificity that gives the metaphor its force leaves little hope that the entire architecture of a theological system can be rebuilt from nothing but the joists and beams of science-based concepts. Just like there are many scientific concepts that are more or less irrelevant to theology, the same is true in the opposite direction. Irrelevance to science does not mean that such concepts are vacuous, but we have to be aware that concepts that are largely internal to one field are of limited use in the science-religion dialogue.

This consideration should also serve as a caution that exporting the idea of constructing models from science into theology does not necessarily alleviate the problem of misunderstanding, nor avoid the charge of vacuity. When Ian Barbour made this proposition twenty years ago (Barbour 1974) it was more imperative than today to stress the similarities rather than the differences in conceptual constructs used by science and theology. The situation is different now, when one of the main proponents of "metaphorical theology" talks about "models of God" (McFague, 1982; 1987). The issue of using metaphorical and formal symbolisms in different areas requires a separate, more detailed investigation. It is obvious, however, that normalisation plays rather different roles in science and theology, respectively.

If the function of models in theology is patterned too closely on its use in science, another semantic problem similar to the one affecting creation can arise. We would do well to remember that constructing the complex, sophisticated theoretical systems that are the pride of science is exactly the kind of development that has in the past turned religion into repression when used by theology.

Our consideration of the limits of possible mutual understanding leaves us with some practical conclusions for the science-theology dialogue: (1) Not all theological systems can be partners in a genuine dialogue. (2) Misunderstandings, as in the case of *creation*, can happen, but are potentially resolvable with careful conceptual spadework. (3) Introducing highly specialised concepts into the dialogue may be counterproductive on either side; if they are used at all one must first ascertain how the other side understands them. (4) Potential vagueness of concepts is not a deficiency on the part of the dialogue partner, but a necessary feature of concepts used across fields that have very different contextual matrices. (5) Concepts derived from science can provide fruitful metaphors, but they do not necessarily reduce the conceptual gulf between scientists and theologians. (6) It is important to be as clear as possible as to what kind of job conceptual constructs such as models, metaphors, parables, etc. are doing in each of the fields.

Acknowledgements. Most of the changes that this paper has undergone since its presentation at the 6th European Conference on Science and Theology are due to the stimulating discussions in workshop 2b, for which I am grateful to the discussion partners. Michael Bishop helped to clarify several philosophical issues. Robert Hollinger was a wellspring of philosophical resources and provided much-needed encouragement.

NOTES

1. Murphy refers to "scholasticism" rather than neo-scholasticism, but the context makes clear that what she has in mind is a competitor of modernism.
2. The following discussion of *light* is based on Bishop (1991), the discussion of creation on Kracher (1994).
3. Calling this *less* restrictive may seem counterintuitive. A more limited definition is less restrictive, inasmuch as it allows for a larger range of phenomena to be included.
4. To be sure, a logical positivist would regard the statement as neither true nor false, but meaningless. The situation envisaged in this paper, viz. a dialogue between scientist and theologian, presupposes that both sides attach at least *some* meaning to the statement.

REFERENCES

Barbour, Ian G. 1974: *Myths, Model and Paradigms*. San Francisco: Harper & Row.

Bishop, Michael A. 1991: Why the Semantic Incommensurability Thesis is Self-Defeating.

Philosophical Studies 63, 343-356.

Feyerabend, Paul K. 1981: *Problems of empiricism* (collected papers, vol. 2). Cambridge University Press.

Feyerabend, Paul K. 1988: *Against Method* (2nd edition). London: Verso.

Kracher, Alfred 1994: The Concept of 'Creation' as Epistemological Critique. *Studies in Science and Theology* 2, 174-181.

Kuhn, Thomas S. 1970: *The Structure of Scientific Revolutions* (2nd edition), University of Chicago Press.

McFague, Sallie 1982: *Metaphorical Theology*. Philadelphia: Fortress Press.

McFague, Sallie 1987: *Models of God*. Philadelphia: Fortress Press.

Murphy, Nancey 1990: *Theology in the Age of Scientific Reasoning*. Ithaca, NY: Cornell University Press.

THE ROLE OF
METAPHYSICAL & RELIGIOUS BELIEFS
IN SCIENCE

JITSE M. VAN DER MEER
(*Ancaster, Canada*)

Abstract: Studies on the relationship between religion and science often focus on making religious beliefs and theological doctrine consistent with scientific explanations of reality. The presupposition underlying this approach is that science provides objective knowledge while religion and theology provide subjective beliefs, and that, therefore, science carries more weight than theology. Using examples from Christian theology and the natural sciences, I argue that Christian religious beliefs involve objective fact, and that scientific fact involves metaphysical and religious belief. I conclude that both Christian religious beliefs and science involve complexes of knowledge and belief, that it is through these complexes that they relate to each other, and that this ought to level the playing field between religion and science. I propose a model in which the interaction between religion and science is mutual and respects the integrity of both. This model is designed to replace the Enlightenment polarisation between objective science and subjective religion with a post-modern view of their interaction.

Keywords: Religion, relationship with science; religion, factual dimension of; religion, relationship with mathematics; religion, relationship with physics; religion, relationship with biology; objectivity, of science; objectivity, of Christian religious belief; subjectivity, of science; subjectivity, of religion; belief, metaphysical; belief, religious; Christianity.

INTRODUCTION

If the relationship between Christianity and the natural sciences (science for short) is to be constructive, each will have to respect the other's integrity. However, studies on the relation of Christianity and science are often one-sided, promoting tension by adjusting religious belief to science. This assumes that science provides objective knowledge, to be taken more seriously than the subjective beliefs of religious individuals. These assumptions have been questioned independently in two schools of thought in which it was recognised that so-called extra-scientific factors shape scientific knowledge. The exploration of religion as a force shaping knowledge first became an influential research program in The Netherlands through the work of the theologians Abraham Kuyper (1837-1920) and Herman Bavinck (1854-1921), the philosophers Dirk Vollenhoven (1892-1978) and Herman Dooyeweerd (1894-1977), and the historian of science Reijer Hooykaas (1906-1994) (van der Meer 1996b). The claim of a role for Christian faith in science was grounded by both Kuyper and Bavinck in the comprehensive effect of Christ's redeeming work.

Independently, similar work in Poland (Fleck 1935, tr.1979), the United Kingdom (Foster 1934, 1935-36; Polanyi 1946, 1958) and the United States (Kuhn 1962) led to a recognition of the role of so-called extra-scientific factors in shaping scientific knowledge. This development destroyed positivism (Suppe 1977) and triggered the relativism of the social consensus view of truth. Within the current philosophy of science this relativism has been eclipsed by the new semantic theory of theory (Suppe 1989; van Fraassen 1980), which entails the complete metaphysical and religious neutrality of theories and explanations in science. On this view there are no relations between religion and science to be concerned about.

The semantic theory of theory is a reaction against the relativism of the social consensus view of truth, but it leaves untouched the original idea of the relativity of scientific knowledge. The implications of this original idea for the interaction of religion and science have been pointed out by only a small group of scholars including Michael Polanyi (1946, 1958), Thomas Torrance (1996), and James Loder and Jim Neidhardt (1992). However, their view has been lost in the critique of relativism or has not been distinguished from the latter. In this paper, I re-emphasise that Christian religious beliefs are about transcendent reality as objective fact, and argue that scientific fact involves metaphysical and religious belief. I conclude that both Christian religious beliefs and science involve complexes of knowledge and belief. It is through these complexes that they relate to each other. Therefore, talk about the interaction of subjective religion and objective science is not only polarising but also simplistic.

THE ACTOR IN THE INTERACTION OF RELIGION AND SCIENCE

Before proceeding I need to clarify some distinctions. I distinguish, but do not separate, belief *in* God (trust, love), conceptual beliefs *about* God (theology), and conceptual beliefs *about* nature (science). The interaction between religion and science occurs in a person. Only people stand in a personal relation to both God and nature. In relating to God or to nature the whole person functions in a variety of capacities or ways such

as loving, trusting, imaginative and knowing ways. These ways of functioning can be theoretically distinguished as aspects of the relation, but
they are mutually irreducible (van der Meer 1995). Further, a person can
direct one of the functions to take the lead. For instance, for the believing
theologian as believer love and trust normally lead his or her relationship
to God while for the believing theologian as theologian this is the conceptual way of functioning. Again, for the scientist, it is the conceptual
aspect of his or her relation with nature that takes the lead. A person
freely determines which particular capacity will lead the others. Therefore,
no capacity dominates the others. Rather all capacities are regulated by
one's religious orientation.

When one capacity of human nature takes the lead, the others contribute. For instance, the conceptual aspect of one's relation with God
qualifies this relation in theology without excluding any other aspect.
Therefore, trust in God and imagination have a role to play in Christian
theology. Likewise, the conceptual aspect of one's relation with nature
qualifies this relation in a scientist, but without excluding, among others,
the imaginative and the religious aspect. The continuing role of the sub-
ordinated capacities means that a person's relation to God or to nature
cannot be reduced to one (leading) aspect of the relation. Neither can the
products of these relations such as concepts and theories be reduced in
this way. Concepts and theories in science and theology are not the purely
logical objects they are made out to be in the syntactic theory of theory
of neo-positivism or in the current semantic theory of theory (Suppe 1989,
82, 84, 86, 270-71). Such reductions are quite common. The scientist's
relation to God and nature is reduced to a conceptual relation while the
religious relation with God is commonly reduced to trusting or feeling.
This strategy of reductionism leads to the separation of religion and science because there is no relationship between pure emotion and pure
logic.

To avoid this separation I use a multi-aspectual conception of knowing. In this conception the unity of the whole person preserves interaction
among the aspects of one's relation to God and nature. I use the concept
of religion to refer to the relation of the whole person to God. It is an
umbrella concept because in referring to a person's relation to God I refer
to all the capacities which together contribute to the functioning of the
leading capacity of loving and trusting. Therefore, in a religious belief
proper both content and function are qualified as religious. However, a
religious belief can be directed to a substitute for God. For instance, a
belief in nature as divine has a metaphysical content, but a religious function. I will use the term metaphysical belief to refer to a person's non-
religious relation to nature.

FACTUAL COMPONENT OF CHRISTIAN RELIGIOUS BELIEF

The Bible connects spiritual reality with events that also have an historical and a material dimension. Therefore, trust in God as well as conceptual beliefs about God have a factual basis in matter and history, and Christians are realists with respect to the existence of God.

This has always been recognised by the great theologians who emphasised that Christian faith is a personal commitment (*fiducia*) grounded in factual truth (*notitia*). As Barbour (1990, 72) observes: "If no Exodus took place, and if Christ did not go willingly to his death, the power of the stories would be undermined." Jesus said: "Which is easier to say to the paralytic, 'Your sins are forgiven,' or to say, 'Rise, take up your pallet and walk'? But that you may know that the Son of man has authority on earth to forgive sins"-he said to the paralytic-"I say to you, rise, take up your pallet and go home." (Mark 2:9-11, RSV). This factual basis is essential to Christianity. Why would one believe in the redeeming power and authority of Christ if it was not grounded in His victory over biological death as a sign of His victory over spiritual death? Why would a Christian conform to what is spiritually the case, if spiritual fact is merely a reflection of his or her own subjective spiritual needs?

This needs to be said to counter the continuing denial of the historical and material dimensions of the reality of Jesus Christ as ordinarily understood. That is, as understood in everyday life, without presupposing either objectivist or relativist conceptions of truth. Both objectivists and relativists assume that a combination of reason and observation is the only way to truth with objectivists believing it works and relativists it has failed. The "third alternative" I have referred to as 'ordinary understanding' denies their common assumption and holds that truth can be known holistically or intuitively. In Christianity, the integration of spiritual, material and historical truth makes it possible to establish spiritual truth or to reject it using this ordinary understanding. It is the factual basis of trust and conceptual knowledge that makes Christianity both cognitively and spiritually meaningful.

BELIEF COMPONENT OF SCIENTIFIC FACT

Does scientific knowledge also involve a personal commitment grounded in factual truth? During the last half-century, a scientific fact has come to be seen as an abstract entity constructed from observations, terms, concepts, theories, metaphysical and religious beliefs. Here, I stress the belief component of scientific fact for three reasons. It is not known among the majority of practising scientists. If it is known, it has been dismissed in reaction to the relativistic extremes of the sociology of science school. Finally, in philosophy of science the social construction view of theory has been replaced with the semantic theory of theory which views theory as entirely neutral. Against both relativism and neutralism in epistemology I maintain with Hesse (1994) that it is possible to distinguish between arbitrary and responsible roles of beliefs in science, i.e., between bias and considered belief. These can be distinguished by criteria for good and bad interpretation and inference. To make these distinctions, the role of beliefs in science must be exposed.

Since I am dealing with religious belief and science, I will focus briefly on examples in which religious belief functions as a component in the facts of mathematics, physics and biology.[1] This could involve a religious belief proper in which both content and function are qualified as religious. Or it could be a belief with a metaphysical content, but a religious function.

Beliefs in Mathematics.[2] The equations: $3 + 4 = 7$ and $3 + 4 = 5$ appear to contradict each other. How can we know which is "true" and which "false"? You say, we can count on our fingers and see? But that answer already qualifies the equation by requiring that it means numerical addition instead of, for instance, spatial addition. In a spatial context such as a vector sum on a graph, $3 + 4 = 5$.

For instance, in moving three units to the north and afterwards four units to the east one will be five units away from the starting point (a vector possesses both *distance* and *direction*). There is no logical contradiction between the two equations provided they are taken to refer to two different *kinds* of facts, namely numerical and spatial facts. These facts represent a numerical order of succession in which $3 + 4 = 7$, and a spatial order of simultaneity in which $3 + 4 = 5$. Numerical and spatial facts are mutually irreducible in the same way as motion is an irreducible state of being that does not need explanation. A metaphysical belief that denies this difference, i.e., various forms of reductionism, would affect the content of mathematics by creating contradictions. This is what has happened in the three historic crises of mathematics. The crises involved the metaphysical beliefs that reality is nothing but number (is discontinuous) or nothing but space (is continuous; Pythagoras).

If religious belief is a belief in something or other as divine, Clouser (1991, 23) and Strauss (1996 a,b) argue, then these metaphysical beliefs have functioned as religious beliefs in mathematics. This is exemplified by the Pythagoreans who left us a prayer to the number ten (Clouser 1991, 17). The history of mathematics has not seen a nonreductionist metaphysics in which there would have been no contradictions. However, such a nonreductionist metaphysics could be provided by the Christian belief that reality was created with irreducible diversity (Wolters 1996). The implications of such a nonreductionist metaphysics for mathematics have been developed by Strauss (1996a,b).

Beliefs in Physics[3]. The dominant world-view during Newton's life was mechanicism. Mechanicism can be characterised by beliefs about reality, about explanation and about scientific method. Concerning reality the belief was that matter is composed of particles and has the properties of size, shape, motion, inertia and impenetrability. Explanation must make phenomena intelligible in terms of these five properties. Methodologically, the aim to find invisible particles required the use of hypotheses or conjectures which led to an attitude of probabilism towards theories and explanations.

Newton's theism affected beliefs about the world that guided his theorising, and led him to reject the strict "mechanism" of predecessors such as Boyle, Hooke and Huygens (Wykstra 1996). The effect of religious beliefs on science, Wykstra shows, passes through three levels of decreasing generality: that of world-view, of guiding belief and of theorising. At the world-view level, Newton's belief that God is active in the material world led him to understand matter in terms of God's action. For instance, whereas Descartes believed impenetrability is an essential property of matter, Newton saw it as a property of space dependent upon God causing some space to be impervious to matter and thus to reflect light and impinging bodies. Wykstra (1996) observes that matter then may have further, undiscovered properties that, despite the proscriptions of the mechanists about what matter alone can do, are entirely plausible in a God-sustained universe. He concludes that a world-view produces expectations about the world in light of which some theories appear more plausible than others. Such expectations or guiding beliefs inclined Newton to accept action at a distance not only as a manifestation of God's action, but also as an intelligible explanation of gravitational attraction.

Wykstra (1996) offers three conclusions. First, world-views set standards of intelligibility that produce dispositions toward certain types of theory. Second, this effect is mediated not by logical entailment, but by making one theory more likely than another as a result of articulating specific world-view considerations. As Newton saw it, God's being everywhere sustaining his creation did not entail the existence of forces acting at a distance, but it did not make them surprising. It made them far less surprising than if matter acting on its own, as mechanists specified it, were all that exists. Finally, if world-views affect the selection of broad classes of theory for further development, it follows that this limits the content of future theories. Therefore, the effect of world-views extends from the selection to the constitution of theories.

Beliefs in Biology[4]. A major question in biology is how to account for the complexity of structure and function of organisms. The complexity of structure is generally seen as hierarchically organised, but the nature of such hierarchy is debated. One type of hierarchy is the hierarchy of material composition. It is characterised by nesting, for instance, of atoms in molecules, cells in tissues and galaxies in the cosmos.

This nested view of reality and philosophical materialism are the metaphysical beliefs that have shaped the biological explanation of human sociocultural behaviour by C.J. Lumsden and E.O. Wilson. Materialism enters the explanation not by entailing the nested hierarchy, but by excluding hierarchies that would admit non-material phenomena. The nesting also introduces a relation between microlevel and macrolevel. This relation is applied universally in physical, biological and social systems, creating analogies between them. This offers the possibility of reducing social macrolevel phenomena (culture) to social microlevel phenomena (gene frequencies) using statistical mechanics. The nested hierarchy is seen to channel the effects of materialism down to the theories about the biological basis of sociocultural behaviour.

The metaphysical role of Wilson and Lumsden's materialism shows, Van der Meer (1996a) argues, in their insistence upon theory reduction despite its failure. It fails to account for the downwardly causal role of cells in the production of genes and of optically active populations of molecules. They lump genes and molecules of water together at one level even though genes do not occur independent of cells, whereas water does. Wilson claims that an optically active *population* of molecules can emerge spontaneously from an optically neutral population (a racemate) independent of cells (Wilson 1977, 1978, 11-12). However, only optically active *individual* molecules exist independent of cells, whereas optically active *populations* of molecules occur only in organisms due to downward causation which involves the selection of optically active molecules of one kind.[5] Clearly metaphysics affects the content of biological explanation. Metaphysical materialism assumes a religious function when Wilson (1980) applies it to explain the existence of god(s).

CONCLUSIONS

One reason for conflicts between Christianity and science has been the polarisation between subjectivism and objectivism as attitudes towards knowledge claims. Such attitudes must now be recognised as abstractions of dimensions of all knowledge. Christian religious beliefs involve objective fact and scientific fact involves subjective belief. Both Christianity and science involve complexes of knowledge and belief. It is through these complexes that they interact.[6] This removes one of the main reasons for conflict between Christianity and science. It also suggests their interaction should be mutual.

Mutuality of interaction requires, among others, that the internal integrity of both be respected. The complex of knowledge and belief called science must be protected from false religious and metaphysical beliefs. For instance, Christianity could protect science from a self-destructive materialistic interpretation of nature. Likewise, the complex of knowledge and belief called religion needs protection from false scientific beliefs. This may be achieved by allowing each to *trigger* new understandings in the other. A trigger is a cause that sets in motion a sequence of operations whose lawfulness is not affected by the cause. For instance, in a conditioned reflex the condition can be anything that can be learned from a whistle to a light flash while the resulting reflex always unfolds in the same way. The trigger releases a process that it does not determine or control. Analogously, a science & belief complex can provide reasons to develop new insights or affirm old ones in religion and theology. The content of this knowledge is not prescribed by the science & belief complex because it is developed following religious and theological norms and sources. A Christianity & belief complex can have the same effect in science. That is, there can be mutual effects on content without each prescribing the content of the other.

The relation of a scientific fact to beliefs does not entail relativism (Suppe 1977, 208-209). Relativism holds that reason and observation are the only ways to absolute truth, but that they have failed. This view leaves no other constraints on a fact than beliefs, which are arbitrary so that one cannot agree on them. Instead, I have argued that the relativity of a scientific fact, theory or explanation simply means that it is related to, *among others*, beliefs. Together with observation and reason, trust and creative imagination, belief plays a necessary role on the way to truth about nature.[7] Thus both in science and in theology knowledge requires a personal commitment (*fiducia*) grounded in factual truth (*notitia*). This does not make public agreement impossible, only harder to achieve.

NOTES

1. For other examples see: Brooke, John H. (1991); Buchdahl, Gerd (1969, 147-180); Cantor, Geoffrey N. (1991, Chs.7, 8); Dobbs, Betty J.T. (1991); Lindberg, David C., Numbers, Ronald L. eds. (1986); Osler, Margaret J. (1994); Funkenstein, Amos (1986); Torrance, Thomas F. (1984, 229-231; 1989, 150-151).
2. Based on Strauss, D.F.M. (1996a, b).
3. Based on Wykstra (1996).
4. Based on Van der Meer, J.M. (1996a).

5. This is pointed out by the source of Wilson's example who uses the term "living matter": see Anderson, P. W. (1972).

6. For an explanation of interaction, see: van der Meer, Jitse M. (1995); Wykstra, Stephen J. (1996).

7. On the place of the human subject in knowledge, see Torrance (1996, 85-100).

REFERENCES

Anderson, P. W. 1972: "More is Different: Broken symmetry and the nature of the hierarchical structure of science". *Science* 177: 393-396.

Barbour, Ian 1990: *Religion in an Age of Science.* San Francisco: Harper & Row, Publishers.

Brooke, John H. 1991: *Science and Religion.* Cambridge: Cambridge University Press.

Buchdahl, Gerd 1969: *Metaphysics and the Philosophy of Science.* The Classical Origins: Descartes to Kant. Cambridge, Mass.: The MIT Press.

Cantor, Geoffrey N. 1991: *Michael Faraday, Sandemanian and Scientist.* A Study of Science and Religion in the Nineteenth Century. London: Macmillan.

Clouser, R. 1991: *The Myth of Religious Neutrality.* Notre Dame: University of Notre Dame Press.

Dobbs, Betty J.T. 1991: *The Janus Faces of Genius: The Role of Alchemy in Newton's Thought.* Cambridge: Cambridge University Press.

Fleck, Ludwig 1979: *Genesis and Development of a Scientific Fact.* (eds. T.J. Trenn, R.K. Merton; trs. F. Bradley, T.J. Trenn). Chicago: University of Chicago Press.

Foster, Michael B. 1934: "The Christian Doctrine of Creation and the Rise of Modern Natural Science" *Mind* 43: 446-468.

Foster, Michael B. 1935/1936: "Christian Theology and Modern Science of Nature" *Mind* 44/45: 439-466/1-27.

Funkenstein, Amos 1986: *Theology and the Scientific Imagination from the Middle Ages to the Seventeenth Century.* Princeton: Princeton University Press.

Hesse, Mary 1994: "How to be Postmodern Without Being a Feminist", *The Monist* 77 (4): 445-461.

Kuhn, Thomas S. 1962: *The Structure of Scientific Revolutions.* Chicago: University of Chicago Press.

Lindberg, David C., Numbers, Ronald L. eds. 1986: *God and Nature.* Berkeley: University of California Press.

Loder, James E., Neidhardt, W. Jim 1992: *The Knight's Move: The Relational Logic of the Spirit in Theology and Science.* Colorado Springs: Helmers and Howard.

Osler, Margaret J. 1994: *Divine Will and the Mechanical Philosophy.* Cambridge: Cambridge University Press.

Polanyi, Michael 1946: *Science, Faith and Society: A Searching Examination of the Meaning and Nature of Scientific Inquiry.* Oxford: Oxford University Press.

Polanyi, Michael 1958: *Personal Knowledge: Towards a Post-Critical Philosophy.* Chicago: University of Chicago Press.

Strauss, D.F.M. 1996a: "A Historical Analysis of the Role of Beliefs in the Three Foundational Crises in Mathematics" In: *Facets of Faith and Science.* Volume 2, edited by J.M. van der Meer. Lanham, MD: University Press of America / The Pascal Centre for Advanced Studies in Faith and Science [in print].

Strauss, D.F.M. 1996b: "Primitive Meaning in Mathematics: The Interaction between Commitment, Theoretical World-view, and Axiomatic Set Theory." In: *Facets of Faith and Science*. Volume 2, edited by J.M. van der Meer. Lanham, MD: University Press of America / The Pascal Centre for Advanced Studies in Faith and Science [in print].

Suppe, Frederick 1977: "The Search for Philosophic Understanding of Scientific Theories." In: Suppe, F. (ed.) *The Structure of Scientific Theories*. 2nd ed. Urbana: University of Illinois Press.

Suppe, Frederick. ed. 1977: *The Structure of Scientific Theories*. Urbana: University of Illinois Press.

Suppe, Frederick 1989: *The Semantic Conception of Theories and Scientific Realism*. Urbana: University of Illinois Press.

Torrance, Thomas F. 1984: *Transformation and Convergence in the Frame of Knowledge. Explorations in the Interrelations of Scientific and Theological Enterprise*. Grand Rapids: Eerdmans.

Torrance, Thomas F. 1989: *The Christian Frame of Mind. Reason, Order, and Openness in Theology and Natural Science*. Colorado Springs: Helmers and Howard.

Torrance, Thomas F. 1996: *Theological Science*. Edinburgh: T & T Clark.

van der Meer, Jitse M. 1995: "The Concept of Human Nature in Science and Theology". In: *Studies of Science and Theology* Volume 3, edited by N.H. Gregersen, M.W. Parsons. Geneva: Labor et Fides.

van der Meer, J.M. 1996a: "Religious Belief in Sociobiology: How a Physical Analogy Introduces Materialism in Human Sociobiology." In: *Facets of Faith and Science. The Role of Beliefs in Mathematics and the Natural Sciences: An Augustinian Perspective*. Volume 2, edited by J.M. van der Meer. Lanham: University Press of America / The Pascal Centre for Advanced Studies in Faith and Science [in print].

van der Meer, Jitse M. ed. 1996b: *Facets of Faith and Science. The Role of Beliefs in Mathematics and the Natural Sciences: An Augustinian Perspective*. Volume 2. Lanham: University Press of America / The Pascal Centre for Advanced Studies in Faith and Science [in print].

van der Meer, Jitse M. ed. 1996c: *Facets of Faith and Science. The Role of Beliefs in the Natural Sciences*. Volume 3. Lanham: University Press of America / The Pascal Centre for Advanced Studies in Faith and Science [in print].

van Fraassen, Bas 1980: *The Scientific Image*. Oxford: Clarendon Press.

Wilson, Edward O. 1977: *Biology and the Social Sciences*. Daedalus 106 (4): 127-140.

Wilson, Edward O. 1978: *On Human Nature*. Cambridge: Harvard University Press.

Wilson, E.O. 1980: "The Relation of Science to Theology", *Zygon* 15 (4): 425-434.

Wolters, A.M. 1996: "Creation and Separation." In: *Facets of Faith and Science. Interpreting God's Action in the World*. Volume 4, edited by J.M. van der Meer. Lanham: University Press of America / The Pascal Centre for Advanced Studies in Faith and Science [in print].

Wykstra, Stephen J. 1996: "Should World-views Shape Science? Toward an Integrationist Approach of Scientific Theorising." In: *Facets of Faith and Science. The Role of Beliefs in Mathematics and the Natural Sciences: An Augustinian Perspective*. Volume 2, edited by J.M. van der Meer. Lanham: University Press of America / The Pascal Centre for Advanced Studies in Faith and Science [in print].

HERMENEUTICS, NATURAL SCIENCE AND THEOLOGY: REASONS FOR INTEGRATING NATURAL SCIENCE IN THEOLOGICAL NARRATIVE

JAN-OLAV HENRIKSEN
(Oslo, Norway)

Abstract: We should try to formulate the outcome of the dialogue between science and theology in narratives which integrate, reframe and reconstruct the results of the disciplines in a more comprehensive framework. The theoretical reasons for establishing such narratives can be found in the pragmatic understanding of theology and science, which stress their common background in human interests and values. By expressing faith and self-understanding in such narratives, the dialogue between science and theology offers a concrete way of giving people a comprehensive understanding of themselves. Such a narrative gives the results of natural science a place in a structure of beginning, end, actor, actions, basic motifs, connections etc., that explicitly interprets and at least implicitly evaluates them. This could help people to see clearer the relationship between faith and science, and hence get a better grip on their lives.
Theology should be interested in such constructions in order to take the conviction seriously that this world is God's world, and science should do it in order to recognise the pragmatic background of its own practice, and its relation to the broad sphere of human interests.
Keywords: Narrative, K.O. Apel, community, pragmatic, meaning, hermeneutic, interpretation, integration of science and theology

INTRODUCTION

During the last decades, many models of how theology and natural science could interact have been presented. This paper will not deal with such models, but with the understanding and use of the *outcome* of the use of such models. It focuses on some presuppositions for how the languages and understandings in the different realms could be related to each other, and on a way to use the results, which is closely linked to this. I will sketch a proposal for the understanding of the interaction and its outcome that is based on a *hermeneutical* approach.

Science and theology have some common backgrounds, which become obvious if we define their activities well. Both are parts of human activity. This seems important to stress in order to raise my first point: The two realms are both expressions of the pragmatic character of human existence. By the notion "pragmatic," I do not mean anything sophisticated, but simply that both areas are results of a need for humans to articulate, make meaningful, and understand the reality around us so that it helps us to cope better with life. Theology as well as science have no meaning outside the relation to such needs and interests. We need and use their contributions for specific purposes.

To state this "pragmatic" aspect means also to suggest that the two realms have their specific contexts, in which their results make sense. To be able to see the difference between these contexts belongs to the gains of the differentiations of modernity, and is itself an expression of the pragmatic background of these realms. However, in spite of the gain of these differentiations, today there exists also a recognised need for a fruitful dialogue between the two. This is necessary in order to integrate a proper understanding of nature in a theological discourse.

An attempt to provide for such an integration is offered here. The attempt is partly inspired by some elements in the work of the German philosopher *Karl Otto Apel.* He argues that in order to give an explanation of a natural phenomenon, we need first some kind of understanding of the phenomenon we are approaching. *Understanding precedes explanation.* From this point of view, we can see how different approaches to human and natural phenomena are rooted in the needs and interests of the interpreter to deal with different phenomena in different ways.[1]

From Apel, I will go on and propose that such an integrated understanding of science and theology has some advantages, if they are expressed in a narrative form. Hence, my reading of Apel in the following is also an implicit argument for the use of narrative in this integrative enterprise.

THEOLOGY - DEFINED PRAGMATICALLY

At the pragmatic level, theology is an enterprise to clarify the implications and consequences of what the Christian community believes. It has its point of departure in the content of the Christian tradition, as it is witnessed in the Scriptures and the history of the church. From this, it also offers a framework for understanding and evaluating present experience. Strictly speaking, the task of theology is to understand the reality of God, including the ways in which God has expressed himself in history. To this reality the Scriptures and the traditions also bear their witness. It follows from this that *systematic theology* has its main emphasis in offering an interpretation of the present world as the realm of God.

This also implies that theology must relate to the results of natural science as part of the creation of God. Hence, anyone who works in the theological field in order to relate theology to science, not only has the task of appropriating the tradition, and develop statements that reformulate its content in a valid form for the present age. What can be appropriated in this tradition must be able to interact with natural science, and one has to take scientific results into account, if they can have impact on the present (re-)formulation of doctrine, faith or self-understanding. Thus, the theologian relates himself to a larger horizon of questions than the one he can formulate through knowledge of the Christian tradition alone. He also relates himself to questions within the context of modern science. But he does this from a theological point of view, expressing a theological interest. This paper advances the thesis that the *outcome of this process* is best understood as a narrative in which the results of natural science are re-integrated in another context than its own.[2] This narrative stands closer to theology than it does to science. To provide a more detailed understanding of what this means will be the task of the rest of this paper.

Usually, theological texts, historical events and other elements that belong to the usual theological field of investigation, achieve meaning by being related to a broader horizon of intentions, language, tradition, etc.[3] The meaning of theologically relevant phenomena is constituted by interpreting them in their relation to this horizon. If they cannot be understood inside this horizon, they have no meaning at all. Thus, to make a theological statement means basically to relate what happens in the world to elements inside this horizon. This horizon is usually expressed for us in a narrative framework, or is at least based on an implicit narrative basis. So, to interpret an event, an experience or a statement theologically means that it is *integrated into a narrative* about what is going on in the world from a theological point of view.

The pragmatic interests behind this are to develop "updated" understandings and evaluations of what happens in the world, to help us cope better with it, and to understand ourselves in more comprehensive ways. Such understandings are also expressions of faith. The *basic* expression of such an understanding or belief is, to my mind, a *narrative*, which unfolds different elements of both "how", "why", "what" and "who"-questions, as well as implicit evaluative elements in a comprehensive way. At the same time the narrative opens for rational reconstruction of the different elements in the story. Such a narrative has a beginning and an end, and also some kind of actor.

THEOLOGICAL HERMENEUTICS AND NATURAL PHENOMENA - SOME
PROBLEMS

Turning the attention to natural science, the theologian will see that
here one does not operate with a hermeneutical framework in order to
develop an understanding of natural phenomena. To put it simply: A
causal nexus is not something we usually say that we *understand*. We
observe it, and explain it. The same goes for the behaviour of salmon or
whales. It cannot be linked to - and methodologically it should not - be
linked to a horizon of intentions, traditions etc. like the one who makes
theological statements meaningful. Thus, it turns out that natural science
apparently does not have the same kind of structure and pragmatic framework as theology. In short, this has to do with the fact that the interpretative element is put in brackets (or not recognised at all). One can also
say that in theology, the *object* of study is already symbolically structured
in a way that nature is not (cf. Clayton 1989, 88).[4]

To see this difference clearer, we can turn to hermeneutics, where it
is more generally recognised, e.g. by Dilthey and Gadamer. In the general
discussion on theory of science, they help us to make the distinction between the *understanding* of human and cultural phenomena, and the *explanation* of natural phenomena. This distinction is well established and
has won broad acceptance. Taken literally, this seems to imply that we
do not *understand* nature as we understand intentional or symbolically
structured action, or at least that the understanding of natural phenomena
is of quite another kind than the understanding of human and cultural
phenomena.

Thus, a traditional hermeneutical approach will imply that nature has
no meaning, and that the elements that constitute meaning (intention or
purpose, context of reference etc.) are lacking in nature. But to many
people this seems to be contrary to their experience: We do not see nature
as meaningless, but we conceive its meaning in another way than "the
culturally based meaning". This is visualised by many of the attempts to
transcend the concrete results of research in natural science and expand
them to a cosmological vision. Thus, also here we see the establishment
of a more general framework than the methodologically very restricted
one of natural science.

Hence, my thesis is that some kind of hermeneutical horizon, like
the one I said was necessary for theology, is also a necessary condition
in order to make results from science (including natural science) relevant
to theology, and vice versa. If such a horizon is not developed, the two
realms (natural science and theology) are unable to influence each other.

How shall we understand this need to "frame" concrete phenomena or experiences into a larger horizon? Here, I think, Karl Otto Apel offers us some help.

APEL'S NOTION OF THE A PRIORI COMMUNICATIVE COMMUNITY

Apel has developed an understanding of the function of the a priori communicative community for the development of language and science. He says that language cannot be understood in the strict semantic way, achieving its meaning through a "this is that" announcement. Instead, he claims that every language has its meaning in relation to its development for specific aims, and these aims are dependent upon the understanding of the community in which the language is situated. Thus, it is not the world denoted that gives language its basic meaning, but the community that uses the language. Hence, Apel stresses the pragmatic meaning of language, pointing out that no language can have any meaning independent of the meaning given to it by the community.[5] This implies that the intersubjective communicative action between human beings is a priori to the use of other kinds of language.

> ...die Gegenstände der Humanwissenschaften [können] sich ohne eine gewisse moralische Wertung nicht konstituieren. Zwar konnte die moderne, experimentelle und theoretische Naturwissenschaft ihren Gegenstand erst unter der Voraussetzung des prinzipiellen Verzichts auf ein kommunikatives Verstehen und entsprechendes Bewerten im Sinne eines normengerechten oder normwidrigen Verhaltens [...] konstituieren. *Der phänomenkonstitutive Anfangsverzicht auf das Verstehen und Werten entspricht hier dem vorgängigen Erkenntnisinteresse an der möglichen Verfügbarmachung kausalgesetzlicher Prozesse als Mittel im Dienste menschlicher Zwecksetzungen* (Apel 1993, 379, my italics).

This means that before we come to the actual act of differentiating between languages for different pragmatic purposes, we are already "living in" and communicating on the basis of a pre-scientific and pre-theological language. We participate in a community and experience the phenomenon of life a long time before we start reflecting upon it. Our understanding is rooted in this pre-reflective life in community with others.[6]

Let me illustrate this with some examples: In order to try to clarify and develop for scientific use concepts such as "God", "miracle," "causal nexus," "law" etc., we need to have some basic or pre-theoretical sense already of what these notions are all about. These notions never exist isolated from larger horizons where they are used for different purposes. The use of the word "God" is different in the Sunday service and in a book by D.Z. Phillips. However, they are interconnected through their common basis in the a priori communicative community. This does not imply that there need be much identity between them, but some identity has to be assumed. If not, we find other and different words for what we worship in the service or write about in a book.

Apel states that we can never make this pre-scientific evaluative and pragmatic element of language and science disappear completely. It is always there, because we, as humans, do what we do within a wider framework, which cannot be understood as simply pre-scientific, but also expresses the values on which science is based:

> Selbst wenn der Historiker sich um eine objektiv-geschichtsim-manente Begründung der Bedeutungsurteile bemüht, bleibt doch eine selektive Vorstellung und narrative Darstellung der Geschichte ingesamt [...] wesentlich durch die Wertungsperspek-tive bestimmt, die aus der praktischen Zugehörigkeit des Histo-rikers zur Geschichte stammt [..] (Apel 1993, 381).

The most important thing for Apel is not to state this, but to find out what is the meaning of the methodological neutralisation of such evalu-ative aspects in scientific work. He sees this as an attempt to establish a new understanding of phenomena - not determined by traditions and for-mer history - by critically examining the objective connections in reality, thereby also making possible a new and critical evaluation (1993, 381f.).

Thus, Apel opens up for a critical hermeneutical reconstruction of the function of scientific ideas and scientific knowledge. For him, the moral points in this are just as important as the methodological. But he admits that this hermeneutical reconstruction of the "objects" of science, although determined by their pragmatical context, is not based on an ethi-cal-normative commitment only.[7] It has also a *methodological* normativity rooted in the same context (Apel 1993, 383f.). I think it is right to say that this normativity is what defines science in general. It is the normative presuppositions of the scientific community who defines regularities, what contingency is, what regularity is, what a natural law is, how a cause-ef-fect-connection should be defined etc. (cf. Toulmin 1982, Nordgren 1994, Müller & Pannenberg 1970).

Therefore, the alleged neutral, empirical-analytical sciences have a normative basis, which is closely connected to their function and use in relation to a specific community. In this sense, they need an "ethic", says Apel, because

> ... diese monologischen Operationen der Wissenschaft eine dia-logische Sinnverständigung und Geltungsrechtfertigung in einer

Kommunikationsgemeinschaft voraussetzen. Kurz: Die normative Wissenschaftslogik (Szientistik) setzt normative Hermeneutik und mit dieser zugleich normative Ethik voraus, weil "einer allein" nicht Wissenschaft treiben [...] kann (Apel 1993, 402f.).

It follows from Apel's reflections that to be able to understand something as a scientific fact, we first have to operate with specific ideas that themselves are not solely based on experience, but precede experience in the sense that they reflect our interests in what we need to or want to experience.[8] So, the concepts have a formative impact on what we see. To explain how a bird can fly, presupposes a certain understanding of the words "bird" and "fly". Without such a contextual clarification of what the words mean, we would not know in which cases the statement "a bird can fly because..." is meaningful. This understanding is developed in the pragmatic context(s) where these words occur. Scientific progress is however at least partly linked to the abstraction from and neutralisation of this context in the concrete application of the concepts.

However, to say that such concepts have a background in the meaning-creative activity of human communities is different from saying that the phenomena they describe are meaningful in themselves. They achieve their meaning in relation to a broader context of reference and function. That goes for both scientific results as well as theological statements. Apel helps us to see that the lack of a possibility to establish an *understanding* of nature similar to that of culture and human action, is not due to something in nature in itself, but is a consequence of how we find it pragmatically useful to relate to nature. *If we had a chance of relating results of natural science to a broader context of understanding, we could e.g. talk about proposals for narratives which express certain understandings of the results of natural science as well.* My conviction is that this is what happens when we try to link natural science and theology: Then we see what natural science describes within a broader context than its own.[9]

CONCLUSIONS AND CONSEQUENCES

It follows that both theology and natural science are challenged to transcend what their initial frames of context or reference are, in order to understand their relationship to and the relevance of that other part. Both fields need to develop a more comprehensive understanding of reality than the one they have received through the differentiations of modernity. Such a broader horizon can be established more easily if we accept that both realms are anchored in the understandings already tacit to some extent in the a priori community of communication.[10] The a priori of the community includes the pragmatic and contextual in every narrative expression, and thus it opens up for *the revisionary character of both theological and scientifically based narrative.*

When we relate nature, as understood by science, to theology, what happens is that scientific results are *re-established in the broader pragmatic context of meaning that it was abstracted from.* This broader context has as its subject the a priori community and its pragmatic interests, and as one of its expressions the theological narrative. Hence, the context itself should not be identified with the theological narrative, but the theological narrative should be seen as an attempt to manifest this context and its interests by expressing values and self-understanding, providing means for orientation, etc. Theology is thus a possible contributor to the pragmatic context of a community, if it accepts that science as well as theology has a common task in interpreting and understanding the same world.[11]

Asking more concretely, how does such a re-establishing of natural science in the theological realm take place? As mentioned, I suggest that it occurs *by giving the results of natural science a place in a narrative structure of beginning, end, actor, actions, basic motifs, connections etc., that explicitly interprets and at least implicitly evaluates them.*[12] This can give human beings an understanding of their own pre-history and the history to which they belong, and thus give them a help in the development of their self-understanding. Narratives contribute to such self-understanding in a far more concrete way than abstract philosophical explanations.

Hence, theology can appear to be an interpretation of what occurs in the world and of God's relation to it, and give the results of natural science theological significance. Such narratives are not given once and for all, and it belongs to the *constructive* element in systematic theology that they have to be revised, altered and criticised. It is also in the interest of natural science to do this, as this helps to develop an understanding of why we relate to and understand nature in the way we do. Hence, the narrative about the world and about God's relation to nature must constantly be told in new ways, even though it has some basic motifs. *How* to tell it is *a common* task of science and theology.

From what was said, it follows that such narratives should be recognised as experimental and provisional.[13] In a post-modern context, where there is a growing awareness of the many possible perspectives from which it is possible to construct expressions of religious and scientific experience, this is obvious. This fact, however, also implies that such narratives cannot be understood as Lyotardian "grand narratives" (Lyotard 1984) which serve as *authoritative* contributors to legitimatisation of power, knowledge and practice. They must be understood as a kind of visions, which frame knowledge and human experience in a larger context, and offer a guiding pattern for the interpretation of further developments in knowledge, shaping of life-forms, and new experiences. As such, narratives can help people to establish a more comprehensive understanding of their own lives, which takes both the reasons for belief in God, and the results of (post-)modern science seriously.

To sum up: We should encourage the construction of new, visionary and experimental narratives based on a profound interplay between science and theology, where none of the disciplines have the privilege of saying the last word. One should openly admit the limitations of such narratives. If this could help people to see clearer the relationship between faith and science, and hence get a better grip on their lives, this task should not be neglected. Theology should be interested in this in order to take the conviction that this world is God's world seriously, and science should do it in order to recognise the pragmatic background of its own practice, and its relation to the broad sphere of human interests.[14]

NOTES

1. An earlier attempt to formulate some of these insights and their relevance for the theology-science -debate, can be found in Clayton 1989, 59ff.

2. This means that there is an asymmetry in the interests of theology and science: Theology is more interested in approaching science and making use of it than the other way around. This is partly due to differences in scope, but also has to do with methodology. Cf. Niekerk 1993, 162-165.

3. Cf. the work of Wilhelm Dilthey, who made this clearer than anyone else in his work on the differences between natural science and the humanities.

4. It should be added that these are not the only differences between the two realms. E.g., natural science is orientated towards the law-like, regular and common, while theology and history have put more emphasis on the idiosyncratic and contingent. However, as the work of Pannenberg (1970, 1978) shows, the two approaches should not be seen as mutually exclusive.

5. This implies that no language is free of evaluation: Since every language is rooted in a community, it also expresses the values and the interests of that community. If one develops a language which strives to be free of evaluation, this is in itself an expression of the interests and values of the community. The bottom line of this seems to be that a community is not possible to sustain without grounding it in some values and interests. Or, to put it pragmatically: No community without the need for acting in specific ways, and following specific interests.

6. See for a development of this Hübner 1990, 176ff.

7. On the basis of this, Apel can say that he assumes that "die Objektivität der wertfreien Wissenschaft selbst noch die intersubjektive Geltung moralischer Normen voraussetzt" (1993, 395).

8. Cf. van Huyssteen 1996, 4: "This fact reveals that the reasons, arguments and value-judgements employed by the community of scientists, are fundamentally related to, or 'grounded' in social practices."

9. I think one can see two basically different models in the history of the relationship between natural science and theology: Either integration of science in theology (ending in narratives approaching some kind of metaphysics) or theology being integrated in science (ending up in narratives expressing reductionist naturalism, e.g. E.O. Wilson's socio-biology).

10. Although I cannot develop it here, this concurs with the results in Clayton 1989.

11. I stress this also because the scientist himself has an individual interpretation of the theories and their presuppositions. This opens up for pluralism in interpretative contexts on science, and an idiosyncratic element also in the individual scientists work. See Nordgren 1994, 130. This also implies that we rule out any possibility for establishing a comprehensive explanation and understanding of the world solely based on natural science. Such an explanation would exclude its own presupposition: The fact that we tend to understand and interpret everything around as part of an already given and meaningful structure, and not qua something (what would that be?) that is given first, and then is given meaning by us. For this see further Pannenberg 1984, where he develops an argument which I think is possible to combine with what is said here about Apel.

12. Cf. Pannenberg 1978, 155f.: "Dabei läßt die Erklärung aus der Systematik einer naturgesetzlichen Theorie als Spezialfall des Entwerfens von Bedeutungs- und Sinnzusammenhängen verstehen, das in einem anderen Modus in den Formen

historischer und hermeneutischer Erklärung vorliegt, in allgemeiner Form aber Aufgabe der philosophischen Theoriebildung ist." See also Toulmin 1982.

13. An attempt to formulate such a narrative can be found in Mortensen 1989, 166ff.

14. Van Huyssteen 1996, 6, with reference to the work of Parnusnikova, writes on this that scientists seem to appreciate the more open attitude of post-modernism concerning scientific practice: "Post-modernism [...] allows for unconventional approaches in doing science and for greater flexibility in various organisational and administrative arrangements concerning scientific life." If this is the case, my proposal here should not be out of place.

REFERENCES

Apel, Karl Otto 1993: "Das Apriori der Kommunikationsgemeinschaft und die Grundlagen der Ethik". *Transformation der Philosophie II*, Frankfurt: Suhrkamp, 358-435.

Clayton, Philip 1989: *Explanations from Physics to Theology*. New Haven: Yale University Press.

Hübner, Jürgen 1990: "Science and religion coming across." J. Fennema & J. Paul (Eds.): *Science and Religion*. Dordrecht: Kluwer, 173-181.

Lyotard, Jean-François 1984: *The Post-Modern Condition. A Report on knowledge.* Minneapolis: Manchester University Press.

Nordgren, Anders 1995: *Evolutionary Thinking. An analysis of Rationality, Morality and Religion from an Evolutionary Perspective.* (Studia Philosophiae Religionis 14) Stockholm: Almquist & Wicksell.

Mortensen, Viggo 1989: *Teologi og Naturvidenskap. Hinsides ekspansion og restriksion.* København: Munksgaard.

Müller, A.M.Klaus & Pannenberg, Wolfhart 1970: *Erwägungen zu einer Theologie der Natur.* Gütersloh: Gerd Mohn.

Niekerk, Kees van Kooten: 1993: "Teologi og fysik". N. H. Gregersen (ed.): *Naturvidenskab og livssyn*. København: Munksgaard, 155-174.

Pannenberg, Wolfhart 1978: *Wissenschaftstheorie und Theologie*. Frankfurt: Suhrkamp.

Pannenberg, Wolfhart 1984: "Sinnerfahrung, Religion und Gottesfrage." *Theologie und Philosophie* 59, 178-190.

Toulmin, Stephen 1982: *The Return to Cosmology. Post-modern Science and the Theology of Nature.* Berkeley: University of Calif. Press.

Van Huyssteen, Wentzel 1986: "Is there a post-modern challenge in theology and science? Some postfundationalist reflections." Paper at ECST VI, Cracow.

NEITHER A PAGAN SCIENCE
NOR A HOLY METHODOLOGY:
KARL BARTH
AND THE SUSPENSION OF FRAMEWORKS
WHICH CAUSES BIAS IN THE INTERPLAY
BETWEEN SCIENCE AND THEOLOGY

GERBEN J. STAVENGA
(*Groningen, The Netherlands*)
and
AXEL W. KARLSSON,
(*Uppsala, Sweden*)

Abstract: As a matter of fact, many participants in the debate between science and theology allow frameworks derived from current culture, philosophy and science to play a part in their characterisation of theology. Form and content of theology might thus be determined beforehand by frameworks derived from current "pagan" science, i.e. science impregnated by current world-views and ideologies. The risk is obvious that the intended object of inquiry is not seen at all, or at the best seen in a distorted way. An unprejudiced investigation into the relation between science and theology would then be impossible. Preconceived notions about theology have seemingly endless variety of views and speculations as a consequence. Is this not a main cause of the confusion and stagnation in the science-theology debate?

Our article discusses some problems in connection with this fact, crucial to the whole science-theology debate. It is argued in accordance with general standards of scientific inquiry that we first have to suspend current frameworks, even if they claim to be scientific, in order to determine the proper object and task of theology. A pivotal question, of course, is if such a suspension is at all possible.

In Karl Barth's programme for theological research, all decisive concepts (e.g. revelation, God, faith, religion) are derived from empirically given documents, not from general frameworks. His programme emphasises that theology, just as every science, should be determined exclusively by its object of research as it presents itself. For this reason — and not in order to immunise itself against criticism — it has to take as much distance as possible from the influence of current intellectual frameworks, and especially those who claim to be scientific.

We investigate briefly Barth's theological research programme in order to see if it can fulfil this task. We especially take into consideration the "suspensive" methodology that motivates this programme.

As a conclusion we claim that new possibilities for the science-theology debate will emerge if this methodology and research programme are taken seriously.

Barth claimed that "All the sciences at their acme could be theology," and if this happens, it will "render a separate theology superfluous" (Barth 1932, 3-5, CD 4-6). What remains to be investigated is which way will take us to this goal, and how what this state of affairs would be like.

Keywords: Fallibility, rigorous research, exact science, Nazi science, proper theology, questions as result of dogmatics, God as subject of theology.

A FUNDAMENTAL METHODOLOGICAL PROBLEM IN THE RELATION BETWEEN SCIENCE AND THEOLOGY

As a matter of fact, many participants in the debate between science and theology allow frameworks derived from current thinking to play a part in their characterisation of theology. This holds true concerning various strategies for handling the relation between science and theology. It applies to those scholars who claim a separate domain for theology by marking it off from science, as well as to those who strive to achieve an integration between them by giving theological notions a meaning suitable for this end. It goes without saying that in order to understand the relation between science and theology, and how these two influence on each other, we must first have some consensus concerning scientific methodology, including an answer to the question about the proper "object" of theological inquiry. Here we come face to face with a fundamental methodological problem. It seems obvious, that in many notions of what theology ought to be, and in particular of what *the object* of theology is, basic frameworks and world-views, often derived from science, play an important part.

Some scholars, like e.g. Barbour, delimit the science-theology debate to a description and classification of standpoints like conflict, independence, dialogue and integration (Barbour 1990). Others accept for the sake of a friendly conversation whatever definition of theology is maintained. Still others take, more or less consciously, current scientific frameworks for granted and use them to assign the answer of the questions. For an investigation aiming at rigorous scientific insight into the science-theology relation, however, these cannot be taken for granted.

The nature of the proper object of theology can be determined on the basis of frameworks taken from current science in several different ways. E.g., the main theological notions are beforehand endowed with such a meaning that integration with science can easily be achieved. Or a separate domain can be claimed for theology by marking it off from ordinary science. In the latter case the determination is an indirect and negative one; nevertheless, a delimitation makes the influence of preconceived frameworks no less radical.

Possibly, current intellectual paradigms and scientific frameworks play a part in all main strategies for characterising theology. The problem is that the tacit assumptions of such frameworks might function like a pair of glasses, entailing that the intended object of theology is not really seen at all, or at the best seen distorted. An unbiased inquiry into the relation between science and theology would thus be impossible. The consequences are the existing seemingly endless variety of views and speculations, arbitrariness, confusion and stagnation in the science-theology debate.

Can this methodological problem be avoided? Is it possible to break away from the intellectual frameworks and world-views permeating the culture of our epoch? Can we escape the implicit influences of current scientific frameworks, or are we condemned to muddling on and to accept confusion and stagnation?

A PLEA FOR A CRITICAL RESEARCH PROGRAMME

Being decisive for the whole science-theology debate, a solution of these issues is urgent and must be attempted. It thus seems advisable, first and foremost, to try to find a *concept of theology* under the condition of an explicit suspension of all current scientific frameworks and world-views. Of course, the pivotal question is whether such a suspension is possible at all. In any case, determining what theology should be, cannot be done simply by falling back on existing theological conceptions. There is a confusing diversity of them, and all kinds of preconceived ideas seem to interfere. Nobody can claim to have recourse to a theology independent of prevailing intellectual frameworks. Those who advocate a radical de-limitation between science and theology - which often is an immunisation strategy - often prove that they are influenced by current science. Science does not produce results lifted above the flux of time.

Theology thus must be aware of the possibility of being not only influenced, but actually based by current frameworks, cultural as well as scientific. *We propose that the influence of these frameworks are counteracted by the attempt to incorporate a temporary suspension of them in the theological research programme.* The suspension in question must in no way be an immunisation strategy, and it need only be *temporary*, for what the relation between theology and science finally will prove to be, remains to be seen until after the content of theology has been determined. Then one can clarify if there are conflicts on certain points, or if some integration is possible. We thus propose a rigorous research programme according to the following guidelines:

A. First of all one should acknowledge this basic methodological problem.

B. Next one must try to design or find a theological research programme incorporating a temporary suspension of current scientific and cultural frameworks.

C. After critically scrutinising such a possible theological research programme, one can investigate the relation between science and theology, and its possible interplay with world-views and cultural, philosophical and scientific frameworks.

KARL BARTH ON SCIENTIFIC METHODOLOGY

Karl Barth's theological research programme attempts to achieve a critical suspension of predetermined frameworks causing bias on the basis of the specific object of research. He was aware of the fact that no science is without presuppositions. E.g. hermeneutical assumptions are inevitable in the process of the exploration of the biblical documents (Barth 1921, 10). Barth never developed a methodology for all kinds of sciences, but he formulated some fundamental ideas in this field. The most comprehensive principle of general scientific methodology is that *every scientific methodology must be governed by the specific character of the object of inquiry.* (Barth 1932, 2f, 9). The predominance of the object is crucial, according to Barth, because there must always be a possibility of correction by deeper insight into the object. Like Paul Feyerabend, Barth is against formal methodological procedures imposed from the outside and thus inappropriate to the object of inquiry (Feyerabend 1975).

Barth acknowledged science a "a good enterprise, as good as man himself" (Barth 1948, 25). He criticised the science of his days for being "pagan" or even quasi-religious (Barth 1932, 9f). Therefore the special science of *theology is a practical necessity.* Its very existence is a protest against every "pagan" concept of science. This criticism of science, however, does not mean that Barth claims that theology, in a medieval manner should take the position of "queen" over the other sciences, and that they be regarded as mere servants. Theology has no privileged position and is not in possession of truth or of an ultimate criterion of truth which other sciences are deprived of (Barth 1932, 9). "In reality theology does not find itself in possession of special keys for special doors! ... *All sciences at their acme could be theology*", and if this happens, it will "render a separate theology superfluous" (Barth 1932, 3-5, CD 4-6). In his Church Dogmatics, Karl Barth claims that everything must be understood in relationship to God if it is to be fully and properly understood at all (Link 1990).

By locating itself in *solidarity* among all human endeavour for knowledge, under the common designation "science", *theology shows that it does not take their "paganism" seriously*. Barth is concerned about the *distinction* between science, theology included, and the *truth*, which in the end is always the *truth of God*: he is eager that provisional and relative scientific knowledge might not be turned into an *ideology*, or a *world-view* (Weltanschauung), If "exact science" (Barth 1948, 25, CD 23) really is and remains "exact science", it will never make its conclusions, hypotheses and axioms stiffen or treat them as revealed dogmas (Barth 1948, 25 f, CD 23 f). On the contrary, real science will remain open. "Exact science" has in common with theology that it does not enclose a world-view (Barth 1948, 12). Theology and science thus have common counterparts to fight: misleading ideologies and world-views.

Barth sees problem as acute when it comes to the sciences of man. The factual sciences, e.g. social sciences and psychology, deal with all kinds of aspects and possibilities of man, but *not yet - as Barth emphasises (Barth 1948, 26, 236; CD 23, 198) - with man as he reveals himself and is called by name*, which is dealt with in theology. Therefore a sharp and essential separation between non-theological science and theology is *temporarily* necessary, due to the present deficiencies in the sciences.

It should not be forgotten that Barth issued his criticism against "pagan science" in the light of the great disaster for German science. In fact, many of his ideas about science were formulated before the beginning of Nazi rule, and so far there is something prophetic about his criticism. During Nazi rule, biological sciences became permeated by racism, nuclear physics was denigrated as "Jewish", in the humanities one strove for "Aryan" ideals. Nazi ideology was legitimised by theologians as well as professors of law.

THE OBJECT OF THEOLOGICAL INQUIRY

In this limited paper it is of course impossible to perform an extensive analysis of Karl Barth's theology and research programme. (For a more elaborated analysis see Stavenga 1991, esp. Chapt. III.) Here only some main points can be presented. Barth's most fundamental claim is that a critical theological research programme must be determined exclusively by the "object" of its research. Access to that object of study is offered by a particular collection of documents: they form the empirical data, and all information will therefore be derived from them. This object reveals itself in the biblical documents.

Theology is a methodologically ordered way to knowledge and deserves thus to be called a science (Barth 1932, 6; CD 7). As Barth understands it, its criteria rest in the content of revelation. In his lecture "The first commandment as the theological axiom" Barth claims that theology must start from a "theological axiom" in the form of a commandment, an address, constituting the relationship between God and man: "You shall have no gods except me!", but that he uses the term "axiom" in another sense than in mathematics (Barth 1933, 298). The commandment is said to have the same content as the reconciling Gospel about Jesus Christ (Barth 1933, 299). *The object of theological inquiry Barth thus describes as the Word of God made available to man by the revelation of God* (Barth passim, e.g. Barth 1940, 1-65). All concepts of theology (such as God, faith, revelation) must be derived from the empirical data, the specific documents, not from general frameworks. Barth found that many traditional terms had to be given a radically new meaning on the basis of the relevant documents. These concepts, however, are to be regarded as hypothetical. The process of investigation runs from preliminary to more well-founded concepts. "The *real* results of dogmatics ... can themselves only be new questions ..." (Barth 1932, 284; CD 308). This, however, does not mean that dogmatics cannot produce definitive results. But it cannot be proclaimed once and for all what these results are. They can only be found again and again by critical research. This is one example of a built in "suspension" of predetermined intellectual frameworks in Barth's research programme. This critical potential is due to the very object of inquiry.

The only way to know the reality of this "object" is through the *unique event* in which it reveals itself completely. This implies that *we do not have this reality at our disposal*. It thus possesses an intrinsic hiddenness. For the same reason it cannot be objectified and its is impossible to make a model or image of it. The designation "object of inquiry" is to be understood under this provision (Stavenga 1991, 32). Therefore Barth concludes that the knowledge of this reality differs from all other knowledge (Barth 1940, 21; CD 21). The specific structure of this knowledge is also reflected in a specific subject-object relation: both subject and object, distinguishable conceptually, participate completely in the cognitive event. So it is not a particular aspect of this reality that is known in this way; no, in such an event this reality manifests itself completely. Hence, all information about what is known has to be and can be derived from the unique event, i.e. from the effect that result from it, as recorded in the document. So, as far as informational content is concerned, these three, viz. *What* is known, *the event* and the *effect* - distinguished conceptually - coincide completely (Barth 1932, 311-318; CD 339-346). It is this specific cognition which Barth terms "*revelation*". It has nothing subjective, esoteric or authoritarian about it: revelation is true cognition, although possessing an exceptional structure.

The discipline that deals with this specific revelational reality and knowledge is *theology*. Christian theology, according to Barth, either deals with the World of God in his revelation as its criterion, or is not Christian theology. "True theology" is realised by man when his being is determined and taken into service by God. This becomes an event by God's gracious turning towards man: the free personal presence of Jesus Christ becomes an event in man's acting (Barth 1932, 18 f). Theology thus does not have the inner power to pronounce the veracity or falsity of its own assertions.

It appears that the theological research programme here described fulfils the conditions set above and thereby offers a genuine possibility for further investigation.

CONCLUSION

Barth clearly saw the ever present danger that a subjective concern encroaches upon the scientific objectivity. Religious or existential "experience" must not be made the criterion for theology. There is no ultimate human remedy for the weakness and vulnerability of man-made theology. It is one of the great advantages of the theological thinking of Barth, that he does not hide these conditions, which all kinds of theology is exposed to. He did not take refuge to any rational foundation, e.g. in the form of natural theology, but showed openly how susceptible theology, his own included, is to error and human mistakes.

Feuerbach's criticism, that all theology is but a projection out of the human mind, was accepted by Barth as a possibility for all theological projects. In the last resort, Barth can only refer to the secret that God reveals himself when and where he wants to - and to pray: "I do believe, dear Lord, help my unbelief!" He took into account that the Spirit of God - i.e. the proper 'object' of theology - could make Himself to be the ultimate subject and reality behind theological reasoning.

God, as he is in himself, cannot be the object of human knowledge and human science. Every concept of God is by human design and must thus be open, i.e. the theologian must be willing to test new hypotheses. Every concept of God is explicitly or implicitly finished by the clause that God is Otherwise, greater than our thoughts about him. A consequence is that there can be *no canonical, "holy" methodology, determined once and for all*. A deeper insight into the nature of the object of theology is always possible and could demand changes in methodology.

Theology must always, because of its object, be unfinished.

Barth envisaged an integration of all human knowledge, as a protest against every "pagan" science who denies this possibility (Barth 1938, 291). Because of the internal unity of all truth, a dialogue between science and theology is a necessity. As a theologian, Barth was thus eager to be in close dialogue with non-theological science.

The truly "exact sciences" and theology, in Barth's view, share insight about their limitations; they are human projects and thus fallible, tentative and hypothetical in character (Barth 1948, 25f). Science and theology fight a common struggle against "pagan" ideologies and world-views with false pretensions. Thus there is hope for what might be called a "sanctified" science. There is no methodology above criticism, the object of theology must always be free to correct our results.

To Barth, in the end there should be neither a pagan science nor a holy methodology, but an interplay between revelational theology and science - not always a harmonious one, but one marked by tensions and mutual challenges. We conclude that the insight obtained from Barth's theological research programme allows us better to understand and to judge existing ways of relating science and theology, as well as the actual influence on theology of the current scientific world view.

Insight into the described connection between science and theology comes about thanks to the temporary suspension of current intellectual frameworks, be they scientific or in the form of world-views. There is a kind of "suspension" also of the theological concepts in Barth. *This suspension takes place in the light of the object of theology.* The process of investigation in his theology runs from preliminary concepts, without which there of course could be no research at all, towards more profoundly grounded concepts. This process is in principle never ending. (Barth: "Wir müssen immer wieder mit dem Anfang anfangen" — we must always start anew from the beginning).

FOR FURTHER INVESTIGATION

Barth draws a radical consequence from his conviction that the most comprehensive principle of all scientific methodology is that it must be governed by the character of the object of inquiry. *If the world was a better place, there would be no theology at all!* There is no necessity in principle to show any autonomy for theology. He saw theology as an "emergency arrangement". But as such, it must be truly scientific. All sciences, in the final analysis, could end up in theology (Barth 1932, 5). All truth and all knowledge ought thus to form a unified whole.

A problem, however, is how this merging of theology and other sciences should be envisaged. How shall we imagine the state of affairs when all sciences are theology? If all sciences at their acme can be theology, and a separate theology therefore in principle is made superfluous, there must follow far-reaching consequences for theology as well as for the other sciences.

Does this mean that it is possible to express in entirely secular terms what theology deals with (Stavenga 1991, 43)? Or is it Barth's intention that nothing is really understood if its relation to God is not clarified? Shall the knowledge the sciences produce be seen in an overarching and integrating theological horizon? Or is Barth talking about knowledge in an eschatological future?

What could be meant in concreto remains to be elaborated. This is one of the most important possibilities for further investigation. We claim that if the various sciences attuned themselves to the specific "theological" reality and the knowledge gain from it, a new kind of interplay between science and theology would appear.

Another problem concerns the ultimate reason behind the idea of theology becoming superfluous. Is it the belief that there is but one single world - God's world? Is the object of theology and the object of the non-theological sciences in the end one, because the world as well as the truth about it is one and the same? Has it something to do with Barth's ideal that God is objectively known in the world, although this knowledge of God is not realised subjectively (KD IV)?

REFERENCES

Barbour, Ian G. 1990: *Religion in an Age of Science*. San Francisco.

Barth, Karl 1921: *Der Römerbrief.* München.

Barth, Karl 1933: "Das erste Gebot als theologisches Axiom". *Zwischen den Zeiten*, 1933, 297-314. Also in: *Theologische Fragen und Antworten*. Gesammelte Vorträge. 3. Band, Zollikon 1957, 127-143.

Barth, Karl, 1932: *Kirchliche Dogmatik*, I/1.

Barth, Karl, 1938: *Kirchliche Dogmatik*, I/2.

Barth, Karl 1940: *Kirchliche Dogmatik*, II/1.

Barth, Karl 1948: *Kirchliche Dogmatik*, III/2.

Barth, Karl 1951: *Kirchliche Dogmatik*, III/4.

The abbreviation CD refers to the corresponding pages in Church Dogmatics, the English translation of *Kirchliche Dogmatik*.

Feyerabend, Paul 1975: *Against Method*. London.

Link, Christoph 1990: Spørgsmål i omkredsen af Karl Barths skabelsesteologi, in *Karl Barth og den lutherske tradition*. Aarhus 1990, 153-171, 163. Also in: *Zeitschrift für dialektische Theologie*. 1987 S. 65-85: Fragen im Umkreis der Schöpfungstheologie Karl Barths.

Stavenga, Gerben J. 1991: *Science and Liberation. A Blind Spot in Scientific Research — Exploring a New Structure of Reality*. Amsterdam.

TO SEE MORE CLEARLY:
PHILOSOPHY IN THE DIALOGUE
BETWEEN SCIENCE AND THEOLOGY

CHRIS WILTSHER
(*Sheffield, England*)

Abstract: This paper claims that philosophers should be welcomed as equal and essential participants in the dialogue between science and theology, and warns of the dangers of ignoring the particular contribution of philosophy to the dialogue. Three ways in which philosophy can contribute to the dialogue are discussed in detail: the analysis of language, the study of metaphysics, and thought experiments. In each case it is shown that by ignoring the contribution of philosophy, however critical and disturbing it may be, participants in the dialogue run the risks of superficial agreement, cheap consonance and incipient scientism. The paper argues that constructive dialogue involves an openness to change in both partners, and that openness depends on a clear grasp of the scope, the strengths and the weaknesses of one's own position as well as the positions of others. It is claimed that without the assistance of philosophers, neither side in the dialogue between science and theology can achieve the necessary openness to make the dialogue constructive.
Keywords: analysis of language, dialogue, metaphysics, philosophy, science, theology, thought experiment

1. INTRODUCTION

Philosophers are parasites. They surge round the doctrines of other disciplines, feeding voraciously on the ideas of others and drawing nourishment from probing in depth the tiniest particle of utterance. They ask questions without giving answers, raise mountains of problems where all was plain, and delight in discovering paradox and inconsistency. But, like other parasites, philosophers have their uses. Indeed, I want to suggest in this paper that philosophers are more than useful, they are indispensable to any rational inter-disciplinary dialogue, particularly where the disciplines involved are as different as the disciplines of science and the discipline of theology.

To show this, I shall look very briefly at three of the many ways in which philosophers might assist in the dialogue between science and theology. In each case I shall attempt to show both what philosophy can usefully do and the difficulties which arise when philosophical considerations are ignored.

2. THE ANALYSIS OF LANGUAGE

Language is necessary for rational thought and is a significant means of communication. Consequently the analysis of language has always been of great interest to philosophers. What words mean is important; what the author intended the words to mean is important; what the recipient understood by the words is important. Each of these aspects of language usage raises large philosophical questions, particularly about how we determine meanings.

Beyond these questions there are other issues too, for we do not use words in isolation. Round the words we use hangs a great cloud of meanings and ideas and concepts, many of them not properly formulated or apparent, even to the user of the words. These half-hidden meanings and nuances change with time and circumstance as natural languages develop, and often the changes are recognised only when disputes arise.

Let me give an example. All over Europe, indeed all over the world, we now find "Greens", people who claim to be environmentalist in their thinking. Greens apparently are in favour of conservation, against pollution, seek an eco-friendly policy of sustainable development, and so on. But in different places, the Greens are seen differently. Some associate them with political extremism, others with a kind of romantic liberalism. To some, Greens are saying no to progress, to others, the Greens are progress. Time makes a difference too: in the 1980s, Greens were seen by many as political catalysts; in the 1990s they seem to many of the same people to have become political pawns. Everything depends on what you mean by Green and who you include under the Green banner. And what you mean by Green is not just a matter of the objective, clinical application of a particular word, it is a question of what associations that word has for you. If your image of "Green" is bad, for whatever reason, you are unlikely to give your full support to a Green campaign!

The problem here is to separate the different meanings and implications of Green, and to isolate and acknowledge our reasons for taking up a particular stance in relation to Greens. Only then have we a chance of making sure that our reactions to one aspect of greenness are not coloured by reaction, or over-reaction, to another aspect. It is precisely this kind of analysis of words, and the ideas and concepts surrounding them, which is the philosopher's business.

What is true of a word and concept such as "Green" is just as true of the words and concepts used in the dialogue between science and theology. Here words like creation, reality, evolution and life are used with very precise technical meanings in particular disciplines, and very imprecise meanings in general discourse; and the more imprecise the meaning, the greater the conceptual baggage which is brought along without acknowledgement. Thus the word "life" sounds very different to a theologian steeped in the Eastern Orthodox traditions of Christianity and to a biologist trained in modern Darwinian evolutionary biology.

If such conceptual differences remain hidden and unacknowledged, there is a great danger that the dialogue between science and theology will become easy, because superficial, with real divisions disguised and ignored. Let me illustrate the point with the term "intelligibility". We are told by numerous participants in the dialogue between science and theology that both scientists and theologians are concerned with the search for intelligibility. But are they concerned with the same search for intelligibility? For the scientist, to make something intelligible is to give an account of its nature, of how it came to be as it is, and its role in the natural order. For the theologian, to make something intelligible is to give an account of its nature as God sees it, to give an account of how by divine providence it came to be as it is, and to say what divine purpose is fulfilled by its being and what it may become. Certainly both scientist and theologian are engaged in a search for intelligibility and their searches overlap: but the criteria for intelligibility at least suggest that they are engaged in different searches. It is the demonstration and delineation of such cosy but potentially disastrous confusions that philosophical analysis offers the dialogue between science and theology.

3. THE STUDY OF METAPHYSICS

Language is one means of expressing thought. All our thinking requires the ability to classify, and a framework of ideas or assumptions within which the classification works. Such a framework involves metaphysical ideas and assumptions, often so basic and so much a part of our thought that they are unnoticed.

Take for example the idea of causality. For most people trained in the Western intellectual tradition the idea of causality is a basic category: wherever there is an effect, an occurrence, we expect to find a cause. We may be aware of the celebrated sceptical attack by David Hume, in which he denies the connection between cause and effect: but most of us (including Hume in non-philosophical mode) work with the idea of cause and effect, even if we cannot explain it. The idea of causality has become so deeply embedded in us that we automatically look for causes; and we automatically distrust any suggestion of a non-natural cause. Note I say distrust, not dismiss: we may accept a non-natural cause in the end, but our first move is to distrust the suggestion. This is because there is a very close connection for us between the idea of cause and effect, the requirement that all explanations have a causal element, and the claim that the natural world offers sufficient causal explanation for all events within it. The three notions are separable, but they have become so united in our frameworks of thought that we take them all for granted as a package.

Now it is part of the philosopher's business to help us examine our metaphysical frameworks and become aware of the ease with which we slip from one idea to another. It is also part of the philosopher's business to point out that there are many metaphysical frameworks, and to draw out the implications of each, for each framework commits its holders to certain ideas if they are to remain coherent in their thinking. This is especially important in a dialogue between disciplines which might be expected to have different metaphysical presuppositions, as in the dialogue between science and theology. We tend to assume that others share our unexamined metaphysics, and do not state all our assumptions. When our partners in dialogue do the same, it is easy to rejoice over shared ideas without realising that it only the silence that is shared.

For example, Stephan Körner has shown, convincingly in my view, that different categorical frameworks lead to different conceptions of what counts as a reasonable or satisfactory explanation (Körner 1970, 61). Arthur Peacocke is one writer who has recognised the importance of this particular issue for the dialogue between science and theology, with his discussion of criteria for reasonableness (Peacocke 1993, 17). Nancey Murphy too pays attention to this question (Murphy 1990), and shows the benefits of philosophical discussion. However, both Peacocke and Murphy concentrate their attention on the justification of knowledge, and both take scientific knowledge and its justification as their paradigm. Now they may be right to do so; it may be that scientific knowledge provides the going standard of evidence in the modern world, as Murphy claims (Murphy 1990, 192). But it is not obvious that they are right; and the only argument advanced in favour of their approach is the "success" of science. A philosopher asks immediately what metaphysical assumptions are being made here.

In such cases, philosophical analysis comes to the aid of the dialogue between science and theology by uncovering metaphysical assumptions, pointing out their implications, noting alternatives and indicating dangers (including in many cases an incipient scientism). It is so easy for those who are engaged on an exciting intellectual quest to forget the wider world and re-invent the square wheel. The square wheel does not work very well in our everyday world, and nor will a dialogue between science and theology which loses sight of its own metaphysics.

4. THOUGHT EXPERIMENTS

So far we have looked at two ways in which philosophy can help in the dialogue between science and theology by asking critical questions of both partners. In the analysis of language and the exhibition of meta-physical frameworks, philosophers will provide a critical and searching scrutiny of what is being said, and left unsaid, and the metaphysical bag-gage that is being dragged, often unconsciously, into the dialogue. How-ever, while these critical operations accord with John Locke's view "it is ambition enough to be employed as an under-labourer in clearing ground a little, and removing some of the rubbish that lies in the way to knowl-edge" (Locke 1960, 58), they are not sufficient. Philosophers can be crea-tive as well as critical (as Locke was!). So what more creative role can philosophy play in the dialogue between science and theology?

One answer is that philosophers can conduct thought experiments which promote new thought possibilities. This is important, because one of the many factors affecting break-throughs in thought, in any discipline, is what it is possible to think at a given time. For example, if you work at a time when all your training and all your culture combine to insist that space and time are given and fixed, you can be forgiven for not thinking of the relativistic universe: it is, literally, unthinkable. Unthink-able, that is, until somebody trying to make sense of a number of disparate elements conducts a thought experiment which shows that the unthinkable is at least conceivable.

My claim is that this is one of the services which the philosopher can offer. Analysing language, considering metaphysics, the philosopher is well placed to see the cracks between different frameworks of thought and to point out the difficulties of holding certain ideas within a given framework. Having done so, the philosopher is also well placed to collect elements from different places and put them together in new ways, of-fering new possibilities for others in their own disciplines to try out and amend.

An example of this process is the beginning of process thought. Here is a thought experiment, carried out by a mathematician and philosopher, which took off. Whitehead analysed the metaphysical basis of claims about the world and about God, and found then flawed. His response was to carry out a thought experiment in an attempt to develop a new framework which could include all that he saw as worth preserving. His thought experiment has been taken up and developed by others, and now process thought has an effect in many disciplines, not least theology and philosophy.

The example of process thought is particularly instructive for the dialogue between science and theology. It shows that the philosopher is particularly well-placed to make this contribution to the dialogue because the philosopher has apparently less attachment to the metaphysical structures of science and theology than scientists or theologians. I say apparently, because philosophers too carry their metaphysical baggage; they are just expected to be more aware of it and to acknowledge its influence!

Such thought experiments are, I suggest, particularly required at present in the dialogue between science and theology. For while there is much talk of consonance, it is also clear that in a very practical way science sets the agenda for the dialogue, while many in theology turn their backs on it. The theologians justify their attitude by accusing the scientists of unscientific speculation, having themselves largely abandoned the speculative theology which has carried religion forward in every age. To move from a science-dominated consonance to a fruitful and creative dialogue, we need some fresh thought possibilities and that means we need some rigorous thought experiments.

5. CONCLUSION

There are other ways in which philosophy might contribute to the science-theology dialogue. Enough has been said to show both that philosophy is a useful partner in the dialogue, and that it is foolhardy to ignore the philosopher's contribution. Unfortunately, both science and theology are in danger of neglecting philosophy at present. Many scientists seem to think that the undoubted achievements of science make redundant the close scrutiny of concepts, methods and frameworks of thought, as though science is its own justification. In theology (which has much less excuse), there is a rush away from the hard examination of ideas to the reverent turning of old leaves, as though religion could be preserved as it was in some Golden Age. When science and theology come together in dialogue, those concerned are eager to avoid any suspicion of hostility, eager to respect one another's expertise, eager not to erect unnecessary barriers. Consequently hard questions which might provoke sharp answers and expose fundamental conceptual divides are eschewed, in favour of gentle disagreements about details. This is not a plea for a return to the bad old days of the so-called war between science and religion, which was largely a dialogue of the deaf. It is a plea for recognition that the dialogue between science and theology, like any genuine dialogue, requires clarity and honesty as well as respect: cheap consonance is as bad as cheap grace.

In calling on philosophers to help avoid cheap consonance, those engaged in the dialogue between science and theology must be ready to treat philosophy with respect. Philosophy is a discipline with its own methods, presuppositions and rules of procedure. It is not a handmaiden, concerned only with questions of meaning and validity, employed to mediate between those who might otherwise fail to understand each other; nor is philosophy the source of some transcendental viewpoint from which science and theology might be united in some kind of higher reality. Philosophy is pursued by people who have a passion for truth, a dislike of the constraints of dogmatism and a constantly critical curiosity expressed in the question "why?".

Philosophers therefore bring their own specific perspectives and resources to the dialogue between science and theology, and come as equal partners in the dialogue.

They will not always be welcome partners, for their contributions will challenge all participants to examine, develop and defend their own perspectives as well as those of others. Close examination of one's own standpoint is not always comfortable or welcome, but it is necessary if true dialogue is to take place. For true dialogue carries the risk of change, even fundamental change, on all sides, and the openness required for change to take place cannot be achieved until participants are ready to recognise and acknowledge the roots, shape and constraints of their own positions as well as others'. True dialogue is constructive, as is the better understanding of our own perspectives, our own science, our own theology, even our own philosophy. True dialogue is also creative and exciting, as the best discussions between scientists and theologians show. It is to make the dialogue between science and theology ever more creative and exciting that I urge the inclusion of those parasites, the philosophers.

In a much-quoted statement, Albert Einstein said, "Science without religion is lame, religion without science is blind"[1]. Perhaps the role of philosophy in the dialogue between science and theology is just to help the lame to walk a little more easily, the blind to see a little more clearly. And there are good precedents for trying to do that!

NOTE

1. As far as I have been able to discover, this famous statement was first made in a paper presented to a conference on religion and science in New York in September 1940 and later published in a volume entitled *Science, Philosophy and Religion: A Symposium*, published in 1941. The statement then reappears in later works by Einstein, such as *The World As I See It* (1949) and *Out Of My Later Years* (1950)

REFERENCES

Einstein, Albert, 1949: *The World As I See It*.

Körner, Stephan 1970: *Categorical Frameworks*, Oxford, Basil Blackwell.

Locke, John 1960: *An Essay Concerning Human Understanding*, London, Fontana.

Murphy, Nancey 1990: *Theology in the Age of Scientific Reasoning*, Ithaca, Cornell University Press.

Peacocke, Arthur 1993: *Theology for a Scientific Age* (enlarged edition), London, SCM Press.

PARUTIONS RECENTES
CHEZ LABOR ET FIDES

Thomas Römer, *Dieu obscur*
Hubert Auque, *Renoncer*
Pierre-Olivier Monteil, *La grâce et le désordre*
Anne Marie Reijnen, *L'ombre de Dieu sur terre*
Christian Grappe et Alfred Marx, *Le sacrifice*
Collectif, *Jésus de Nazareth*
Lytta Basset, *« Moi, je ne juge personne »*
Bernard Reymond, *De vive voix*
Collectif, *Dieu s'approche*
Henry Mottu, *Le geste prophétique*
Marc-André Charguéraud, *Tous coupables ?*
Hubert Doucet, *Les promesses du crépuscule*
Rémy Hebding, *L'espérance malgré tout*
Mokhtar Ben Barka, *Les nouveaux rédempteurs*
Marga Bührig, *L'avenir de l'homme*
D. Marguerat et Y. Bourquin, *La Bible se raconte*
D. Müller et C.-A. Keller, *La spiritualité protestante*
Pierre Gisel et Serge Molla, *Images de Jésus*
André Gounelle, *La mort et l'au-delà*
Konrad Raiser, *Quelle Église pour demain ?*
Jacques Waardenburg, *Islam et Occident face à face*
Paul Tillich, *Le courage d'être*
Jean-Marc Chappuis, *Ecclesiastic Park*
Dietrich Bonhoeffer/Maria von Wedemeyer, *Lettres de fiançailles*
Jean-Christophe Attias et Pierre Gisel éd., *Enseigner le judaïsme à l'Université*
Élisabeth Parmentier, *Les filles prodigues*
Jean Anderfuhren, *Pour relancer l'œcuménisme*
Kathy Black, *Évangile et handicap*
Jean-Pierre Bastian et Jean-François Collange éd., *L'Europe à la recherche de son âme*
Collectif, *Éthique chrétienne et médecine moderne*
Éric Fuchs, *Le désir et la tendresse*
Robert Grimm, *Luther et l'expérience sexuelle*
Félix Moser, *Les croyants non pratiquants*
Denis Müller, *L'éthique protestante dans la crise de la modernité*
Marc-André Charguéraud, *L'étoile jaune et la croix rouge*
Bernard Reymond, *Le protestantisme en Suisse romande*
Liliane Crété, *Le protestantisme et les femmes*
Pierre-André Stucki, *Le protestantisme et la philosophie*
Michel Leplay, *Le protestantisme et le Pape*

Achevé d'imprimer par Corlet, Imprimeur, S.A.
14110 Condé-sur-Noireau (France)
N° d'Imprimeur : 37648 - Dépôt légal : mars 1999

Imprimé en U.E.